IDENTIFYING HOLLYWOOD'S AUDIENCES

Cultural Identity and the Movies

Edited by

Melvyn Stokes and Richard Maltby

 Publishing

First published in 1999 by the
British Film Institute
21 Stephen Street, London W1P 2LN

The British Film Institute is the UK national agency with responsibility for
encouraging the arts of film and television and conserving them in the national
interest.

Cover design: ketchup
Cover image: Sharon Stone as Catherine Tramell in *Basic Instinct*
(Paul Verhoeven, 1992).

Set in Minion by Fakenham Photosetting Limited, Fakenham, Norfolk
Printed in Great Britain by St Edmundsbury Press, Bury St Edmunds

British Library Cataloguing-in-Publication Data
A catalogue record for this book is available from the British Library
ISBN 0–85170–738–6 hbk
ISBN 0–85170–739–4 pbk

Contents

Notes on Contributors

Robert C. Allen is James Logan Godfrey Professor of American Studies, History and Communication Studies at the University of North Carolina at Chapel Hill. He is the author of *Speaking of Soap Operas* (University of North Carolina, 1985) and *Horrible Prettiness: Burlesque and American Culture* (University of North Carolina, 1995), the co-author (with Douglas Gomery) of *Film History: Theory and Practice* (McGraw-Hill, 1985) and the editor of *Channels of Discourse* (Methuen, 1987), *Channels of Discourse Reassembled* (Routledge, 1992) and *To Be Continued: Soap Operas Around the World* (Routledge, 1995).

Thomas Austin is Lecturer in Media Studies at the University of Sussex. His work has appeared in the *Journal of Popular British Cinema* and *Framework*. He is currently working on a book tracing the marketing and reception of recent Hollywood films in Britain.

Martin Barker is Reader in Media Studies at the University of Sussex. Among his recent publications are (with Roger Sabin) *The Lasting of the Mohicans: History of an American Myth* (University Press of Mississippi, 1996) and (with Kate Brooks) *Knowing Audiences: Judge Dredd, its Friends, Fans and Foes* (University of Luton Press, 1998). He has recently completed an ESRC-funded project into the responses in the UK to David Cronenberg's 1996 film, *Crash*.

Kate Brooks is a research assistant based at Sheffield University. She has lectured on criminology, media and cultural studies and is co-author (with Martin Barker) of *Knowing Audiences* (1998). She has also worked on readers of men's lifestyle magazines and is currently researching second-hand retailing and consumption in British cities.

Brigid Cherry recently completed her doctorate in Film and Media Studies at the University of Stirling. Her research was carried out with female fans of the horror genre. She teaches film and media studies classes at the University of Edinburgh and Queen Margaret University College, Edinburgh.

Annette Hill is Senior Lecturer in Mass Media at the University of Westminster. She is the author of *Shocking Entertainment: Viewer Response to Violent Movies* (John Libbey, 1997), the co-author of *Living Media: Television, Audiences and Everyday Life* (Routledge, 1999), and has published several articles on media audiences. She is also the editor of *Framework: the Journal of Cinema and Media*.

Peter Kramer teaches Film Studies at the University of East Anglia. His essays on various aspects of American film and media history have appeared in *Screen*, *The Velvet Light Trap*, *Theatre History Studies*, the *Historical Journal of Film, Radio and Television*, *History Today*, and numerous edited collections. He is the editor (together with Alan Lowell) of *Screen Acting* (forthcoming from Routledge). He is currently working on a study of contemporary Hollywood cinema.

Annette Kuhn is Reader and Director of Graduate Studies in the Institute for Cultural Research at Lancaster University and an editor of *Screen*. Her publications include *Cinema, Censorship and Sexuality, 1909 to 1925* (Routledge, 1988), *Family Secrets: Acts of Memory and Imagination* (Verso, 1995) and, as editor, *Queen of the Bs: Ida Lupino Behind the Camera* (Flicks Books, 1995) and *Screen Histories: a Screen Reader* (Oxford University Press, 1998).

Richard Maltby is Professor of Screen Studies and Head of the School of Humanities at Flinders University, South Australia. He is the author of *Harmless Entertainment: Hollywood and the Ideology of Consensus* (Scarecrow Press, 1983) and *Hollywood Cinema: An Introduction* (Blackwell, 1995). He is co-editor (with Melvyn Stokes) of the previous volume in this series: *American Movie Audiences: from the Turn of the Century to the Early Sound Era* (BFI, 1999).

Susan Ohmer teaches media history and criticism in the Department of American Studies at the University of Notre Dame. She has published articles in the *Journal of Film and Video*, the *Velvet Light Trap* and *Film History*. She is currently writing a book on George Gallup in Hollywood.

Robert Sklar is a Professor of Cinema in the Department of Cinema Studies, Tisch School of the Arts, New York University. His book *Film: An International History of the Medium* (Abrams/Thames and Hudson, 1993) won a Kraszna-Krausz Foundation award. His other recent books are *City Boys:Cagney, Bogart, Garfield* (Princeton University Press, 1992) and *Movie-Made America: A Cultural History of American Movie* (Vintage, revised and updated, 1994).

Melvyn Stokes teaches American and film history at University College London, where he has been principal organiser of the Commonwealth Fund Conference in American History since 1988. His co-edited books include *Race and Class in the American South since 1890* (Berg, 1994), *The Market Revolution in America* (University of Virginia Press, 1996), *The United States and the European Alliance since 1945* (Berg, 1999). He is co-editor (with Richard Maltby) of *American Movie Audiences*.

Introduction

Richard Maltby

Leo A. Handel, former director of audience research at MGM, claimed in 1953 that 'the movie industry is still the only major business in the United States which has never made a serious attempt to study its potential market'.[1] Hollywood's apparent ignorance of its audience, indeed, plays a prominent role in the industry's self-mythologisation, which presents multinational corporations as dream factories and helps to disguise the brute determination of the economic in the production of mass entertainment. The history of movie entertainment is consequently often itself presented as a form of entertainment, and the catalogue of surprise hits, unexpected flops and moguls' intuitions constantly reinforces the industry's self-representation that show business is really no business. Central to this perception is the persistent belief that audience tastes and preferences are inherently unpredictable.

The unpredictability of audience taste is itself no myth: as economists Arthur De Vany and W. David Walls suggest, 'nobody knows what makes a hit or when it will happen', since audiences make hits 'not by revealing preferences they already have, but by discovering what they like'.[2] In most other acts of repeated consumption, purchasers' expectations are met exactly by a standardised product identical to those previously consumed. Audience behaviour, however, is shaped by the difference between viewers' expectations of any given movie before they see it and their evaluation of it afterwards. De Vany and Walls have produced a theoretical model of how the random factor of what the industry calls 'word of mouth' governs the stochastic commercial life-cycles of movies. Consumers searching for new variations of familiar pleasures transmit information to other consumers, and 'demand develops dynamically over time as the audience sequentially discovers and reveals its demand'. Differences among levels of audience satisfaction at a picture's opening are compounded by information feedback through the run, growing at exponential speed: 'A broad opening at many cinemas can produce high and rapidly growing audiences; but it can also lead to swift failure if the large early crowd relays negative information.'[3]

De Vany and Walls argue that the contemporary distribution and exhibition industry's flexible contractual arrangements over rental prices and the supply of theatrical outlets are highly adapted to exploiting the economic opportunities provided by the industry's particular demand dynamics.[4] Economic historians investigating Classical Hollywood's production and distribution practice similarly argue that the industry was run by rational economic agents making commercial decisions according to recognisable business criteria. John Sedgwick and Michael Pokorny, for instance, have argued that the annual production schedule of the major vertically integrated film companies can be viewed as an investment portfolio, with each production seen as an individual asset incurring some level of risk and generating some rate of return. Dividing a company's output into three broad budget categories, they argue that A and B features were primarily designed to fill the screen time of the parent company's theatres with company product, as well as servicing the secondary markets of lower-run theatres throughout the country. Their rates of return were relatively stable as, consequently, was the risk involved in producing them. Risk, profit and competition between the majors was concentrated on the production of a relatively small number of high-budget 'super-specials' designed to play for extended periods in the company's own first-run theatres and also to gain access to the screens of rival corporations.[5] These pictures were most likely to become commercial hits, but in any season only a handful of pictures – no more than 2.5 per cent of those in release, and far fewer than the industry's total output of high-budget pictures – earned more than five times the mean box-office take.[6] While some high-budget pictures would generate higher box-office revenues, they also carried a substantially higher risk of commercial failure than medium- or low-budget movies.[7] This analysis reveals a much closer degree of continuity between Classical Hollywood's production economics and those of the blockbuster syndrome which came to dominate the industry after the Paramount decision required the divorcement of exhibition from production and distribution.

In contrast to these accounts of the motion picture industry's economic rationality in the face of the random variables of audience choice, Hollywood's discourses about itself have put the unpredictability of audience behaviour to other uses, positioning it at the causal centre of the industry's atmosphere of permanent crisis and instability.[8] The emphasis on the role of what appears to be chance in the success or failure of an individual picture has frequently substituted for the uncertainties of creativity. It has also encouraged the use of strategies of formula and imitation as rational procedures to contain the unpredictability of the audience. Critical comprehension of these strategies has, however, remained relatively undeveloped, in part because of a reluctance to regard Hollywood's output as 'product'. While it is a commonplace in the analysis of television to argue that programmes exist in order to deliver viewers to advertisers, it is as yet considered a form of vulgar economism and an undervaluation of the aesthetics of production to observe that Classical Hollywood's motion pictures existed to deliver audiences to exhibition sites.

The persistence of concepts of film genre constructed with little reference to commercial and industrial history has also hindered critical comprehension of Hollywood's production strategies and their relation to audiences. The economic models described above suggest that a major box-office success will lead its producers to pursue their competitive advantage by producing sequels or quasi-sequels, while other producers seek to imitate its mixture of ingredients. Sedgwick and Pokorny argue that the key determinant of aesthetic trends in Hollywood has consistently been the characteristics which make up each season's most commercially successful films. Such films have a seminal influence on the next season's productions, but that influence is usually short-lived.[9] Rather than describing a cinema of stable, rule-bound genres, their account suggests a cinema of cycles within what Tino Balio has called 'production trends' (one example would be the 'family film' of the late 1980s and 1990s described by Robert Allen in Chapter 7 of this book).[10] If genre criticism were to transfer its concern from ideas of essence and boundary to the analysis of a more fluid system constructed around the assembly of interchangeable component parts – from a cinema of genres to a generic cinema – the critical attention given to the role of the audience in studies of Hollywood would necessarily increase.[11] Explaining why the industry produced the pictures it produced will require looking more closely at the historical specificities of audience choice, season by season.

Until recently, critical study of Hollywood has taken little interest in movie audiences, concentrating its attention on the relatively abstract entity of the 'film-as-text'. The emphasis on interpreting individual motion pictures as aesthetic objects has also served to confirm the mythological account of Hollywood's ignorance of its audience, by proposing a series of interpretative strategies that implicitly marginalise – and on occasion explicitly demean – the majority audience. Critical misperceptions of the 'woman's film' as a low-status product in Classical Hollywood provide perhaps the most prominent examples of the critic assuming the role of the resistant or 'sophisticated' viewer 'reading against the grain', in opposition to the mass of duped spectators constituted by the apparatus of the text – spectators such as the 'women [who] ply their handkerchiefs' in Douglas Sirk movies, in Jean-Loup Bourget's notorious phrase.[12]

In a recurrent vein of hostility to the aesthetic consequences of market research in post-Classical Hollywood, criticism has also reiterated the prevailing mythology's belief in a relation between the unpredictability of audience taste and ideas of artistic achievement in Hollywood. What Thomas Doherty has called the 'juvenilization' of American cinema since the 1950s has often been blamed on the industry's catering to the demographic majority of its audience.[13] Critical accounts habitually describe the changes made as a result of audience previews in negative terms: no one has suggested that the revised ending of *Blade Runner* actually improves the picture, for example. Inherent in such accounts – and indeed in the promotion of 'the director's cut' as a marketing device – are underlying cultural assumptions about the autonomy of art and the aesthetic poverty of mass taste. These assumptions also account for the separation of Hollywood's sphere of production from any direct concern with the audience. For both the production industry and most critical practice, Hollywood's claims to be taken seriously as an aesthetic or cultural phenomenon are interwoven with a denial of the importance or the influence of the mass audience.

This is, to say the least, a perverse argument, perhaps only matched by the apparent critical belief that an industry driven by the question 'What do audiences want?' would choose not to study its potential market. The essays in this volume engage in a variety of ways with the consequences of recognising these critical perversities, and with the concomitant recognition that, as Janet Staiger has suggested, 'looking just at celluloid texts will no longer do in writing film history'.[14] A cultural history of cinema must take account of both Hollywood's actual audiences and the discursively constructed audiences its movies addressed. A history of Hollywood's audiences must, by the same token, be a history of its products and its institutions. The remaining six chapters in Part 1 explore, in chronological sequence, aspects of Hollywood's conception of, and discourses on, its audiences from the 1920s to the 1990s. The five chapters in Part 2 examine what viewers do with their experience of cinema.

In the first chapter, I argue that Leo Handel exaggerated the industry's ignorance of its audience's composition. Writing at a moment of genuine industry crisis, as domestic audiences fell to barely half the numbers they had reached only seven years previously, and as the major companies struggled with the changes brought about by divorcement, Handel was addressing the fact that production companies had not yet replaced the mechanisms that vertical integration had provided for knowing the domestic audience. Within the major companies' divisions of labour, it was not specifically the business of production personnel to know much about their spectators. That responsibility fell to the Sales Department and to the managers of the company's theatre chain, who had the financial data of previous box office performances to guide them.[15] We may well recover a more complete picture of how the industry as a whole understood its audiences when film historians explore the archival records of distribution and exhibition, and produce more accounts of the specific contexts of picture-going to amplify our understanding of the diversity both of Hollywood's audiences and of the programmes they viewed.[16] We also need to reassess our understanding of the industry's perception of its audiences, and this reassessment forms the common element of the essays in the first part of the present volume.

In my chapter, I suggest that from the mid-1920s to the 1940s the industry held a generic conception of its audience that was closely interwoven with its conceptions of its pictures and its theatres. Pictures were conceived by the industry and evaluated by the trade press as suitable for exhibition in different types of theatres, which were attended by different types of 'community and class ... of patronage'.[17] Although the undifferentiated audience was a rhetorical trope vital to the industry's claims to practice a form of cultural democracy, in actuality the exhibition sector recognised and operated a symbiotic system of 'classification of both theatres and product with reference to audiences and markets'.[18] Distributors classified theatres hierarchically from first-run picture palaces to neighbourhood double-bill houses, allocating each theatre a position in a movie's commercial life-span on the basis of their potential audience. By this process, audience tastes were categorised implicitly by income and class as well as explicitly by gender and age.

Classical Hollywood thus recognised a number of quite clearly differentiated groups of viewers, and organised its output to provide a range of products that would appeal to different fractions of the audience. Movies were assembled to contain ingredients appealing to different generically-defined areas of the audience, so that their marketing and exploitation could 'position' each picture in relation to one or more of those 'taste publics'. While the ideal picture would succeed in appealing across the range of audience groups, this was a rare and apparently unpredictable event. But the season's whole portfolio, and indeed each block of pictures that distributors sought to sell to exhibitors, contained ingredients that would between them appeal to the entire range of 'taste publics'.

The industry's generic typology of its audience may or may not have been an accurate description of actual movie audiences, but it did provide a means through which Hollywood could negotiate the generic organisation of its products. The categories of difference within this typology were not rigidly demarcated, and shifted over relatively short periods of time to accommodate the variations in audience response recorded at the box office. Apparent changes in the generic tastes of audience groupings were often invoked to justify shifts in production policy, such as the deliberate creation of a 'family' audience for a bourgeois cinema of uplift in the mid-1930s. Classical Hollywood thus periodically reinvented and reconfigured its audience, typically discovering a 'new' audience who had previously not attended, and devising products that would unite this audience with the existing ones.

Some audiences were, however, more important than others. Questions of gender are prominent in this volume, but readers will find little discussion of race and spectatorship, principally because the topic was largely absent from the industry's classification and construction of its audience. Issues of race and spectatorship will, however, feature in the third volume in this series.

In his chapter, Melvyn Stokes argues that in its construction of the female spectator as a concept rather than a person, feminist criticism has concealed and underestimated the centrality of the female audience to Classical Hollywood's imagination. Surveys in the 1920s and early 1930s supported the industry assumption that women formed the dominant part of its audience, and Stokes disputes the contention of later audience surveys that the female-dominated audience was a myth, at least in the period preceding the introduction of more formalised audience research. What is clear, he argues, is that during the 20s and early 30s the motion picture industry assumed that women were its primary market, both through their own attendance and through their roles as opinion leaders, influencing the males with whom they attended. In an industry dominated by men, the assumption that in order to be profitable its products had to appeal mainly to women had profound effects on Classical Hollywood's development of the star system, on the growth of the discursive apparatus of fan culture, on the rise of an increasingly elaborate system designed to use movies to sell consumer goods, on the employment of women screenwriters to craft mainly female-centred stories, and on the eventual emergence of the 'woman's film'.[19]

Underlying many of these approaches, of course, was the assumption that women differed from men in terms of viewing practices and in terms of the types of movies they preferred. Stokes traces how these divergences were documented by social scientists working during the 1920s and early 30, most notably in the Chicago survey conducted by Alice Miller Mitchell and the two surveys of Muncie, Indiana, organised by Helen and Robert S. Lynd.

Most of the work on theoretical female spectatorship has assumed the essential passivity of such a spectatorship. Moreover, as Kathryn Fuller has pointed out, fan magazines of the 1920s insistently promoted the image of a 'new and improved' female movie fan – the flapper – who was also regarded in primarily passive terms, being constructed as an idealised consumer, fascinated by the star system and dependent on movies to generate her needs and desires.[20] Stokes, however, uses the 'movie autobiographies' that Herbert Blumer collected in the late 1920s for his work on the Payne Fund Studies in order to analyse the responses of 'real' female viewers to the films they saw. He argues that, in contrast to theoretical models of female spectatorship or fan magazine constructions, 'real' women revealed themselves to be active rather than passive spectators, using movies in complex ways to negotiate their own identities, appearance and behaviour.

In her chapter, 'The Science of Pleasure', Susan Ohmer describes the development of George Gallup's methodologies of audience research and the arguments he used to persuade motion picture companies to adopt his practices as a means of defining and manipulating the most unpredictable element of 'the whole equation of pictures', audience desire.[21] She argues that audience research, like fan magazines and Classical Hollywood's classification of theatres, constructed a discourse of spectatorship which attempted to describe, explain and control audience reactions. Locating the origins of Gallup's work in the development of applied psychology in the 1920s, Ohmer emphasises that his surveys of public taste and opinion were 'administrative' in that they were intended to serve the marketing interests of his employers, not those of consumers. Her argument concurs with James Beniger's identification of the 'market feedback technologies', such as retail statistics and opinion surveys developed in the first decades of the twentieth century as instruments of the 'Control Revolution', by which consumers were regulated through the information they provided.[22]

Gallup's rhetorical claim to scientific objectivity, buttressed by the quantitative certainties of charts and graphs, was central to his critique of Hollywood's existing procedures for ascertaining audience preferences as 'haphazard' and 'inaccurate', because they relied on sources that were not representative of their actual audiences. In practice, however, his methods largely duplicated the results of those procedures. Although Gallup attributed the resistance he encountered from senior production executives in the major companies to their hostility to any challenge to their authority, they may have declined to enter into contracts with his Audience Research Institute (ARI) less because they were attached to conservative business practices than because they already knew what he was offering to tell them.

ARI identified three key components in the composition of Hollywood's audience: age, gender and income or class, and argued that the audience was younger, more male and poorer than the industry had previously assumed. This survey evidence, and ARI's assumption that the tastes of the actual audience should be appealed to, ran counter to the industry's deliberate attempts to promote a more bourgeois cinema. As evidence of this conflict, Ohmer cites ARI's critique of Paul Muni, one of the most prominent icons of Hollywood's late 30s cinema of respectability.

Some of ARI's conclusions, such as the suggestion that stars needed to make at least three pictures a year to maintain their 'marquee value', clearly served the studios' interests. In other results, Gallup reinforced existing industry wisdom: for instance, that men preferred action films and women were drawn to romance. In arguing that movies needed to contain elements to appeal to both audience groups, Gallup also confirmed the existing industry practice by which the overwhelming majority of Classical Hollywood pictures combined a love story with another plot.[23] Indeed, the centrality of Hollywood's recognition of its audience as made up of distinct taste groups can hardly be more clearly demonstrated than in the construction of the Classical plot, and one can readily extend this argument to account for much of the textual ambiguities of Classical Hollywood movies. A mass cultural form has little use for textual ambiguity unless it serves some purpose in relation to multiple audiences or viewing possibilities. Classical

Hollywood's recurrent 'drama of false appearances', in which the central characters appear to have enacted a forbidden desire but are eventually exonerated, fulfilled the requirement that, as commodities, the movies had to play simultaneously to 'innocent' and 'sophisticated' audiences. So long as the characters never became 'committed to any irretrievable act whose consequences they must bear', a movie's inclusion of contradictions, gaps and blanks meant that it could be consumed as at least two discrete, even opposing stories going on in the same text.[24] This capacity was constructed into the movies as a necessity of their commodity function, to sell the same thing to two or more audiences at the same time.

Ohmer concludes that audience research served as a tool of managerial control during the 1940s, as debates about the composition and desires of film audiences become the discursive site of attempts to manage change and uncertainty within the industry as a whole.[25] Robert Sklar's chapter explores these debates from a different perspective, concerned with their explanations for the precipitous decline in movie attendance in the fifteen years after 1946. While the principal causes for this decline were external to the industry, Sklar focuses on contemporary discussions of possible intrinsic factors, including changes in audience composition and taste, and shifts in movie content. Contrary to Handel's assertion that the industry knew little about its market, Sklar draws attention to a number of studies of audience composition, of the effects that pictures had on their audiences and of the social function of movie-going.

Studies of the effects of movies in general retreated from the claims of the previous two decades. There was widespread scholarly acceptance that the claims of the Payne Fund Studies concerning the effects of movies on audiences had been overstated. Comparable anxieties, however, surfaced in the 1950s about the effects of movies, television and comic books on juvenile delinquents, and led directly to the 1956 revisions in the Production Code.[26] Research concluding that media effects were conditioned by viewers' predispositions and socio-economic circumstances implied a much more active spectator than had earlier been envisaged. Some analyses of what viewers used movies for, particularly those of sociologist Eliot Friedson, moved tentatively toward rejecting Blumer's concept of the audience as an anonymous, heterogeneous, unorganised and spatially separated mass – a concept which continues to govern pschoanalytically based analyses of spectatorship. Friedson argued, rather, that membership of a movie audience was a social activity; spectators shared expectations and attitudes. But in a research climate concerned to demonstrate that media messages had negligible effects on the formation of opinions, the suggestion that viewers were capable of restructuring the thematic content of a media text to suit their needs and beliefs was not developed into a concept of active or resistant spectatorship. Viewers were presented as responding (or not) to the stimulus of the text, and in its concern with how a text might produce a desired effect, the emphasis of the research remained predominantly 'administrative'.[27]

Some 1950s research into attendance also contradicted earlier findings. While ARI had suggested in 1941 that the great majority of movie tickets were purchased by people on low or average incomes, surveys in the 1950s indicated that people in higher socio-economic brackets attended more frequently than did others. These results were, however, subjected to little or no analysis, so that no conclusions were drawn about whether the composition of Hollywood's audience had actually changed. Rather, the new data were again offered as 'facts' to discredit previous assumptions. Most attention was paid to the most familiar result: that the majority of the audience was young – as Gallup had found it to be, and as the major companies had in practice assumed it to be in the 1920s and early 1930s. The conclusions drawn from this finding varied considerably, however. Critic Gilbert Seldes attributed the loss of the 'Great Audience' to Hollywood's over-attention to the tastes of adolescents, something which other writers blamed on the influence of audience research on production decisions.[28] Sociologists David and Evelyn T. Riesman argued, on the other hand, that contemporary movies might be too 'mature' – too fast, too 'insubordinate' and too formally complex – for older audiences to follow. Using the writings of critic Manny Farber, Sklar opens a discussion of the extent to which historical reception studies can chart changes in audience expectations, demands and social relations, and how these changes might be related to shifts in the content, style and address of Hollywood's products.

One conclusion that the post-Paramount-decision industry drew, gradually and apparently with great reluctance, from the audience research and scholarly studies in the 1950s was that its target viewer – the opinion leader making decisions about which movie to attend on behalf of a group – had changed gender. This was, perhaps, the key change in Hollywood cinema, the real marker of the shift between Classical and post-Classical Hollywood. *Motion Picture Herald* editor Terry Ramsaye christened the target viewer of the mid-1930s 'Tillie the Toiler';[29] film historian Charles Eckert described her thus:

> Out there, working as a clerk in a store and living in an apartment with a friend, was one girl – single, nineteen years old, Anglo-Saxon, somewhat favoring Janet Gaynor. The thousands of Hollywood-assisted designers, publicity men, sales heads, beauty consultants and merchandisers had internalized her so long ago that her psychic life had become their psychic life. They empathized with her shyness, her social awkwardness, her fear of offending. They understood her slight weight problem and her chagrin at being a trifle too tall. They could tell you what sort of man she hoped to marry and how she spent her leisure time.[30]

By the mid-1960s, however, the industry's conception of its audience had shifted to accommodate what American-International Pictures called 'the Peter Pan Syndrome', which proposed that younger children would watch anything older children would watch, and girls would watch anything boys would watch, but not vice versa. Therefore, 'to catch your greatest audience you zero in on the 19-year-old male'.[31] Peter Krämer's chapter explores some of the consequences of this shift. He cites a 1972 *Variety* article articulating the then-operative Hollywood wisdom that women preferred television to cinema, and that their visits to the movies were now 'dominated by the male breadwinner's choice of screen fare'.[32] Men, it was assumed, were predominantly interested in stories about men, and after 1968 Hollywood largely abandoned the production of big-budget movies aimed at the female-led 'family' audience, such as *The Sound of Music* (1965). The abandonment of the Production Code for the ratings system made the movie theatre an increasingly uninviting venue for women, and female stars no longer occupied the top positions as box-office attractions. In the three decades since 1969, barely a handful of actresses have been regarded as 'bankable'.

Krämer argues that, contrary to the claims of some industry figures and statements in the trade press, Hollywood is still dominated by the economics of male-oriented blockbusters. Since 1970, women have rarely been specifically addressed as an audience, and then only by modestly budgeted pictures. During the 1980s, the most successful female-oriented pictures – *Tootsie* (1982), *Flashdance* (1983), *Rainman* (1988) – tended also to be male-centred, and at best earned only half the revenue of their male- or family-oriented competitors. The exceptional box-office performance of two 1990 movies, *Pretty Woman* and *Ghost*, indicated the commercial potential of female-oriented pictures, which the industry identified as romantic comedies and 'dating movies', capable of generating repeat viewings, the key feature of post-*Star Wars* (1977) box-office success. Despite this success, industry executives in the 1990s continued to target young male viewers, believing that young women could not persuade their boyfriends to see a picture without a bankable male star.

Although his use of information from industry research on audiences demonstrates the centrality of this activity to post-Classical Hollywood's production, Krämer still finds it necessary to ask 'What is actually known about the female audience and its cinema-going habits and preferences in recent decades?' His analysis, therefore, suggests that post-Classical Hollywood, replete with its armoury of audience research statistics, is as reluctant to revise the identity of its twenty-year-old male target viewer as Classical Hollywood was to abandon Tillie the Toiler. Krämer attributes this avoidance of demographic facts to the 'basic sexism' of most studio executives. An alternative account might attribute it, along with Classical Hollywood's commitment to the female audience, to a basic commerical conservatism. The success of *Titanic* (1997), which drew record audiences composed 60 per cent of women,[33] and which Krämer has suggested not only returned women to the cinema but also returned the cinema to women, may lead Hollywood away from its commitment to the young male audience. But as Krämer himself observes, the likelihood is that 'much like the Titanic, Hollywood's inertia may well be too big for the industry to be able to change course.'[34]

Hollywood's acceptance of the 'demographic vistas'[35] of audience research is also, in part, an acknowledgement of its close interrelationship with television, where the measurement of audiences and the identification of 'lifestyle' groups through statistical factor analysis is an integral aspect of both programme production and economic organisation. Hollywood's orientation toward youth in the late 1960s and 1970s evidenced the industry's awareness of the demographic imperative of the baby boom, the members of which reached their prime movie-going years in that period. When that generation passed beyond the age of most frequent attendance in the late 1970s, the industry sought to narrow the gap it had previously maintained between cinema as an entertainment for the young and television as a product for older people. As Robert C. Allen discusses in the chapter which concludes Part 1, this was in practice most fully achieved through the video recorder and the extraordinarily rapid development, between 1984 and 1990, of a secondary market for video release.

Allen's chapter investigates another of Hollywood's demographic vistas: the production of what he calls 'postmodern family entertainment' as a cultural response to the technological and social changes that have accompanied the baby-boomers' middle age. Hollywood, he argues, re-oriented itself in the late 1980s, exploiting the potential of the video rental and 'sell-through' markets by producing a new variant on the family movie, targeted at the diverse array of relationships among baby-boomers and their 'echo boom' children which comprise the postmodern family. As Allen describes it, the postmodern family movie, archetypally represented by *Home Alone* (1990), ceased to identify pictures addressed exclusively at children, instead becoming 'the discursive marker for a set of narrative, representational, and institutional practices designed to maximise marketability . . . by means of what we might call cross-generational appeal'. In the 1990s, 'family' movies, rated PG or PG-13, were three times more likely than an R-rated picture to take over $100 million at the box office. With most video purchases being made by parents for their children, they also dominated video sales.

Allen's account of the family movie as not constituting a genre 'in the traditional sense' chimes with the argument made in this book's first chapter, that the generic elements of the content of Hollywood movies are best perceived as distinct and separable features rather than as packages demarcated from each other by strictly delineated boundaries. In that sense, the 'family' movie's existence across a number of generic groupings – comedy, animation, adventure, fantasy – replicates the Classical industry's deployment of such terms as 'melodrama' or the 'woman's picture'.[36] The term itself also indicates that the contemporary industry's concepts of generic product and content are in a symbiotic relationship with its generic conceptions of its audiences.

In some respects Allen's account may appear to be at odds with Krämer's, but only if the reader presumes that Hollywood, as a synecdoche for the American entertainment industry in general, has a single demographic understanding of its audience. Allen's figures showing the numerical decline of the prime movie-going sector of the population in the 1980s support Krämer's contention that the industry should have made product to appeal to an older audience. As Allen argues, however, Hollywood's principal response was to manufacture product that not only had a cross-generational appeal, but also stimulated a range of other dispersed markets through product tie-ins, licensing and 'synergistic brand extension'. The target consumer for these movies, and even more clearly for the raft of toys, clothes, home furnishings and other merchandising tie-ins that accompanied them, was the 'echo-boom' child. Tillie and the nineteen-year old male were joined and perhaps supplanted in Hollywood's portfolio by pre-adolescent Kevin, who succeeded in dragging whatever now constituted the rest of the family to a 'non-drop-off' movie before taking them shopping.[37] The need for not only the movie, but also its ancillary product range – what Allen's daughter Madeline calls 'the movie on the lunchbox' – to appeal to this audience group shaped Hollywood's increasing use of animation and digital effects technology by requiring family movies to have a distinctive and reproducible iconography that its producers could copyright and license, preferably without incurring financial obligations to movie stars: as Disney has long understood, animated creatures have no legal interests to conflict with those of their copyright-holders.

For the major players in contemporary Hollywood, John Sedgwick's concept of a portfolio of investments balancing risks across a range of products targeted at different groupings in the potential audience now includes franchises, tie-ins and licensing as elements in that product range. Allen suggests that the high-budget movie has become a 'narrative and iconographic field through which old licenses are renewed and from which new licenses can be harvested', existing as toys and Happy Meals in advance of its theatrical release and surviving on video and as computer games long after it has left the shopping-mall multiplexes. As a result, he contends, Hollywood cinema – the institutional, cultural, and textual apparatus we have known since the 1910s and studied since the 1960s – is dead.

Allen concludes his essay by emphasising the ambivalence and indeterminacy of the 'family' films he has been discussing, formal qualities which he attributes to their postmodern status as texts subject to refashioning as commodities. This indeterminacy, he suggests, calls into question not only the hermeneutic strategies employed within media and communication studies, but even our ability to identify the audience for 'post-Hollywood cinema' in any way other than as a set of markets. Yet 'interpretative polyvalence' and an 'overabundance of meanings', to use Zygmunt Bauman's characterisation of postmodern culture, have always been present in Hollywood movies as a necessary design component of products that had to play to a range of audience interests.[38] The indeterminacy of Hollywood's contemporary output is more readily visible to us because we have the opportunity to interrogate audiences other than ourselves, rather than having largely to imagine them, as we have to do for Classical Hollywood's spectators. Allen is, of course, right to observe that film studies' preoccupation with the analysis and interpretation of the text has ignored or concealed the extent to which audiences have always engaged in polysemic interpretations, and the extent to which movies have always been produced with opportunities for different audience groups to consume differently. As Ruth Vasey has persuasively argued in *The World According to Hollywood*, Classical Hollywood production practices have always required the 'principle of deniability' through a system of representational conventions by which 'conclusions might be drawn by the sophisticated mind, but which would mean nothing to the unsophisticated and inexperienced'.[39] Movies have thus always been at least partially free of 'adjudicating authorities': it is part of their claim to be a particularly democratic cultural form.

While the essays in Part 1 are mainly concerned with Hollywood's identification of its audiences, the contributors to Part 2 discuss a number of different processes by which viewers use movies both to negotiate their identities and to invest their identities in the activities of cinema-going and viewing. All employ a common strategy most remarkable, perhaps, for the infrequency of its use in earlier accounts of audience: quite simply, listening to spectators describing their experience of viewing. To paraphrase Jackie Stacey's account of her methodology in her study of female film-goers of the 1940s and 1950s, if we are interested in the issue of spectatorship, which has dominated film theory for the past twenty years, then it is important to find out what spectators say about Hollywood. Listening to audiences is, however, not a methodologically straightforward matter. As Stacey argues, spectators' accounts of their viewing behaviour are 'forms of representation produced within certain cultural conventions', and the interpretation of those conventions forms part of the interpretation of the viewing experience.[40] David Buckingham has observed that media consumption is neither simply nor directly structured by pre-existing identities, but rather articulates those identities. Identity is, therefore, 'actively produced and sustained' through discourse, and leaves its traces in the texts of viewers' letters, questionnaires and interviews.[41] These texts themselves may be constrained by the extent to which viewers can articulate what they understand, and they are also necessarily subject to a process of multi-layered translation: viewers translate their experience into stories; in interpreting these stories 'symptomatically' and situating them within the social contexts of their production, researchers translate them into accounts of the cultural processes undertaken by sub-cultures or interpretative communities.[42] Although Virginia Nightingale has recently expressed some scepticism about whether such work is better described as applied tex-tual research than as ethnography, John Corner is surely right to insist that the 'researching together of interpretative action and textual signification' – as demon-strated in the essays in Part 2 – remains 'the most important thing for audience research to focus upon'.[43]

Annette Kuhn's chapter examines what she terms 'enduring fandom': loyalty to a star which continues throughout the life of the fan, even surviving the star's death. Kuhn's larger project uses oral histories to investigate British cinema-going in the 1930s and shares Stokes's and Krämer's concern to challenge the silencing of women in historical accounts of cinema. Kuhn seeks to differentiate between varying types of fan behaviour, exploring how fans construct their identities as fans, and how the fan identity forms part of an individual's whole persona. Building on the work of Henry Jenkins, Kuhn describes fans as providing each other with a social community within which pictures are re-viewed and related to the fans' emotional lives, dreams are discussed, and mem-ories are kept alive.[44]

Most of the participants in Kuhn's larger study recalled the social activity of 'going to the pictures', rather than individual movies or stars. For them, cinema-going was an everyday activity, usually shared with a peer group for a short but significant period of their lives. For the enduring fan, however, the cinema-going past is constantly present as part of contemporary daily life. Enduring fandom, she maintains, involves distinct modes of remembering. Such fans speak of their moment of 'falling in love' with the star as the departing-point for their narratives of life-long devotion, and Kuhn's chap-ter focuses on a number of female fans who have sustained such an attachment to Nelson Eddy, star of a series of MGM musicals including *Maytime* (1937). The oral his-tories offer poignant insights into how these fans integrate their allegiances with their personal lives. As re-viewings of the films become overlaid with personal memories and associations, their conversation moves constantly between the past and the present. Indeed, they use memory to link the two, even if they examine what is to them a living past very much through the eyes of the present. In their treatments of time and mem-ory, Kuhn argues, the discourses of enduring fans around *Maytime* offer intriguing par-allels with the movie's own narrative construction of nostalgia.

The other contributors to Part 2 listen to contemporary audiences discussing their relationships to particular kinds of cinematic experience. All acknowledge a debt to Janice Radway's seminal piece of media ethnography *Reading the Romance*, but both the authors of these chapters and their audiences are British, and their methodologies refer primarily to the empirical tradition of British cultural studies.[45] At least in relation to cinema, Radway's approach seems to have been relatively little taken up in the United

States, her own country. Contemporary Hollywood is not, of course, in any significant sense a national cinema, and it is certainly not unreasonable to assume that, barring evidence to the contrary, the identities that British viewers construct from their experiences of Hollywood might correspond closely with those negotiated by comparable American spectators. But the issue of translation arises here as elsewhere, and without a suitable body of comparable American research it is a matter of speculation as to whether the transatlantic difference is a matter of audience behaviour or research methodology. Virginia Nightingale has emphasised the contrast in audience studies between a British preoccupation with 'defining the realism of media experiences as cultural experiences' and an American preoccupation with 'capturing the realism of consumption', while David Morley, among others, has warned of the dangers of transplanting British cultural studies as a 'free-floating transnational academic paradigm'.[46] Such caveats should, perhaps, principally serve to remind us that, while Hollywood's products accommodate the shifts in signification that occur when they cross borders, the same is not necessarily true of the methods for their study.

While Annette Kuhn's larger project is concerned to challenge the silencing of women in historical accounts of cinema, Thomas Austin's chapter explores the responses of an audience group neglected by academic research on audiences, although not by Hollywood itself: the straight white male target audience of the Peter Pan syndrome, which Austin describes as 'the normative, unmarked identity category of western culture'. He focuses on how this audience group responded to *Basic Instinct* (1992), which in its explicit treatment of sex and sexual violence brought the conventions of the low-budget 'erotic thriller' – a genre often only released direct to video – to mainstream Hollywood production. Rather than perceiving this response as simply a reflection of patriarchal and heterosexual attitudes, Austin uses it as an example of the complex way in which these viewers actively negotiate their self-images and the meanings of the texts they consume, in a manner comparable to the 'reading' practices ascribed to minority audiences by feminist and queer theory.

Austin also examines how the movie's promotion and media coverage shaped its reception. While he acknowledges that there is no straightforward fit between marketing assumptions and audience response, he argues that by paying attention to the industrial procedures of market research and advertising in forming audience expectations we can avoid the overly simplistic polarity that exists in theoretical models of spectatorship between a notion of textual power on the one hand, and spectator freedom on the other. Marketing, merchandising and media 'hype' construct plural identities for a picture by 'raiding' it for commodifiable features – versions of Allen's 'movie on the lunchbox' – that circulate independently of the movie itself. As Justin Wyatt has suggested, these features are constructed into 'high concept' movies such as *Basic Instinct* during production.[47] Using Barbara Klinger's concept of the 'dispersible text', which views a movie as 'a potentially polysemic package of component parts designed to both facilitate and benefit from promotional processes', Austin argues that these promotional and merchandising strategies increase the movie's capacity to address a multiplicity of viewers with diverse tastes.[48] Polysemy, multiple viewing positions and contradictory interpretations are, therefore, as much part of the product design of such pictures as they were in Classical Hollywood's construction of movies that simultaneously addressed 'sophisticated' and 'unsophisticated' audiences.

In his analysis of audience responses to *Basic Instinct*, Austin observes that some female viewers interpreted the movie as a narrative of female desire and agency, driven by the Catherine Tramell character played by Sharon Stone. Male respondents, however, often gave primacy to the sight of the female body, suppressing Catherine's narrative agency in order to position her largely as an erotic object. For these viewers, the pleasures of *Basic Instinct* lay in the combination of the sexual and pornographic elements of an 'erotic thriller' with the high production values of a big budget mainstream production. Looking in particular at the uses to which *Basic Instinct* was put by male adolescents, Austin suggests that 'under age' males saw viewing the film as both a means of acquiring status within their peer group and as an initiation into adult heterosexual male desire. The manner in which male viewers focused on some elements of the movie as enjoyable (the 'good sex') and filtered out others (violence and 'bad sex') can be seen as a negotiation with the movie's representation of masculinity and a construction, on the viewer's part, of a heterosexual male identity. Austin suggests that these accounts demand a more flexible model of identification than is provided by theories which propose the masculine spectator's total and unquestioning absorption into voyeuristic and sadistic pleasures. The norms of everyday masculine identity and behaviour affect both the encoding and the decoding of movies such as *Basic Instinct*, but even within these dominant norms a range of conflicting but not mutually exclusive responses are available to the male viewer, from the construction of femininity as a sexual spectacle to the embarrassment of watching sex scenes in a public cinema and the rejection of an unstable, violent masculinity driven by heterosexual desire.

Martin Barker and Kate Brooks share Austin's concern that most recent qualitative audience studies have concentrated on women as audiences, leading to a tendency to treat the male audience as occupying a position that is already understood. Like Austin, they argue that their research into audiences for *Judge Dredd* (1995) suggests some weaknesses in current theorisations of text–audiences relations, particularly those associated with the British cultural studies tradition. Arguments constructed within this paradigm, they suggest, alternate between the two poles of textual determinism, in which the spectator is an automaton constituted by the cinematic and ideological apparatus of the film-as-text, and a polysemic perversity, in which there are no limits to the boundaries of meaning and any interpretation is understood to be as valid and valuable as any other. Arguing that in fact audiences, and fans in particular, care about, and make demands upon their chosen materials, Barker and Brooks seek to consider what people do with their cinematic experiences, and what common elements can be identified within the diversity of audience responses. What do people gain from going to the cinema, and how does this experience interact with their other projects, hopes, understandings and identities?

On the basis of their interview material and the discourse analysis techniques they use to interrogate it, they argue that viewers demonstrate a range of modalities of response, which vary according to the degree of involvement viewers have in the world of the picture, and according to their perception of its realism. Female and middle-class viewers who saw *Judge Dredd* without any particular preparation, commitment or expectation of the picture were likely to experience it as an ephemeral and 'unrealistic' entertainment unconnected to their everyday existence, but they were also least likely to be disappointed by it. By contrast, young working-class viewers were more likely to engage richly with the movie, even if that resulted in their being disappointed by it. These viewers' pleasure in what they termed 'Actions' combined the experience of uninhibitedly sharing a common response with a physical delight in being 'done to', sensually assaulted by the percussive soundtrack, spectacular images, pace and special effects. They also saw a way of imagining their own class situation in Judge Dredd's bleak presentation of a dystopic future. Fans of the comic book on which *Judge Dredd* was based were disappointed by the movie's infidelity to its source material, but these young viewers' objections were rather that it failed to deliver the impact they demanded of an 'Action', and instead required them to pay attention to the plot. These viewers vociferously deny the primacy of narrative. For them, plot is only the vehicle that moves the picture from one action to the next.

Barker and Brooks suggest that spectators have a strategy of viewing which governs how they prepare for seeing a picture, what their expectations of it are, and how they use the experience of viewing. Further, they argue, viewers can decide either to commit themselves to the act of viewing, sticking by their strategy and choosing to have their expectations fulfilled or disappointed, or else they can disengage from their strategy, discarding the viewing experience as 'unrealistic' or merely entertaining. Some viewers who were untroubled by the 'unrealistic' violence in *Judge Dredd* declared their simultaneous admiration for and discomfort with pictures which they saw as representing violence in a very realistic way. Annette Hill's chapter is concerned with such viewers, who are conscious of the risk they take in watching screen violence. Audiences for pictures such as *Natural Born Killers* and *Reservoir Dogs*, which Hill labels the 'new brutalism', know from their marketing and media coverage that they have been identified as disturbing or dangerous. Attending them, therefore, involves two kinds of risk: one concerns the viewer testing how he or she will respond to such violence on screen, and the other relates to the wider society's negative perceptions of film violence.

Hill's participants' perception of these movies as challenging and controversial reinforced their opinions about the type of viewer they perceived themselves to be. Rather than accepting the opinion of themselves frequently disseminated in the media as emotionally deficient or socially dysfunctional, these viewers were more likely to regard themselves as sensitive to film violence.[49] Their desire to be perceived as both intelligent and critically aware prompted them to an aesthetic defence of the movies, and also of their own taste. They tended also to be highly aware of both their own responses to representations of violence, and to those of others. Male viewers, especially, wanted to be seen as socially prepared for it, and had clear opinions on appropriate responses to it. For them, therefore, viewing is a social situation involving a patrol of the self, in which spectators regulate their response according to their perception of others' reactions to the 'risks' of such violence.

Like some of Barker and Brooks' respondents, Hill's participants revealed a dissatisfaction with Hollywood's ultra-high budget projects as being 'too cartoony', and too often no more 'realistic' than a 'kids' comic adventure'. A concept of realism, however vaguely defined, haunts these responses, along with a notion of 'sophistication' as

something equally absent from big budget product. Hill's respondents combined a
desire to take greater aesthetic risks in their entertainment with a desire to take
emotional and social risks in their own reactions to the content of more 'realistic' and
violent pictures. One summed up this perceived relationship between aesthetic and cultural expressiveness and viewer response in his observation that 'off beat' pictures such
as *Reservoir Dogs* and *Man Bites Dog* 'make you scream inside' and 'can get away with
saying more'. What seems to be at stake in these discussions of 'realism' is more a matter of generic convention than of thematic content: the 'more' that is 'said' is a form of
attempted explicitness akin to the 'frenzy of the visible' that Linda Williams discusses in
relation to pornography, as well as an element of arbitrariness in the movies' events,
which seems to make them resemble the randomness of 'real life'.[50]

Viewers use these movies, and their own reactions to them, as opportunities to display their cultural competence, and as forms of cultural capital. Their distinction
between types of movies also functions to discriminate between groups of viewers on
the grounds of their own powers of discrimination: as Pierre Bourdieu argues, 'taste
classifies and it classifies the classifier. Social subjects, classified by their classifications,
distinguish themselves by the distinctions they make, between the beautiful and the
ugly, the distinguished and the vulgar'.[51] The distinction that Hill's participants make
between action movies as fun, playful and unrealistic and 'new brutalism' pictures as
serious, intelligent and realistic also reinforces a distinction between what Barker and
Brooks term 'modalities of viewing': the aesthetic appreciation of a picture worthy of
critical seriousness represents an alternative modality of response to the playful engagement with 'unrealistic' entertainment; the aesthetic classification is, simultaneously, 'a
recognition of the value of the work which occasions it' and an assertion of its own
legitimacy as an act of cultural discrimination.[52]

In the final chapter, Brigid Cherry also examines the responses of an audience group
making a particular investment in the activity of viewing and in activities related to
viewing: women who 'refuse to refuse to look' at what is conventionally assumed to be
the predominantly masculine cinema of horror movies. Like Annette Kuhn, Cherry
takes Jackie Stacey's study as a model which highlights the need to interpret generic
films in relation to their audience. She also shares the concern of Kuhn (and Stokes and
Kramer) to draw attention to the hitherto invisible experiences of women with some
forms of popular culture, in order to allow the voice of an otherwise marginalised audience to be heard, and their pleasures identified.

Although women have been a willing audience for the 'female Gothic' tradition in
literature, Cherry suggests that they have been a less visible audience in the more con-
spicuous setting of the movie theatre, under social pressure to repress a pleasure in horror because such a response has been seen as unfeminine. The horror movie's attack on
the symbolic order has to an extent been prohibited to women not, she suggests,
because of the content of the pictures themselves nor because of women's socially
unmediated reactions to them, but through the operations of the social constructions
of femininity that the pictures themselves may have challenged. Fans simultaneously
resist and reproduce these constructions in their frequent self-identification as outsiders and their enduring empathy for grotesque or supernatural monster figures. The
female following for horror is most likely to be private, viewed watching on television

or video rather than in the constraining environment of the cinema itself. Marketing horror pictures as Gothic romances, however, stages their appeal to a female audience more acceptably.

Like Hill's respondents, these fans recognised the need to defend their taste preferences against anticipated social and cultural criticism. Generally, they most admired the horror movies they were able to think of as intellectualised, imaginative, literary or thought-provoking. They used their categories of distinction among film types and individual films as agencies of self-assessment: notions of 'quality' were used to distinguish films from each other, and also to elevate the respondent's own taste. They also shared with Radway's readers of romance a propensity to ignore narrative events that contradicted their own interpretative framework, again indicating that actual consumers may be less concerned with narrative coherence than film theory conventionally suggests. Their behaviour precisely fits the profile of 'committed fan' identified by Barker and Brooks, of which Annette Kuhn's 'enduring fan' would be one category.

In many ways, the main concern of this book, and of the series to which it belongs, is to challenge the dominance of text-based constructions of 'the spectator' in scholarly discussions of film spectatorship. Historical spectators – unlike theoretical constructs – were influenced in their viewing habits by their own social and cultural identities. Hollywood, as discussed in the first part of this book, knew and exploited this fact by aiming particular kinds of movies at certain identifiable groups. Yet historical spectators were also active in creating meanings from the films they saw and putting their constructions to social use. Part 2 of this book, containing empirical studies of actual audience groupings, explores a variety of ways in which such meanings were created. Interpretive activity by viewers, they suggest, is considerably affected by pre-existing social constructions and gendered and social determinations. It seems very likely, of course, that such processes played as large a part in historical spectators' experience of cinema as they do in the experience of contemporary audiences.

Notes

1 Leo A. Handel, 'Hollywood market research', *Quarterly of Film, Radio and Television* vol. 7, Spring 1953, p. 308.

2 Arthur De Vany and W. David Walls, 'Bose-Einstein dynamics and adaptive contracting the motion picture industry', *The Economic Journal* 106 (November 1996), p. 1493.

3 Ibid., pp. 1493, 1501.

4 Ibid., p. 1513.

5 John Sedgwick and Michael Pokorny, 'The risk environment of film making: Warner Bros in the inter-war years', *Explorations in Economic History* 35 (1998), p. 197.

6 John Sedgwick, 'Cinemagoing preferences in Britain in the 1930s', in Jeffrey Richards, (ed.), *The Unknown Thirties: An Alternative History of the British Cinema, 1929–1939* (London: I. B. Tauris, 1998), p. 6.

7 Sedgwick and Pokorny, 'The risk environment of film making', p. 205.

8 For accounts of Hollywood as an environment of perpetual crisis, see Hortense Powdermaker, *Hollywood the Dream Factory: An Anthropologist Looks at the Movie-makers* (Boston: Little, Brown, 1950), and Leo Rosten, *Hollywood: The Movie Colony, the Movie Makers* (New York: Harcourt, Brace, 1941).

9 Sedgwick and Pokorny, 'The risk environment of film making', pp. 219–20.

10 Tino Balio, *Grand Design: Hollywood as a Modern Business Enterprise 1930–1939* (New York: Scribner's, 1993), pp. 179–312. See also Barbara Klinger's discussion of the 'adult film' as a 'local genre' in *Melodrama and Meaning: History, Culture and the Films of Douglas Sirk* (Bloomington: Indiana University Press, 1994), pp. 37–51.

11 I discuss this idea in more detail in Richard Maltby, *Hollywood Cinema: An Introduction* (Oxford: Blackwell, 1995), p. 107.

12 Jean-Loup Bourget, 'Sirk and the critics', *Bright Lights* 6 (Winter 1977–8), p. 8.

13 Thomas Doherty, *Teenagers and Teenpics: The Juvenilization of American Movies in the 1950s* (Austin: University of Texas Press, 1988).

14 Janet Staiger, *Interpreting Films: Studies in the Historical Reception of American Cinema* (Princeton, NJ: Princeton University Press, 1992), p. 120. See also Stuart Hall's observation that cultural studies must assume both 'that culture will always work through its textualities – and that textuality is never enough': the text must be studied 'in its affiliations with [quoting Edward Said] "institutions, offices, agencies, classes, academies, corporations, groups, ideologically defined parties and professions, nations, races, and genders" '. Stuart Hall, 'Cultural studies and its theoretical legacies', in Lawrence Grossberg, Cary Nelson and Paula Treichler (eds), *Cultural Studies* (London: Routledge, 1992), p. 284.

15 *Harvard Business Reports Vol. 8: Cases on the Motion Picture Industry*, ed. Howard T. Lewis, (New York: McGraw-Hill, 1930), pp. 516-7.

16 An exemplary starting-point for such accounts is provided by Gregory A. Waller, *Main Street Amusements: Movies and Commercial Entertainment in a Southern City, 1896–1930* (Washington, DC: Smithsonian Institution Press, 1995).

17 *Motion Picture Herald*, 14 May, 1932, p. 9.

18 Ibid.

19 For discussions of women's positions in Classical Hollywood production, see Cari Beauchamp, *Without Lying Down: Frances Marion and the Powerful Women of Early Hollywood* (Berkeley, University of California Press, 1997), and Lizzie Francke, *Script Girls: Women Screenwriters in Hollywood* (London: British Film Institute, 1994).

20 Kathryn H. Fuller, *At the Picture Show: Small Town Audiences and the Creation of Movie Fan Culture* (Washington DC: Smithsonian Institution Press, 1996), pp. 144, 148.

21 F. Scott Fitzgerald, *The Last Tycoon* (Harmondsworth: Penguin, 1974), p. 6.

22 James Beniger, *The Control Revolution* (Cambridge, Ma.: Harvard University Press, 1986).

23 David Bordwell, Janet Staiger and Kristin Thompson, *The Classical Hollywood Cinema: Film Style and Mode of Production to 1960* (London: Routledge & Kegan Paul, 1985), p. 16.

24 Martha Wolfenstein and Nathan Leites, *Movies: A Psychological Study* (Glencoe, Il.: Free Press, 1950), pp. 189, 301. For a more fully elaborated discussion of this argument, see Richard Maltby, ' "A brief romantic interlude": Dick and Jane go to three-and-a-half seconds of the Classical Hollywood cinema', in David Bordwell and Noel Carroll (eds), *Post-Theory: Reconstructing Film Studies* (Madison: University of Wisconsin Press, 1996), pp. 434–59. For a related discussion of how divergent audience interpretations of television drama need not be 'oppositional' in the sense of rejecting the text's normative

ideological framework, see Sonia M. Livingstone, 'Audience reception: the role of the viewer in retelling romantic drama', in James Curran and Michael Gurevitch (eds), *Mass Media and Society*, (London: Arnold, 1991), p. 297.

25 For a related discussion of how audience measurement functions as 'a prime instance for the objectifying, othering, and controlling kind of knowledge that circulates within the institutional context of American commercial television', see Ien Ang, *Desperately Seeking the Audience* (London: Routledge, 1991), p. 4ff.

26 James Gilbert, *A Cycle of Outrage: America's Reaction to the Juvenile Delinquent in the 1950s* (New York: Oxford University Press, 1986), pp. 143–77.

27 Todd Gitlin has observed that the administrative purpose of most audience research – the management or commercially viable delivery of audiences – has actively prevented its use in any form of cultural critique: Todd Gitlin, 'Media sociology: the dominant paradigm', *Theory and Society*, Vol. 6 (1978), pp. 205–53. For a summary history of the administrative trajectory of the communications effects tradition of research, and its domination by what C. Wright Mills called 'abstracted empiricism', see Daniel Czitrom, *Media and the American Mind* (Chapel Hill: University of North Carolina Press, 1982), pp. 122–46; and William D. Rowland, Jr, 'Television violence redux: the continuing mythology of effects', in Martin Barker and Julian Petley (eds), *Ill Effects: The Media/Violence Debate* (London: Routledge, 1997), pp. 102–24.

28 Ernest Bornemann, 'The public opinion myth', *Harper's*, July 1947, pp. 30–3.

29 Terry Ramsaye, ' "Highbrow" Productions – and Tillie', *Motion Picture Herald*, 28 May 1932.

30 Charles Eckert, 'The Carole Lombard in Macy's Window', *Quarterly Review of Film Studies* 3 (Winter 1978), p. 10.

31 Robin Bean and David Austen, 'U.S.A. confidential', *Films and Filming* 215 (November 1968), pp. 21–2. Quoted in Doherty, *Teenagers and Teenpics*, p. 157.

32 'Old 4-hanky "women's market" pix, far, far from 1972 "Year of Woman" ', *Variety*, 30 August 1972, p. 5.

33 By comparison, industry surveys suggest that 56 per cent of *Basic Instinct's* British cinema audience was male.

34 Peter Krämer, 'Women first: *Titanic* (1997), action-adventure films and Hollywood's female audience', *Historical Journal of Film, Radio and Television* vol. 18 no. 4 (October 1998), pp. 613–4.

35 I take the phrase from David Marc, *Demographic Vistas: Television in American Culture* (Philadelphia: University of Pennsylvania Press, 1984).

36 Steve Neale, 'Melo talk: on the meaning and use of the term "melodrama" in the American trade press', *The Velvet Light Trap* 22 (Fall 1993), pp. 66–89.

37 Kevin is named after Kevin McCallister, the character played by Macauley Culkin in *Home Alone*.

38 Zygmunt Bauman, *Intimations of Postmodernity* (London: Routledge, 1992), p. 31.

39 Ruth Vasey, *The World According to Hollywood, 1918–1939* (Exeter: University of Exeter Press, 1997); Colonel Jason S. Joy, the Production Code's first administrator, to James Wingate, 5 February 1931. Production Code Administration Case file, *Little Caesar*, Department of Special Collections, Margaret Herrick Library of the Academy of Motion Picture Arts and Sciences, Los Angeles.

40 Jackie Stacey, *Star Gazing: Hollywood Cinema and Female Spectatorship* (London: Routedge, 1994), p. 76.

41 David Buckingham, 'Boys' talk: television and the policing of masculinity', in Buckingham (ed.), *Reading Audiences: Young People and the Media*, (Manchester: Manchester University Press, 1993) p. 97.

42 Virginia Nightingale, *Studying Audiences: The Shock of the Real* (London: Routledge, 1996), pp. x, 63, 99, 151; Ien Ang, *Watching Dallas: Soap Opera and the Melodramatic Imagination* (London: Methuen, 1985), p. 11.

43 Nightingale, *Studying Audiences*, pp. 50, 109–17; John Corner, 'Meaning, genre and context: the problematics of "public knowledge" in the new audience studies', in James Curran and Michael Gurevitch (eds), *Mass Media and Society* (London: Arnold, 1991), p. 275.

44 Henry Jenkins, *Textual Poachers: Television Fans and Participatory Culture* (London: Routledge, 1992).

45 Janice A. Radway, *Reading the Romance: Women, Patriarchy, and Popular Literature* (Chapel Hill: University of North Carolina Press, 1984).

46 Nightingale, *Studying Audiences*, p. 11; David Morley, *Television, Audiences and Cultural Studies* (London: Routledge, 1992), p. 2.

47 Justin Wyatt, *High Concept: Movies and Marketing in Hollywood* (Austin: University of Texas Press, 1994), pp. 8–22.

48 Barbara Klinger, 'Digressions at the cinema: reception and mass culture', *Cinema Journal* vol. 28 no. 4, Summer 1989.

49 Julian Petley, 'Us and them', in Martin Barker and Julian Petley (eds), *Ill Effects*, pp. 87–101.

50 Linda Williams, *Hard Core: Power, Pleasure, and the 'Frenzy of the Visible'* (London: Pandora, 1990), pp. 34–57.

51 Pierre Bourdieu, *Distinction: A Social Critique of the Judgement of Taste*, trans. Richard Nice (Cambridge, Ma.: Harvard University Press, 1984), p. 6.

52 Pierre Bourdieu, 'The field of cultural production, or: the economic world reversed', in *The Field of Cultural Production: Essays on Art and Literature* (Cambridge: Polity Press, 1993), pp. 35–6.

PART ONE

1 Sticks, Hicks and Flaps: Classical Hollywood's generic conception of its audiences

Richard Maltby

The composition of Classical Hollywood's audiences remains relatively unknown to film historians and, as a topic of research, has yet to attract the same attention as that paid to early cinema audiences. In part, this results from the predominant construction of the history of the American cinema as a history of production, a practice compounded by the tenaciousness of that mythological version of Hollywood as less a business than a kind of sideshow run by comically sentimental or irascible buffoons second-guessing public taste by the seat of Harry Cohn's pants. This underlying tendency has been reinforced by the ready acceptance of the idea, advanced by advocates of audience research in the 1940s, that the motion picture industry then knew 'less about itself than any other major industry in the United States'.[1] Such claims were, however, made by parties with obvious axes to grind: having just taken office, Motion Picture Association President Eric Johnston was seeking to establish a Department of Research in the MPAA. Even more obviously, when audience researcher Leo Handel deplored the scientific inadequacy of sneak previews by comparison with the 'objective' precision of cross-section sampling, he was seeking to sell his product, the Motion Picture Research Bureau, to the major companies.[2]

It is, however, literally true that Hollywood personnel knew little about their audience. In July 1927, director Rowland V. Lee complained that the production departments of the major companies 'have not the slightest idea what happens to our pictures', and a director had no way of finding out 'why his picture didn't do well in the South, why his picture didn't do well in England, why his picture could not be shown in Germany'.[3] In the industry's division of labour, that knowledge was the preserve not of the director but of the sales department. One reason historians have found so little evidence of the industry's perception of its audience is that they have looked mainly in the records of production, rather than in the history of exhibition and in the almost entirely unwritten history of distribution.

This chapter seeks to consider the motion picture industry's discursive construction of Classical Hollywood's audiences during the 1930s and, in particular, to examine the interplay between its typologies of audience groupings, of theatres and of productions. In arguing that the industry grouped audiences, theatres and pictures according to interrelated systems that are best understood as generic classifications, I hope to avoid the limitations of film genre criticism's established concerns with ideas of essence and boundary, and adopt a more fluid conception of generic cinema as describing a system constructed around the assembly of interchangeable component parts.[4]

Rowland Lee has made reference to the major companies' practice of determining the broad shape of the next season's output at conventions of the sales department held in the spring.[5] Such events were vividly described by economist Campbell MacCulloch in a 1931 article in *Motion Picture Classic*:

> The cold, cruel fact is that the real boss of the studio picture production is the sales
> department, in convention at a different city each year, when the film sales clans gather
> from all the thirty-four key cities of the land to decide just what kind of pictures they
> can sell during the coming year ... The erudite and cultivated gang from the exchanges,
> filled with higher culture and a keen psychological insight into what you and the rest of
> the picture patrons are thinking or going to think during the next twelve months, make
> that decision solemnly, and with the calm restraint of a dog fight ... The programme of
> so many Westerns, so many rough-stuff melos, so many comedies with real snappy kick
> in them, so many this, that and the other ... is banged out, and ... the studio chief,
> perhaps a little sorrowful and subdued, goes back to Hollywood and studies his
> typewritten list of fifty-two features and twenty-six 'shorts' with a somewhat jaundiced
> eye. Sighing (sometimes), he gathers his studio cabinet and delivers the ukase of the
> real bosses.[6]

Although MacCulloch's account is obviously coloured by the context in which it appeared (a fan magazine), it does describe one means by which 'the big organizations that are on a quantity production basis' determined how their production schedules would reflect the public's taste.[7] The process by which distribution – the New York-based buyer and the sales department in spring conclave – drove production at least to the extent of apportioning the numbers of each broad generic category of production on the basis of information based on sales records, was not necessarily either as belli-cose as MacCulloch described, or as unscientific – or, at least, unstatistical – as Leo Handel later suggested. More detailed records of these procedures, and with them evidence of theatre chains' or distributors' ideas about their audiences, may still exist in the archives of the distribution companies, but we can also find traces of them in the terminology of trade press reviews and in the 'What the Picture Did for Me' columns of the *Motion Picture Herald*. In addition, descriptions of Paramount-Publix distribution and exhibition practices by Sidney Kent and Sam Katz suggest a great deal of systematic input in, for example, the use of test runs and the information held by Paramount's Sales Statistical Department to establish a sales quota for a particular picture in each of the country's 250 zones.[8]

The composition of a theatre's potential audience – the character of its surrounding population, 'its earning capacity; its saving tendencies; its normal need or desire for relaxation' – was the prime determinant in decisions about its location, architecture and entertainment policy.[9] Once it was operating, 'every detail of that operation', including attendance figures, was recorded and forwarded to the main office to be used in the planning of future programmes.[10] Universal solicited public opinion through Carl Laemmle's weekly column in the *Saturday Evening Post*, eventually developing a mailing list of 60,000 individuals, some of whom were consulted on a regular basis over their preferences in story type, their views on adaptations and the likely popularity of forthcoming productions.[11]

Companies used this information to assess the appeal that the various component parts of their output held for different sectors of the audience and to guide their decisions about the content of future productions. In order to serve its commercial purpose of increasing the efficiency with which the industry's output delivered the maximum number of viewers to exhibition sites, the information about audiences became part of an interrelated system by which pictures, theatres and audiences were categorised and classified. The resulting categories of audience classification may not have been based on any demographic research that would meet Dr Gallup's later standards, but they did serve to construct a generic typology through which the industry constructed its audience discursively and by which it negotiated the generic organisation of its products.

In classifying theatres according to their hierarchical position in the zone-run-clearance system, the distribution divisions of each company also categorised their audiences, collecting a body of generic knowledge about them that was utilised in the generic assembly of movies to ensure that they contained ingredients appealing to different groups within the total audience. Rather than Hollywood maintaining a view of the audience as an undifferentiated mass, the industry sought to provide a range of products that would appeal to different fractions of the audience, and to include a set of ingredients that, between them, would appeal to the entire range of different audience fractions. The evidence of this discourse on the audience suggests that the industry assumed that it addressed a number of quite clearly differentiated groups of viewers, and that the categories of difference altered over relatively short periods of time.

From 1929 to 1933, Hollywood's audience was classified by the discourse of the exhibition sector into a series of overlapping binary distinctions between 'class' and 'mass', 'sophisticated' and 'unsophisticated', 'Broadway' and 'Main Street'. These terms were not exact synonyms, but their differences were matters of emphasis. The terminology distinguished between the clientele in different types of theatre, classifying viewers as part of the process of classifying theatres, and it served consistently to indicate that different audiences required different products. Overlaying this typology of theatre audiences was a terminology designed to distinguish between groups of viewers within any given audience by gender and age, as a guide for exhibitors to the most effective exploitation of a particular movie. The range of classification and the interplay between categories were summarised in *Variety*'s February 1932 review of *The Greeks Had a Word for Them*, Sidney Howard's adaptation of the successful Zoe Akins play, which it described as 'a direct reversal from the feminine side of the McLaglen-Lowe love-'em and leave-'em technique, and from the first to the last an opulent spoof at the male gender on the make'. According to this summary of the picture,

> it's one of those peculiar stories, nearly always by a woman, in which the not-too-good
> heroine eats her cake and has it too, and for the femme trade that formula is generally

and almost fool proof. . . . Wit of the dialog may be a bit polished for the proletariat, but the basic humor of the situations . . . will register universally. The men won't care for it much, but flap and matron will adore its flashy sophistication, certainly in the key towns, even if the whole thing may prove a bit high for the neighborhoods and rural spots.[12]

Within this discursive system, there was a fundamental tension between a rhetorical pose adopted by the production industry, affirming the existence of an undifferentiated and unified audience, and the practical recognition, on the part of distribution and exhibition, of different 'taste publics', and of the practical necessity for film exploitation to 'position' a given picture in relation to one or more of those 'taste publics'. The ideal picture would, perhaps, appeal across the range of audience groups and audiences, but in this period it was a rare and apparently unpredictable event, as was demonstrated by the unexpected success of *It Happened One Night*.[13] At moments of economic or institutional crisis, the undifferentiated audience surfaced as a rhetorical trope by means of which the industry would either claim a higher social status or else assert that it was performing a benign and unifying social function. In late 1934 and early 1935, for instance, the MPPDA distributed 20,000 copies of a series of six posters by M. Leone Bracker, one of the country's leading illustrators, depicting a series of idealised acts of cinematic consumption: an elderly woman escaping a world of cares, a young couple aspiring to the Democracy of Goods, a boy dreaming of heroic exploits. The industry's claims to cultural democracy also relied on the rhetoric of the undifferentiated audience. According to MPPDA official Charles C. Pettijohn,

the greatest part of this business is the fact that the humblest theater in the land can show the same production with the same 40-piece symphony orchestra accompaniment

Two posters designed by M. Leone Bracker distributed to exhibitors by the MPPDA, 1934–5. Reproduced in the *Motion Picture Herald*, 22 December 1934.

that is shown at the Roxy theatre in New York. Pictures will die when they can't be shown at the littlest as well as the biggest motion picture theatres of the country.[14]

The exhibition sector, however, saw a danger in production taking this rhetorical trope too seriously. During the 1930s, the MPPDA was frequently called upon to defend the distribution practice of block booking, and the statistical evidence it produced indicates quite clearly that some pictures circulated much more widely than others. In May 1932, the *Motion Picture Herald* argued that, while producer-distributors operated on 'a policy which presumed that every picture was made to be sold to every exhibitor and shown to everybody', the exhibition sector had been moving hesitantly 'toward classification of both theatres and product with reference to audiences and markets'. The 'community and class and type of patronage' to which a theatre played was, the *Herald* observed, determined primarily by its physical location.[15] In late 1934, a brief controversy arose over the hostile reaction of small-town audiences to *Crime without Passion*, a Ben Hecht–Charles MacArthur script starring Claude Rains, which one exhibitor suggested simply should not be shown in communities of under 4,000 people. New York exhibitor Arthur L. Mayer observed that the picture's appeal was 'consciously directed to metropolitan audiences eager for the unconventional, the subtle and the artistic'. The patrons of small-town theatres, on the other hand, were 'more appreciative of human, conventional stories and of conservative technique in their presentation':

> Neither audience is right or wrong. Each has the privilege of enjoying what it finds
> most appealing and provocative. The basic difficulty arises from the effort of the
> producers to satisfy all types of communities with the same kind of pictures.
> Occasionally this is accomplished. A *Thin Man* or *It Happened One Night* strikes a
> universal common denominator. They appeal to the high-brow and the low, the
> sophisticated and the 'regular guy' alike. Such cases, however, are rare. Time after time,
> pictures which aim to please both classes fall between them and satisfy neither.

The answer, asserted Mayer, lay in the recognition that 'we need different sorts of pictures for publics whose tastes differ very fundamentally. The producers cannot afford to sacrifice either revenue or progress in motion picture construction to the natural conservatism of the rural communities. On the other hand, they are highly ill advised if they antagonize small-town patrons and their legislative representatives by forcing upon them ultramodern and experimental pictures.'[16]

In the early 1930s, small-town exhibitors frequently objected that production was far too heavily weighted toward allegedly 'sophisticated' metropolitan audiences. One exhibitor observed that small communities did not want 'smutty dialogue and nasty suggestions, illicit love scenes and the like', but added that

> I doubt if there is a single exception to the universal complaint against dirty, salacious,
> suggestive pictures that the exhibitors are compelled to play under the block booking
> system. Wherever I go I meet up with the complaint that nasty pictures are driving
> people away from the theatres . . . It is quite evident that pictures are being made with
> an eye singly to city patronage.[17]

Producers and distributors, on the other hand, sought to redefine the term 'sophisticated' through a critique of small-town audiences and independent exhibitors.
Deploring the poor reception given to *Cavalcade* by non-metropolitan audiences, Fox's
head of distribution Sidney Kent complained:

> If we make them too good we just watch them die in the smaller towns. It would make
> a stone man weep to see the way people won't watch some of the best films we turn out.
> ... what do you think people care about our camerawork and our visual beauty? I care,
> you care, Jesse Lasky cares ... maybe several thousand people in the large cities value it
> and react to it. But what does the man in the small-town theatre care? You know darn
> well he doesn't give two cents. And, unfortunately, that's the bird we're selling to -- the
> thousands of men that run small-town theatres ... We make certain films that are of
> highest appeal. You critics go into ecstasies about them. The people in the cities praise
> them. And when we get to the small towns the theatre managers yell blue murder
> because they have to play them.[18]

Such problems were, in part, a consequence of the coming of sound. There is some
evidence to suggest that the industry viewed the silent cinema audience as being
largely undifferentiated in its taste, classifying them primarily by the manner of presentation offered in different theatres.[19] It was commonly assumed that if a picture was
successful in one part of the country, it would be successful in other parts as well. In
particular, it was expected that a success on Broadway would be repeated throughout
the United States, since Broadway's tastes in motion pictures were understood to be
'indicative of the tastes of the rest of the country'. One consequence of this belief was
that all the major companies acquired and operated a number of Broadway
exploitation theatres as showcases for their product prior to national release. Initially,
this treatment was reserved for their superior, roadshow products but, increasingly, in
the late 1920s the practice was employed in the promotion of programme pictures as
well. Following Sam Katz's lead at Paramount-Publix, the centralising policies of the
major exhibition chains also encouraged an emphasis on the opinion of the New York
City audience. Film booking for the entire chain was increasingly concentrated in the
hands of the chain's New York executives, making a successful Broadway pre-release
showing a matter of vital importance to the overall sales potential of an individual
picture.[20]

By 1929, however, the assumptions underlying this policy were being seriously ques-
tioned.[21] The Broadway theatres themselves were almost invariably unprofitable, justi-
fied as loss leaders largely by their value as advertising propaganda. But the failure of
this policy to guarantee the commercial success of more ordinary programme pictures
led some executives to argue that 'Broadway exploitation had passed the period of use-
fulness and that people outside New York City and its adjoining areas were not particularly interested in what New York liked in motion pictures or in what it paid to see
them'. One company sales manager found it increasingly difficult to sell pictures on the
strength of a Broadway exploitation-run, since the public was no longer influenced by
the publicity it generated. Moreover, publicity emanating from New York had little
effect in the Midwest, South and Far West. An alternative strategy emerged in the late

1920s, using pre-release showings of programme pictures and superspecials in key cities other than New York.[22]

For a variety of reasons, the period around 1929–30 witnessed a change in the industry's perception of its audience. Sound played a principal role, initially by dividing viewers into the primarily metropolitan audiences who could experience it, and the audiences in smaller theatres who, for a season or two, had to live with silent versions of talking pictures. Some accounts suggested that sound had brought about a more complete integration of the audience: journalist Reginald Taviner asserted that 'the "sticks" have gone forever'. Silent movies, he suggested, had been made with one eye on the small town theatres, where 60 per cent of all audiences saw them:

> Talkies have changed all that. No longer will any old picture do. Film exchanges and leading theatre-owners say that there isn't a single 'hick' audience left in the country … Ruth Chatterton and the sophisticated type of picture such as *Holiday*, *Monte Carlo*, *Anna Christie*, have taken the place of Tom Mix, Hoot Gibson, Fred Thomson and the other cowboy heroes who used to gallop the box-office trail. The farmers have moved from the corral into the drawing room. Mentally, they'd rather mix cocktails than drink hard cider. Producers say that there is no longer any 'selective' or 'type' audience. All audiences are much the same … *Let Us Be Gay*, a smart, citified Norma Shearer vehicle, drew capacity crowds in the nearest thing there is left to the 'sticks,' just as it did in the big cities.[23]

According to Taviner, the change had been brought about by the closure of many small, late-run venues in rural communities. The movies no longer went to 'the uplands', so the uplands had either to abandon the movies or join the 'huge back-to-the-city movement' among audiences:

> Si and Mirandy, instead of going to the crossroads schoolhouse or the Bijou, now crank up the Ford and drive twenty miles instead of two, pay perhaps thirty cents and up, instead of ten – and demand real entertainment in return for their time, money, and effort. From going to the towns and cities, they have learned to judge entertainment from city standpoints. That is why a picture that is a success among the 'city folks' nowadays will be a success in Gopher Prairie, too.[24]

The elimination of late-run exhibition also meant that a talkie's commercial life was much shorter than that of a silent picture, and its profits lower. 'One medium-sized theater now takes the place of ten former smaller ones, audiences and all', Taviner observed. 'The "sticks" have been annexed into the metropolitan areas, and the "rube" viewpoint has gone the way of all flesh.'[25]

The dying screams of late-run exhibitors recorded in the trade press told a different story, however. The intense antagonism between the majors and independent exhibitors in the early 1930s arose, in large part, from the majors' attempt to use the conversion to sound as a means of concentrating business in their theatres and profiteering from other theatres by greatly increasing film rentals. This antagonism was exacerbated by the independent exhibitors' belief – almost certainly correct – that the major companies had effectively abandoned any interest in serving their sector of the market when constructing their production policies. Instead, they concentrated on producing material that would play with success in the theatres which they themselves owned: first- and second-run theatres in metropolitan areas, playing predominantly to employed urban working- and lower-middle-class audiences in their twenties and thirties. While the immediate general popularity of musicals and musical comedies established a degree of homogeneity, the principal impact of sound was a steep increase – often a quadrupling – of film rental charges, passed on to the audience in higher admission prices. A 1929 *Exhibitors Herald-World* survey found the average top ticket price in theatres equipped for sound to be 50 per cent higher than in theatres with no sound, while the average bottom price was twice as high.[26] Most small exhibitors reported reduced profits on sound films as compared to silents. As one small-town Oklahoma theatre-owner expressed it, 'The exchange houses have taken all the business, and exchanges continue to rob the small exhibitor for all that it is possible for them to get in.'[27] Such comments, together with the pattern of theatre closures, make it clear that, as sound concentrated profit on the upper tiers of the exhibition system, the major companies abandoned the marginal sectors of their audience. This decision was, however, camouflaged as an appeal to the audience, in this case to an audience described by E. B. Derr of Pathé as older and more critical. According to Paramount's B. P. Schulberg:

> We are making pictures today that we would never have dreamed of making two years ago, pictures that wouldn't have been box office successes then. Now there seems to be an audience for them. … We made *The Virginian* for our old familiar movie friends whose tastes we have learned from years of picture making, and we made the *Lady Lies* and the *Laughing Lady* for our new friends, our new audiences, trained to delight in the subtler shades of human motives by books and stage plays.

Journalist Dorothy Calhoun commented that, among the 15 million new patrons the industry claimed were attending the movies each week in 1930, 'there are sophisticates, highbrows even, attracted by the cleverness of a Ruth Chatterton, the delicate irony of a Claudette Colbert, the savoir faire and slightly risqué finesse of a Maurice Chevalier. Horn-rimmed spectacles are now prominent in movie loges'. In addition to the youngsters, the flappers and the family fans, the newcomers – 'theater-trained, music lovers, sophisticated, critical, adult' – were:

> drawn to the movies by the new aspects of the films, by the voice of a Lawrence Tibbett, by the subtlety of Ann Harding or Walter Huston, by the whimsical dialogue of a Barrie, by the new magic of color and song and spectacle of screen musical comedies, more elaborately costumed and expensively cast than any legitimate show could afford. … The most substantial audience in the world has been won over to the most democratic amusement in the world. … They have money enough to gratify expensive tastes, but they have found that the movies, once and still the poor man's entertainment, have something for them also.[28]

This utopian description of the continued bourgeoisification of the audience might have met Will Hays's aspirations for a steady 'improvement in "the standard of demand"', but it was something less than a complete account of the changes in the American audience.[29] If sound was drawing a new patronage from 'business men, college professors, millionaires and highbrow critics', it had also brought about a 40 per cent fall in children's attendance by the end of 1930.[30] Children aged twelve and under had constituted between 6 and 8 per cent of the audience for silent cinema, primarily attending subsequent-run neighbourhood theatres. Parents could 'give the children fifty cents and send two or three of them around the corner to the small theater, knowing them to be safe and close at hand – and from under foot for a few hours'.[31] As these small theatres closed, both cost and distance reduced child attendance, but it was also clear that children 'did not care greatly for dialogue pictures'. The silent cinema of 'broad, easily interpreted action' and 'elemental humor' had satisfied what trade paper editor Rob Wagner called their demands for 'cataclysm, tumult and noise'. But, by 1930, it was apparent that 'sound pictures were not the best possible medium for plots of violent action'.[32] In Campbell MacCulloch's 1930 analysis, children 'do not care much for social problems, emotional reactions, sex, philosophy, politics or education', the somewhat abstract subject-matter of too many talking pictures, which talked too much and moved too little for the juvenile audience: 'Actors stand about on screen, discussing their emotions, arguing, exchanging witty repartee, and performing no more violent action than drinking a cup of tea or using a telephone. ... "When are they going to do something?" the children demand, wriggling with boredom.'[33]

According to industry wisdom, however, the child audience was not in itself large enough to warrant its own line of production, so that whatever was done to secure the child audience 'must have an appeal also for the adult mind'. In addition, as Harold B. Franklin, President of West Coast Theatres, noted, children did not like pictures for children: 'Most of them are quick and bright if you give them something to be quick and bright about, but I doubt if we can expect them to appreciate the subtleties of O'Neill drama. Children are not sophisticates.'[34]

In the terminology of 'sophistication' lies one point of origin for the debates over movie censorship and regulation in the early 1930s. A steady stream of smaller exhibitors wrote to the trade press complaining of too much 'sophistication' in the product. One exhibitor in Saskatchewan observed that the majority of his patrons had been to the sound pictures of a rival, and disliked them: 'Some say that it's bad enough to have to see suggestive pictures, but the talk makes it fifty times worse.'[35] A theatre-owner in Harrisburg, Illinois, wrote that:

All the complaint I have had during the year I have been showing talking pictures has been on this one thing, smut lines and smut gags, placed in the picture by some nitwit who thought it would get a laugh, and it always does from the roughnecks and morons ... [I]t may be okey [sic] for the large cities but I doubt that the city dads and mothers want their kids to listen to any such trash. Anyway, out here in this small town and in all others it's bad medicine for our business and is going to bring down a lot of blue nosed ladies before the local city council wanting something done about the matter ... from the standpoint of the exhibitor in the small town of 50,000 and under, something had better be done about it or there is going to be plenty done by people who do not have our interests at heart.[36]

As this letter indicated, if what publisher Martin Quigley called 'the Voice of Main Street' was not listened to at the box office, it would find other ways to make itself heard.[37]

In marked contrast to the utopia of aesthetic democracy described earlier by Dorothy Calhoun, by 1930 reviews in the trade press were applying a generic typology of audiences which assumed that, in fact, very few pictures would play with equal success in all markets. The primary purpose of these reviews was to provide exhibitors with information about a picture's suitability for their particular situations; once it had been acknowledged that pictures no longer appealed indiscriminately, there was an evident purpose in developing a typology of audiences through which an exhibitor could identify his or her clientele. The examples discussed here come predominantly from *Variety*. To perform its function, the review had to identify the probable audience or audience fraction to whom the movie would appeal, in terms sufficiently familiar for the exhibitor to recognise. *Variety*'s peculiar deployment of language makes this procedure relatively easy to spot. The periodical's reviewers were good structuralists: their categorical system was constructed around a series of binary oppositions, although several of the categories delineated by these binaries overlapped with each other. It was, however, implicit in the reviewing discourse that the tastes and preferences of different sections of the audience were, if not exactly mutually exclusive, at least clearly set against each other. This is, indeed, the feature of the system that makes it appropriate to describe it as a generic typology: particular tastes were ascribed to audience fractions so as to create a correspondence between an identified audience group and a particular production feature, whether that be of plot, casting or story type. The ideal production, however, appealed across a binary opposition, however that opposition was constructed.

The dominant distinction in early 1930s reviews was between metropolitan audiences and 'the hinterland', between 'Broadway' and 'Main Street'.[38] *Melody Man*, for example, was described as a 'good neighborhood film ... for the sticks the picture ought to appeal, but for metropolite Americans there are several inconsistent sequences'.[39] The system of distinction was, in part, a categorisation of theatre types: the Wheeler-Woolsey comedy *Peach O'Reno* was described as 'Okay for the minor spots but out of order in a Broadway deluxer'.[40] The Barbara Stanwyck vehicle *Shopworn* 'sums up to a mediocre picture for the class house, but a prospect of prosperity in the lower strata of cinemadom'.[41] *They Just Had to Get Married*, a Slim Summerville–ZaSu Pitts comedy, was a

pinch booking for houses of Mayfair calibre, on main streets of big keys, but as a lesser situation and small-town attraction okay. Out in the spots where the non-sophisticates exist, whether in A-houses in small communities or B-operations in medium-sized cities, picture should make some money ... Slim Summerville and ZaSu Pitts as a team are strong draws in many of the minor situations where audiences like their homey type of comedy and plain, everyday pans. Neither Summerville nor Miss Pitts, together or individually, carry in the first-runs of the big towns.[42]

In distinguishing between 'the upper strata of fans' and 'the commonality', however, *Variety*'s reviewers laid a classification of audiences conducted in terms of their 'sophistication' over the classification of theatres. Sophistication was understood to be an exclusively metropolitan characteristic.[43] Jean Renoir's *La Chienne* was described as 'Okay for sophisticated audiences that look for a taste of spice in a ritzy spot ... But a few releases of that sort in the neighborhoods will sure detract the masses from helping the grosses'.[44] On the other hand, *Cohens and Kellys in Scotland* was 'full of sure-fire laughs for the Grade-B audience, with the makers probably not intending it for higher consumption', while *Sailor Be Good*, a Jack Oakie comedy that turned out to be one of the *Motion Picture Herald's* box-office champions for 1933, 'may go over with the small-town clientele, and might please in the rough city nabes, but on Broadway it's wearing a straw hat and a linen duster ... It will get by where they are not particular'.[45]

Variety's typology of audiences displayed the paper's Broadway bias, as well as its origins as an organ of the theatrical and vaudeville trade. In the opinion of its reviewers, who evidently believed that 'the only persons qualified to judge of the drawing appeal or value of a picture are those who are in daily contact with Broadway', it was impossible to underestimate the taste or the comprehension of the non-metropolitan audience.[46] They worried that 'the hinterland' might not accept the 'unorthodox presentation' of Maurice Chevalier's occasional direct address to the camera in Ernst Lubitsch's *One Hour With You*.[47] They thought it unlikely that the thematic significance of *Death Takes a Holiday* would be appreciated or understood 'out among the whistle stops'.[48]

Within this classification of types of theatre and the audience types who inhabited them, *Variety*'s reviewers also distinguished among the audience of any given theatre. Here the preponderant distinction was one of gender, followed by that of age. Female viewers were assumed to dominate movie choices: the Barbara Stanwyck vehicle *Forbidden*, directed by Frank Capra, was 'a cry picture for the girls and, on that presumption, stands a good chance of going out and getting itself and the theatres some coin'.[49] *A Farewell to Arms* was 'A woman's picture essentially ... It might be labelled the femmes' "All Quiet" – the romantic side of the great holocaust', so long as exhibitors opted to use 'the alternate ending [the "happy" finale to which the author Hemingway objected]'.[50] The 'femme appeal' of *Fashions of 1934* was 'obvious from the billing, so that takes care of the boys also'.[51] *Private Worlds*, a Walter Wanger production set in a mental hospital and starring Claudette Colbert, Charles Boyer and Joan Bennett, was 'a class flick, but with a femme appeal that should insure fair b.o.'.[52]

Appealing primarily to a male audience, as James Cagney vehicles did, was distinctly problematic. According to *Variety*'s review of *Taxi*, whenever Warners opened a new Cagney picture at the Strand theatre on Broadway, 'the boys start to gather early and a peek at 12.30 noon will reveal a good sized assemblage of 90% male', in the expectation of:

> this player socking all and sundry including all the women in the cast. There's even a distinct tremor of disappointment through the house when no wallop is forthcoming ... That element which delays deliveries to see a picture, and drops over from Eighth Avenue and West, goes in a big way for the manner in which James handles his film women.

But this review also doubted 'if the women are going to like *Taxi* to any great extent'.[53] By early 1934, the 'roughneck character work' and 'you-be-damned personality that Cagney has so assiduously developed in his last half-dozen subjects' was a source of increasing criticism. His enthusiastic and escalating violence against women was 'a dangerous experiment for an established star who has everything to lose and not much to gain by ultra methods of sensationalism ... It will bring the star a lot of startled fan attention, but in the long run the general fan reaction is likely to kick back if they let this sort of thing go to such extremes.'[54] The specifically male audience, 'the boys who go for the gangster stuff', was relatively small and exclusively metropolitan. They would 'either stay away or Bronx' a musical like the Janet Gaynor–Charles Farrell vehicle *Delicious.* 'But that should be okay with *Delicious.* Its potential audience is larger than that drawn by the gun mellers, and it's tradition that a technically mediocre talker of this type will do a lot better than a rougher feature of equal rating.'[55]

The equivalent female audience, on the other hand – young metropolitan women aspiring to the condition of Clara Bow or Alice White – was frequently addressed. These were 'the Woolworth sirens' who made up 'the stenographer trade', and read the fan magazines in largest number. The 'extra saucy lines and business' inserted into movies like *Such Men Are Dangerous*, *Playing Around* and *Beauty and the Boss* – what Main Street called 'smut' – were aimed at them. Every studio turned out 'bunches' of such movies, 'aiming them squarely at the flapper trade and generally hitting the mark'. But the ingredients that gave them 'flap appeal' also caused them to 'suffer censorial shears in other spots'.[56]

The extent to which the undifferentiated audience was recognised as a fiction was indicated in 1932 by a set of proposals formulated by distribution executives at United Artists and MGM/Loew's Inc. to segregate theatres, audiences and pictures by eliminating subsequent runs. The plan, initially devised by UA's head of distribution Al Lichtman, proposed that theatres and product would both be classified as either 'A' or 'B'. 'A' product would show only in 'A' theatres, where tickets were to be priced at a minimum of fifty cents. 'A' product would never be released to 'B' theatres, and was never to be exhibited at less than fifty cents a ticket. According to Lichtman, 'under present conditions, we are selling 50-cent pictures for 10 cents and 10-cent pictures for 50 cents, a system which results in dissatisfaction to the public and terrific losses to the picture industry, as well as in most of the misunderstanding and ill-will between distributors and exhibitors.'[57]

Both Loew's and UA put a version of these proposals into effect in the 1932–33 season. According to the *Motion Picture Herald*, the Lichtman plan was 'a dollar success', but it created a 'storm of protest' among exhibitors. Lichtman's own plan actually only took notice of just over half the exhibition sites in the country: he envisaged around 3,000 Class 'A' theatres and 5,000 Class 'B' theatres. The fate of the others was indicated in alternative versions of the scheme, which proposed restricting the exhibition of some pictures to some theatres on the basis of their admission prices. According to M. A. Lightman, President of the Motion Picture Theatre Owners of America (MPTOA), houses charging 15 cents or less, or showing double features, should only 'show product built for them'.[58] The principle underlying these proposals was summarised by W. W. Hodkinson, the founder of Paramount, who proposed advising the public: 'here is a picture, of a certain class, at a certain house, at a certain time, at a certain price. It is now available. You see it now, or never.' Such a procedure, he suggested, 'does not prevent us from having inexpensive pictures in inexpensive theatres for poor people'.[59] But it was explicitly designed to prevent 'higher class patrons' from attending 'dime houses'. Lightman accused these people of 'cheating the industry out of hundreds of thousands of dollars,' since they were trying 'to buy a Lincoln for the price of a Ford':

> If product built for the 10-cent houses were shown in 10-cent houses then the industry would do two things. It would divorce the high-class patron from the 10-cent theatre, thus making him available to the theatres in the higher bracket and would be doing the exhibitor operating the 10-cent theatre a favor because he would again get busy catering to his old-time patron, the mass that wants that type of picture. It is for him that dialogue should be cut to a minimum and where comedy, action, speed should be used widely. We have allowed two very serious things to happen; we have deprived higher class theatres of their rightful patrons and we have driven out the child patron and the class who formerly filled our theatres on Saturdays.[60]

Opposing all these suggestions, Abram Myers, President of the independent exhibitors' trade association, Allied States, argued that they were simply wrong to assume

> that every patron of a low admission theatre is a potential patron of a grade A house. As a theatregoer I know this is not so. Zoning and protection have diverted as much of the normal patronage from neighborhood houses into first run houses as the latter can hope to get. ... [The patronage of neighbourhood houses in Washington] is so different from the downtown houses that they do not even look alike ... I do not believe the elderly people, the very young people, and the people who do not wish to go downtown – not to mention those to whom a difference of from 15¢ to 25¢ is an item – are going to be clubbed into attending the grade A exclusive run houses.[61]

Other exhibitors denounced these plans as being designed solely to operate to the benefit of the major companies, and likely to provoke public resentment. A New Mexico exhibitor asked, 'Are they going to force such a plan whereby the poor or laboring class could not afford to see a good picture but would have to be satisfied in seeing only cheap and inferior pictures?'[62]

These positions occupied relatively little common ground, but they did acknowledge a common problem in what Lightman called 'the basic principle of our present system ... that all pictures should appeal to all people all the time', an idea he thought 'ridiculous'.[63] While silent cinema audiences had differentiated themselves by choosing among the presentational styles of different theatres as well as between types of production, the conversion to sound meant that the burden of differentiation had fallen more heavily on the picture itself. The production industry had not yet accommodated its output to meet the change in demand, and audiences – particularly less 'sophisticated' audiences – were being lost as a result.

On several occasions in the early 1930s, the *Motion Picture Herald* – Martin Quigley's trade paper – sought to demonstrate that the industry's most profitable pictures were those that played to broader audiences. It argued that 'The sophisticated type of motion picture, however smart it may be, however much of clever, even brilliant dialogue it may contain', may be successful in the largest metropolitan centres, but it:

> cannot draw audiences to the box office window at the theatres of the larger body of subsequent-run theatres. These exhibitors, whose potential audience does not have the same variety of taste found in the large city, cannot realize a reasonable profit, if any at all, from the presentation of the sophisticated film ... On the other hand, the truly unsophisticated, homely type of simple, and perhaps romantic film story, is not only greatly desired by the smaller community exhibitors, but is the sort of film from which they derive their greatest profit, which will draw their particular audience to the box office, and which send that audience from the theatre with a definite feeling of satisfaction.

The *Herald* article quoted B. P. Schulberg's admission that the industry's mistake had been to listen 'all too often to the articulate minority' and to overlook 'the inarticulate majority. The result has been many pictures brilliantly done and praised by the articulate few but without mass appeal.'[64] The 'articulate minority' here conflated the Broadway critics, the slumming highbrows in the 'dime' houses, and the 'flapper' fans whom *Photoplay* had been so assiduously educating into a 'sophisticated' knowledge of Hollywood. The neglected audience identified by the *Herald* and also by the MPPDA was the anxious provincial bourgeoisie, gathering together in their women's clubs and PTAs to worry about what their children were seeing and, with MPPDA guidance, to endorse what they identified as 'Better Films'. The *Herald* quoted Carl Milliken, Secretary of the MPPDA, as arguing in February 1933 that 'the fan audience comprised of only "fans" is finished for the reason that the so-called fan no longer has as much money to spend on entertainment'. Contrary to received industry wisdom, he claimed, unsophisticated box-office pictures, endorsed by various previewing groups, figured prominently in the *Herald*'s roll-call of box-office champions. These lists of endorsed pictures, he maintained, 'in addition to stopping sweeping criticism of films, are building audiences of people who never went to pictures before because of a lack of interest'.[65]

The crucial discursive manoeuvre in persuading both producers and exhibitors to follow this course involved the redefinition of one audience fraction: the redescription of the 'juvenile' audience as the 'family' audience. Along with this came a series of new marketing strategies exploiting the educational potential of prestige productions, particularly literary adaptations. The key events in this cycle were the box office success of *Little Women* in November 1933, and the agreement, a month later, between the MPPDA and the National Council of English Teachers to sponsor English instruction through films, using screen guides for films, of which *Little Women* was the first.[66]

In September 1934, Fox MidWest theatres introduced a system of film classification in advertising, describing pictures as either 'family' or 'adult', using the opinions of the reviewing groups organised by the MPPDA. They hoped that this strategy would 'return to the parents of young theatergoers the responsibility for the selection of films for children'.[67] More importantly than local initiatives such as this were campaigns of educational advertising designed to attract 'the patronage of elements in the community who demand so-called better films, and pictures of special appeal', using Study Guides and other targeted appeal. MGM sent a booklet noting educational points in its 1935–6 product to 35,000 teachers. In 1935, RKO's sales promotion manager Leon J. Bamberger estimated that the recovery in the size of the weekly audience from its nadir in 1932 was due not to the return of the fan audience, but to the increased attendance of 'an element of the population which, up to 1931, had sought its entertainment elsewhere than "at the movies". Our function has been to reach the more cultured people who would appreciate fine entertainment, through channels other than those normally developed by our publicity and advertising departments.'[68]

By 1935, the flapper had disappeared from Hollywood's discourse on its audience. She had evolved into a character Terry Ramsaye called 'Tillie-the-Toiler, the busy, yearning little girl who supports the box office': 'Tillie ... does not want to go home from the show with any more problems than she had when she started out for the evening. Tillie wants action and satisfaction. She wants to feel, not to think and worry and reason.'[69]

Tillie was as much an ideological construct, and as much half of a binary opposition, as her predecessor, but it was a differently configured opposition, just as the claims made for the existence of a unified audience in 1935 differed in tone from those of 1930. Variety's notorious comment 'Sticks Nix Hick Pix' actually headlined a story in July 1935 in which Joe Kinsky of the Tri-State Amusement Corporation of Davenport, Iowa, asserted that films such as The Barretts of Wimpole Street, The House of Rothschild and The Scarlet Pimpernel were among the best grossers in the 'Silo Belt'.[70] Unconvinced, Variety continued to suggest that pictures like The Petrified Forest or The Story of Louis Pasteur would play over the heads of the general audience.[71] 'Sophistication', however, acquired a different tone by mid-decade, no longer commanding such box office attention: The Little Colonel was 'skilful hokum that will please in general, although the sophisticated minority may make a point of being superior to such sentimentality'.[72]

In August 1935, the MPPDA initiated a plan to encourage attendance among non-theatre-goers through a 'Picture of the Month' club involving schoolchildren and women's and men's groups, targeting different pictures at different groups: Peter Ibbetson for women, and Lives of a Bengal Lancer for men. As many as 200,000 study guides had been printed for a single film. Distributors were reported as now realising 'that any study and/or discussion of outstanding photoplays in the schoolroom or clubroom eventually reaches the home, where because of the high type of production under discussion there comes a realization by the family of the high standard of such pictures'.[73] Although this new view of production provoked some exhibitor complaint – Ed Kuykendall, Mississippi exhibitor and President of the MPTOA, described the resulting pictures as 'too arty, too costumy and too morbid' – the films proved, for a while at least, to be highly successful.[74]

Hollywood's generic typology of its audience in the early 1930s thus appears highly differentiated. Some groups, such as Variety's metropolites and femmes, were apparently considered central, while other audience fractions, including the hicks in the hinterland and the character Terry Ramsaye called 'Hollywood's Forgotten Man – the All-American Dad', were marginalised.[75] This pattern fits neither Hollywood's officially-advertised self-image nor our current perceptions of its ideological activity, but it raises interesting questions for both. This discursive differentiation among audiences may well also explain, at least in part, why the stars and the movies which consistently appear at the top of trade paper polls – Will Rogers and Marie Dressler, for example – hardly feature in most histories of the period. Our histories are as biased toward metropolitan sources as the major companies were in constructing their output. In addition, it suggests that the calls for the regulation of film content in this period can in part be understood, as Ramsaye suggested, as 'an awkward expression of demand'.[76]

Extrapolating from the account presented here, I would argue that the Classical Hollywood industry was engaged in a periodic process of reinventing and reconfiguring its audience. These reconfigurations typically sought to discover a 'new' audience who had previously not attended: the urban sophisticates and 'highbrows' in 1929 or the clubwomen and families of 1935, who were also described as 'new millions into the theatres who previously did not attend because of their old attitude toward the motion picture as "low brow stuff".'[77] The strategy of reconfiguration also sought to unite the existing audience with this new audience. In the process of doing this, it constantly addressed Will Hays's proposal to 'improve the quality of demand'. What was created by the new form of address to this enlarged, undifferentiated audience was a bourgeois cinema of prestigious uplift: the costume dramas, biopics and literary adaptations of the second half of the 1930s, accompanied by their Study Guides, through which the bourgeois audience was encouraged to recognise Hollywood's cultural respectability.

Notes

1 Eric Johnston, *The Motion Picture Industry on the Threshold of a Decisive Decade* (New York: Motion Picture Association of America, 1946).

2 Leo Handel, *Hollywood Looks at Its Audience: A Report of Film Audience Research* (Urbana: University of Illinois Press, 1950), p. 9; Susan Ohmer, 'Measuring desire: George Gallup and audience research in Hollywood', *Journal of Film and Video* vol. 43 nos. 1 and 2 (Spring and Summer 1991), pp. 11–12.

3 'Conference between representatives of the Producers branch and representatives of the Directors branch on the subject of economies in motion picture production; meeting being held and authorized by the Academy of Motion Picture Arts and Sciences', Los Angeles, California, 14 July 1927, pp. 40–1; MPA, Reel 3, 1927, Academy of Motion Picture Arts and Sciences file.

4 This conception of Hollywood as a generic cinema is elaborated in Richard Maltby, *Hollywood Cinema: An Introduction* (Oxford: Blackwell, 1995), Chapter 3. See also Steve Neale, 'Melo talk: on the meaning and use of the term "melodrama" in the American trade press', *The Velvet Light Trap* 22 (Fall 1993), pp. 66–89; Tino Balio, *Grand Design: Hollywood as a Modern Business Enterprise 1930–1939* (New York: Scribner's, 1993).

5 Lee, Academy conference, p. 38.

6 Campbell MacCulloch, 'The real boss of the pictures', *Motion Picture Classic*, February 1931, pp. 28–9, 94.

7 MacCulloch, 'The real boss of the pictures', p. 94.

8 Sidney R. Kent, 'Distributing the product', in Joseph P. Kennedy (ed.), *The Story of the Films* (Chicago: A. W. Shaw, 1927), pp. 211–4.

9 Samuel Katz, 'Theatre management', in Kennedy, *Story*, pp. 265–6. Universal, for instance, surveyed a 20-square block area, with a population of 150,000, before deciding to build a 3,000-seat theatre in the New Utrecht Avenue district of Brooklyn. *Harvard Business Reports Vol. 8: Cases on the Motion Picture Industry*, ed. Howard T. Lewis, (New York: McGraw-Hill, 1930), pp. 480–4.

10 Katz, 'Theatre management', pp. 271–2; Douglas Gomery, *Shared Pleasures: A History of Movie Presentation in the United States* (London: BFI, 1992), p. 49; *Harvard Business Reports* Vol. 8, pp. 516–9.

11 *Harvard Business Reports* Vol. 8, p. 133.

12 Review, 'The Greeks had a word for them', *Variety*, 9 February 1932.

13 See Richard Maltby, 'It happened one night: the recreation of the patriarch', in *Frank Capra and Columbia Pictures: Authorship and the Studio System*, ed. Robert Sklar (Philadelphia:Temple University Press, 1998), pp. 130–63.

14 *Motion Picture Herald* [henceforth: *MPH*], 2 July 1932, p. 36.

15 *MPH*, 14 May 1932, p. 9.

16 *MPH*, 12 January 1935, p. 53.

17 'How far is Broadway from the United States?', *MPH*, 3 June 1933, p. 19.

18 'They don't want to show the Cavalcades and Grasses and Tabus. And if we didn't have block booking we'd never get our best films into above 5 percent of the theatres in the country. I know what they'd do without block booking. They'd run sex fifty-two weeks in the year. Don't tell me about selling decent films. Why, man, we make a decent film like *Cavalcade* or *State Fair*. And then we sit down and watch a cheap piece of tripe about a woman of the streets like [Mae West in *She Done Him Wrong*, presumably] come and pack 'em in to standing room all over the country. *MPH*, 3 June 1933, p. 19.

19 *MPH*, 21 May 1932, p. 16.

20 *Harvard Business Reports* Vol. 8, pp. 523, 421–5.

21 Several trade papers conducted surveys to determine industry attitudes to the strategy. *Harvard Business Reports* Vol. 8, p. 421.

22 *Harvard Business Reports* Vol. 8, pp. 421–4.

23 Reginald Taviner, 'What talkies did to America', *Motion Picture Classic*, March 1931, p. 24.

24 Taviner, p. 26.

25 Taviner, p. 105.

26 *Exhibitors Herald-World*, 21 September 1929, p. 21.

27 Ibid., 17 August 1929, p. 42.

28 The quotations from Schulberg and Calhoun are both from Dorothy Calhoun, 'The changing movie audience', *Motion Picture Classic*, July 1930, p. 78.

29 Will H. Hays, 'Annual report to the Motion Picture Producers and Distributors of America, Inc.', MPH, 16 April 1932, p. 22.

30 Calhoun, p. 78; Campbell MacCulloch, 'Menaces of the movies', *Motion Picture Classic*, December 1930, p. 24. According to this account, the loss was noticed in January 1930, although trade papers were commenting on the phenomenon in August 1929. *Exhibitors Herald-World*, 17 August 1929, p. 40; Editorial, *MPH*, 31 May 1930, p. 8.

31 MacCulloch, 'Menaces of the movies', p. 84.

32 This realisation was commonly offered as an explanation for Douglas Fairbanks's decision to retire from production. See, for example, MacCulloch, p. 24.

33 Ibid., pp. 24–5.

34 Ibid., p. 26.

35 *Exhibitors Herald-World*, 17 August 1929, p. 42.

36 Steve Farrer, Colonial Amusement Company, Harrisburg, Ill., ' "Smut" in pictures', *Exhibitors Herald-World*, 11 January 1930, p. 56.

37 Editorial, *Exhibitors Herald-World*, 1 February 1930.

38 Review, '*One Hour with You*', *Variety*, 29 March 1932.

39 Review, '*Melody Man*', *Variety*, 26 February 1930.

40 Review, '*Peach O'Reno*', *Variety*, 29 Dec 1931.

41 Review, '*Shopworn*', *Variety*, 5 April 1932.

42 Review, '*They Just Had to Get Married*', *Variety*, 14 February 1933.

43 *Harvard Business Reports* Vol. 8, p. 523,

44 Review, '*La Chienne*', *Variety*, 12 January 1932.

45 Review, '*Cohens and Kellys in Scotland*', *Variety*, 12 March 1930; Review, '*Sailor Be Good* ', *Variety*, 28 February 1933.

46 *Harvard Business Reports* Vol. 8, p. 523.

47 Review, '*One Hour With You*', *Variety*, 29 March 1932.

48 Review, '*Death Takes a Holiday*', *Variety*, 27 February 1934.

49 Review, '*Forbidden*', *Variety*, 12 January 1932.

50 Review, '*A Farewell to Arms*', *Variety*, 13 December 1932.

51 Review, '*Fashions of 1934*', *Variety*, 23 January 1934.

52 Review, '*Private Worlds*', *Variety*, 3 April 1935.

53 Review, '*Taxi*', *Variety*, 12 January 1931.

54 Review, '*Lady Killer*', *Variety*, 2 January 1934.

55 Review, '*Delicious*', *Variety*, 29 December 1931.

56 Reviews, '*Such Men Are Dangerous*', *Variety*, 12 March 1930; '*Playing Around* ', *Variety*, 2 April 1930; '*Beauty and the Boss*', *Variety*, 5 April 1932.

57 Terry Ramsaye, 'Distributors consider plan to eliminate subsequent runs', *MPH*, 14 May 1932, p. 10. In 1931, there were approximately 14,500 theatres operating in the United States. Of those, 2,250 were in circuits or chains owned by or affiliated with the Big Five major companies. Another 1,200 were run by circuits unaffiliated to the majors. Together they comprised approximately 25 per cent of the theatres, but they also represented approximately 50 per cent of the seating capacity of all theatres, and they paid something like 70 per cent of rental fees to the distributors. The remaining 11,000, which were owned and operated as independent, individual concerns on much the same basis as the corner drug store, thus actually produced only 30 per cent of the distributors' income. Half the people who went to the movies in the US saw them in independently owned theatres, most of them 'Mom and Pop' theatres servicing small towns and suburban areas, but their seeing movies was a matter of peripheral economic importance to the major companies. Indeed, under certain circumstances, it was to the majors' economic disadvantage, and the economic interests of the major distributors and the small independent exhibitors were, therefore, frequently in direct opposition to each other. For the distributors, servicing the small exhibitor could significantly

interfere with their maximising profits. MGM distribution executives cited an example, in the small city of St. Joseph, Missouri. When they sold their pictures exclusively to a first-run theatre, they earned an average of $500 a picture. In a subsequent season, they also sold the pictures to a smaller and cheaper subsequent-run theatre, from which they earned an average of $22.50, but it resulted in their income from the first-run theatre dropping to $100 per picture. *MPH*, 14 May 1932, 11.

58 *MPH*, 21 May 1932, p. 16.

59 *MPH*, 16 July 1932, p. 10.

60 *MPH*, 21 May 1932, p. 16.

61 *MPH*, 28 May 1932, p. 79.

62 *MPH*, 21 May 1932.

63 *MPH*, 21 May 1932, p. 16.

64 *MPH*, 16 April 1932, p. 9.

65 *MPH*, 4 February 1933, p. 14.

66 *MPH*, 9 December 1933 p. 12.

67 *MPH*, 8 September 1934, p. 13.

68 *MPH*, 27 July 1935, p. 13.

69 Terry Ramsaye, ' "Highbrow" productions – and Tillie', *MPH*, 28 May 1932.

70 'Sticks Nix Hick Pix', *Variety*, 17 July 1935, p. 1.

71 Reviews, '*The Petrified Forest*' and '*The Story of Louis Pasteur*', *Variety*, 12 February 1936.

72 Review, '*The Little Colonel*' , *Variety*, 27 March 1935.

73 *MPH*, 31 August 1935, p. 13.

74 *MPH*, 16 November 1935.

75 Terry Ramsaye, 'The forgotten man', Editorial, MPH, 3 September 1932, p. 8.

76 MPH, 14 May 1932, p. 9.

77 *MPH*, 16 November 1935.

2 Female Audiences of the 1920s and early 1930s

Melvyn Stokes

One of the major debates within film studies in recent years has focused on the issue of female spectatorship. This is explicable in terms of a complex synergy of developments, including the rise of film studies itself as a discipline, increasing academic interest in mass entertainment and popular culture, the politicisation of many French film theorists in the aftermath of May 1968, the modern feminist movement in Britain and the United States, and – particularly in Britain – developments in avant-garde film-making. For the most part, however, this work has been devoted to female spectatorship as a theoretical construct. 'The female spectator', Mary Ann Doane pointedly declared, 'is a concept, not a person.'[1] Seen against the background from which it emerged, this theoretical preoccupation is relatively easy to understand. Yet it has helped to conceal (and, in all probability, also to encourage) the comparative neglect of female spectatorship as defined in social, historical and cultural terms.

What work there has been in terms of the analysis of historical female spectatorship has tended to follow one of two main paths. The first focuses on how Hollywood addressed women in particular periods (through films themselves, product 'tie-ups' and licensing deals, advertising, publicity, and fan magazines) as consumers of commodities and/or constructed images of femininity.[2] The second endeavours to investigate the reactions of women spectators to film texts either by contextualising their response historically[3] or by interrogating spectators on their cinematic memories in what have come to be known as 'ethnographic' surveys. While the second pathway seems to offer the prospect of getting closer to an understanding of how women have experienced cinema, and the meanings they created out of that experience, it has so far produced less than a handful of publications.[4] From the point of view of understanding the American female response to the cinema, moreover, ethnography in particular has two major limitations. The studies that have so far appeared have mainly dealt with foreign rather than American responses to Hollywood. They also concentrate, for obvious reasons to do with the availability of source materials, on female film-going since around 1940.

In this chapter, I will examine what available materials there are to construct a history of female spectatorship for an earlier period: the 1920s and early 1930s. In cinema, this was a crucial period: it saw, among many other transformations, the growth of the studio system, the further development of movie 'stardom', the innovation of sound, and the beginnings of more formal self-regulation of the industry. For women, it was the period immediately after the ratification of the nineteenth amendment, giving them the vote (1920). It witnessed the social and cultural changes and conflicts of the 1920s and the enormous and wide-ranging effects of the Great Depression. The analysis of female spectatorship in this era, therefore, might perhaps offer fresh perspectives on both the history of the cinema and the history of women themselves.

The 'Myth' of the Dominant Female Audience

The early exponents of 'scientific' audience research, George Gallup (who founded Audience Research Inc.) and Leo Handel (of the Motion Picture Research Bureau), set out to challenge what they saw as a widespread myth that women made up a decisive majority of cinema audiences. Surveys done by ARI for RKO in 1937–39 discovered that women made up 'only' 51 per cent of movie-goers.[5] In *Hollywood Looks At Its Audience* (1950), Handel – citing surveys conducted in New York City in December 1941 and Iowa in April 1942, as well as ARI findings – insisted that men and women attended the movies 'at about equal rates'. Handel did concede that there was evidence to the contrary, but he dismissed one 1942 survey conducted by the Women's Institute of Audience Reactions, which found women making up 65 per cent of the movie audience, as unscientific and 'unrepresentative'.[6]

There has been a tendency, on the part of present-day film scholars, to assume that Gallup and Handel were making statements that transcended the period in which they were made. Garth Jowett, for example, rather than regarding ARI's findings concerning the proportion of women in audiences as relating to the late 30s (when the surveys were done), saw them as effectively destroying the 'long-held' belief that women constituted a clear majority of the audience.[7] It is highly questionable whether results from one period, even if accurate, can be applied to another. Women may have made up 51 per cent of the audience towards the end of the 1930s and in the 1940s, but there is no necessary presumption that the same is true for earlier or later times. Moreover, while Handel himself was hardly ever reluctant to make claims for the accuracy and 'scientific' nature of his work, he was careful to qualify what he said in dismissing the idea that women made up 65–70 per cent of audiences generally by admitting the possibility (though not the probability) that 'this proportion held true at some time in the past'.[8]

Before the work of Gallup and Handel, the evidence we have in relation to the gender composition of audiences is largely impressionistic. In 1920, a *New York Times* writer estimated that 60 per cent of movie audiences were women.[9] The trade press, in subsequent years, opted for even higher figures. An article in *Photoplay* in 1924 set the proportion of women at 75 per cent; one in *Moving Picture World* in 1927 thought they made up an astonishing 83 per cent of cinema audiences.[10] A local survey of school-children in Evansville, Indiana, in 1923 produced some rare empirical evidence to support the notion of more women than men attending the movies. It suggested, during their teens, that boys' attendance at the movies declined while that of girls increased.[11] Such estimates and surveys may have been inaccurate individually, but collectively they suggest an impressive weight of evidence to buttress the idea of a predominantly female audience. Whether women really formed a considerable majority of the cinema audience of the 20s and 30s, however, may actually be of less importance than the fact that Hollywood itself assumed that, both through their own attendance and their ability to influence men, they were its primary market. 'It has become an established fact', asserted the *Exhibitors Herald and Moving Picture World* in March 1928, 'that women fans constitute the major percentage of patronage or at least cast the final vote in determining the majority patronage.'[12]

The assumption, on the part of an industry dominated by men, that to be profitable it had to appeal mainly to women, had a profound effect on the way that American cinema developed during the 1920s and 1930s. A high proportion of 20s films were female-centred melodramas and romances.[13] They were often written by women scriptwriters, frequently adapting material from popular fiction also written by women mainly for women.[14] They featured female stars, who outnumbered their male equivalents and seemed to spring from an apparently endless pool of talent (the 1920 census listed 14,000 actresses).[15] In the next decade, such films gave place to a whole new genre: the 'women's film'.[16] During the first half of the 30s, according to Tino Balio, films of this type made up over a quarter of all the movies on *Film Daily*'s 'Ten Best' list.[17]

The star system itself was primarily aimed at women (one theatre manager would later describe most movie houses as 'Valentino traps').[18] Women made up the great majority of movie fans and the discursive apparatus attached to the cinema in the form of fan magazines and articles on the stars in newspapers, periodicals and women's magazines, was addressed mainly to them. As Kathryn H. Fuller has observed, the construction of this discursive apparatus from 1915 onward amounted to a major reconfiguration of the images of audiences and fans that had by the 1920s made fan magazines 'the major promoters of the image of a female-dominated movie audience'.[19] As the American economy moved from one based on production to one oriented toward mass consumption, the film industry was also quick to appreciate the importance of women as consumers. Charles Eckert noted that 'statistics widely disseminated in the late 1920s and early 1930s' showed 'that women made 80 to 90 per cent of all purchases for family use'.[20] Through advertising associated with product 'tie-ups' and licensing deals, business and the studios in combination set out to sell a range of commodities to women movie-goers. These included goods (clothes, cosmetics) designed for women's own use, as well as more general household products (for example, appliances). The need to appeal to women as consumers in turn influenced the character of the films being made: 'modern films' offered wider opportunities for showcasing products and story-lines were frequently created or amended in order to facilitate tie-ups.[21] Whether it involved the production of particular kinds of films, the development of the star system, or the attempt to appeal to women as consumers, a weight of evidence suggested that the movie industry of the 1920s and early 30s was clearly oriented towards serving (and therefore making a profit from) a dominant female audience.

The attempt to maximise the female audience also affected local conditions of exhibition. It helped determine *when* films were shown (at one point, Molly Haskell remarked, 'the "matinee audience" had considerable influence on movie production and on the popularity of certain stars'.[22]) It may well additionally have influenced the environment *where* they were shown. According to Jeanne Allen, an article of 1927 in *Theatre Management* emphasised the significance of women as the principal 'component and motivators of film attendance', insisting that theatres as well as films should attract them by appealing to their 'sensibilities' and 'their desire for comfort and relax-

ation'. The magazine's recommendations, Allen noted, included 'art works in the lobbies, attractive fabrics and designs for interior decoration, and subdued and flattering
lighting'.[23]

Early Social Studies

While the movie industry of the 1920s and 30s operated on the assumption that women
were the most significant part of its audience, it did not itself take any public steps to
confirm (or investigate further) that assumption.[24] There are, however, a number of
sources from outside the industry that shed light on women's movie-going habits and
preferences during this period.

From the earliest years of the century onward, many Americans manifested an
increasing concern over the impact of movies on those who attended them. One
expression of this concern was the demand that movies should be censored. Another
was the attempt to investigate movie audiences themselves using the methodologies of
social science.[25] Since children were thought to be especially vulnerable to such influence, most of these earliest investigations (Portland, Oregon, in 1914; Iowa City in 1916;
Providence, Rhode Island in 1918) focused upon them.[26] In 1926, two psychologists
conducted a survey into the viewing tastes of adults in rural New England.[27] Although
these studies seemed to suggest, in general terms, the kinds of movies audiences
(especially young audiences) liked, they did not indicate whether females differed from
males in their cinema-going preferences.

The first real evidence that this might be the case came from the results of a survey
in 1923 of 37,000 high-school students in 76 cities done jointly by the Russell Sage
Foundation, the National Board of Review of Motion Pictures and Associated First
National Exhibitors. While most of the differences turned up in the last part of the survey were *geographical* (boys and girls in New England had as their favourite film *Way
Down East* [1920], while their equivalents in eastern, central and western states preferred *The Four Horsemen of the Apocalypse* [1921]), some evidence of different gender
preferences emerged as well. Girls in the South, for example, also voted for *Way Down
East*, while boys from that section supported *The Birth of a Nation* (1915). In terms of
favourite actors, boys preferred action or Western stars (Douglas Fairbanks was their
first choice); girls opted for stars of romance (Rudolph Valentino, perhaps predictably,
topped the poll in this category).[28]

A survey launched by Alice Miller Mitchell in 1926 into the movie-going practices of
10,052 Chicago children both confirmed and elaborated on such differences. Mitchell's
sample was drawn from three groups: children attending high schools and the last four
years of grade schools, juvenile delinquents, and members of the Scouts. In making her
survey, she relied primarily upon written questionnaires, though she also tested the
accuracy of these against material acquired in a number of 'follow-up' interviews and
held a number of 'group discussions'. Because the survey was conducted under supervised conditions (for example, in classrooms, with teachers present), together with the
fact that the children were asked their names and addresses, it is possible that some children responded in ways they deemed uncontroversial and safe. Yet many obviously did
not feel intimidated by these things and were not inclined to bowdlerise their answers
or respond in ways they may well have felt were expected of them. The questionnaire

From *Movie Weekly*, 11 August 1923.

itself had asked: 'How did the pictures make you feel?' 'On some of the quiz papers', Mitchell coldly remarked, 'unpublishable terms were written after this question.'[29]

Mitchell's team discovered that there was an 'approximately equal' average attendance of girls and boys at the movies, although girl Scouts, in particular, tended to go less frequently than the average (once or twice a week for the majority of children). Very few girls went to the movies alone; like the boys, they usually attended 'in groups and unaccompanied by adults'. Only a minority of girls went to the movies with their parents – the percentages of those who did varied from 31.9 (grade-schoolers) to 44.9 (girl

Scouts) – although 10 per cent of each group attended with an older brother or sister. Most girls of all ages (apart from Scouts, for whom the opposite was true) went to evening rather than afternoon performances. Sixty per cent of their movie-going (or nearly all in the case of the girl scouts) was concentrated at the weekend. Girls, like boys, usually selected which movie to see themselves, independently of their parents, and were most influenced in their choice by reports in the daily newspapers, followed (in the case of high school girls and Scouts) by the title of the film or (among grade school girls) by the posters seen in movie-theatre lobbies. But they were also much more likely than boys to be influenced by the presence in a film of a favourite actor.[30]

The sexes also differed substantially in the kinds of film they preferred. Whereas the boys expressed a clear preference as their first choice for Westerns, followed by adventure films, comedies and mysteries in that order, the most popular films chosen first by girls were romances, followed by comedies and Westerns.[31] Quite apart from the problems of definition involved in distinguishing between some of these descriptive categories, the general preferences concealed many cross-currents. Delinquent girls, for example, liked romances and Westerns better than any other types of movies; girl Scouts, by contrast, preferred comedy, mystery and tragedy as their first choices and were not impressed by romance pictures.[32] Tastes also changed in accordance with age. The most popular type of movie for grade school girls was the Western; for older high school girls, it was the romance.[33] While boys, especially younger boys, dismissed film romances as too 'mushy', girls – perhaps on the defensive against male prejudice – rationalised their preference as a 'practical' choice. One girl approved of romances 'because they show the different ways that people love one another and how some are crooks'. Another preferred them because they 'give me an idea of love'. A third liked watching a romance film 'because it sets a person to thinking about the future'.[34]

Mitchell's survey findings undermined what she described as the 'popular belief' that older children attended the movies more often than their younger counterparts. She found that grade schools girls patronised the movies more heavily than high school girls.[35] This could well be a reflection, of course, of the greater range of activities available to older girls. One of the most pioneering features of Mitchell's work was her attempt to contrast the attractiveness of the movies with other forms of leisure. It should have given considerable pause for thought to those apparently concerned by the all-pervasive effects of movies on children. In terms of physical activities, 89.7 per cent of girl Scouts preferred hiking to the 5.8 per cent who liked movies.[36] For high school girls, the comparable figures were 60.7 per cent to 23.8 per cent and for grade school girls 61.2 per cent to 29.9 per cent. When it came to the choice of riding in an automobile or entertainment at the movies, 69.8 per cent of girl Scouts expressed a preference for auto-riding, as opposed to 22.1 per cent for movies. The comparable figures for high school girls were 65.9 per cent to 17.6 per cent and for grade school students 67.4 per cent to 25.0 per cent. In terms of social activities, the bias was even more obvious: 84.5 per cent of Scouts preferred attending a party to the 6.7 per cent who preferred movies; 68.6 per cent of high school girls and 71.4 per cent of grade school girls shared the Scouts' preference (the vote for movies was 14.8 per cent and 19.3 per cent respectively). More remarkably, girl Scouts (by 57.6 per cent to 29.9 per cent) and high school girls (by 45.5 per cent to 35.7 per cent) preferred reading to movies. Only grade school girls, by 52.7 per cent to 36.9 per cent, preferred going to the movies instead of reading.[37]

When it came to recollections of particular movies, Mitchell pointed out, children's memories tended to focus especially on two categories: films they had seen recently or 'large, important ... superproductions' such as *The Birth of a Nation*, *The Covered Wagon* (1923), and *The Big Parade* (1925). Most of the comments on individual films she actually cited and identified by sex, unfortunately, were by boys and tended to concern 'action' movies like *The Sea Hawk* (1924). One movie that was occasionally cited by girls was *It* (1927), with Clara Bow. A tale of romantic misunderstanding and upward mobility, which finished with salesclerk Betty Lou (Bow) winning the hand of her boss, department store owner Cyrus Waltham (Antonio Moreno), it appealed to one high-school girl because – she improbably asserted – 'it was so like real life'. One of the questions in Mitchell's survey covered the 'thrills' children had had at the movies. *It* was one of the films mentioned by girls in response to this question. At one point, Betty Lou jumps into the water from Waltham's yacht in order (helped by Waltham himself) to try to save his existing fiancée. One girl considered this scene ('when they decided they both had it') had given her the greatest thrill she had ever experienced from a film.[38] Generally, while boys were most thrilled by the action sequences in Westerns and war movies, girls thought films of romance (full of scenes of 'loving and kissing and marrying', as one described it) were far more thrilling.[39]

While pioneering, and shedding some light on the female experience of cinema-going, the Mitchell investigation also had a number of significant drawbacks. The survey was confined to children. (The occasional references to adult movie-going were in the form of impressionistic observations. Mitchell, for example, wrote of the movies as 'a veritable escape for the housewife who, passively submerged in drab realities, finds a brief relief in film dreams that might have come true'.[40]) There were important gaps in the questions asked. The investigation was restricted to one locality only. The same year in which the results of the Mitchell survey were published, however, also saw the publication of the first of two studies which – while also local in character – provided information on the movie-going practices and preferences of women from differing age-groups and social backgrounds.

In 1924–5, Robert Staughton Lynd and Helen Merrell Lynd, assisted by a team of field workers, embarked upon the first detailed anthropological investigation of an American community. In 1935, they conducted a follow-up survey of the same city. The community they selected was Muncie, Indiana. The results of their surveys were published as *Middletown* (1929) and *Middletown in Transition* (1937). The first study confirmed some of the findings of the Mitchell investigation. It noted that the attendance of high school girls at the movies was 'about equal' to that of boys and that both girls and boys more commonly went to the movies without their parents (although, in the three upper years of high school, 33 per cent of girls attended the movies more often with their parents than without them, compared with 21 per cent of boys).[41]

The movies, the Lynds noted, had provoked cultural conflict within the 'Middletown' community. A number of middle-class women's clubs were fighting to 'clean up the movies', while the local Ministerial Association was expressing hostility to the showing of movies on Sundays. In opposition to these forces (according to the Lynds) were the owners and managers of the local theatres (whom they characterised as 'a group of men – a former peanut-stand proprietor, and a sometime bicycle racer and race promoter, and so on – whose primary concern is making money'.)[42]

Whether, and under what circumstances, adult women went to the cinema reflected their social position in the community at large and, if married, the social and religious opinions of their menfolk. One 'Middletown' woman cited by the Lynds had been in the habit of going to the cinema once or twice a week with her working-class husband. He had, however, subsequently been converted to religion and had become a preacher in a revivalistic sect. Neither he nor his wife any longer went to the movies, the woman explained, in a curious blend of moralism and practicality, ' 'cause our church says it's wrong – and it saves money, too'. At the other extreme were a number of liberal husbands cited by the Lynds who 'every week or so' stayed home with the children so that their wives could go to the movies.[43] It is not at all clear who, if anyone, these women went with.[44]

When it came to analysing the tastes of audiences, *Middletown* was largely impressionistic. Its authors cited 'the manager of the leading theater' as the only source for the claim that the most popular stars in the town were, in descending order, Harold Lloyd, Gloria Swanson, Thomas Meighan, Colleen Moore, Douglas Fairbanks, Mary Pickford and Norma Talmadge. In terms of the movies themselves, the authors claimed, the largest crowds were drawn to Harold Lloyd comedies. There were comparatively few popular comedies of this type, however. Expensively-produced Westerns and spectaculars, including *The Covered Wagon* or *The Hunchback of Notre Dame* (1923), 'drew heavy houses'. But the kind of movie that packed the motion picture houses of Middletown 'week after week' was always that 'with burning "heart interest" '.[45] Precisely what was meant by this was reasonably clear: it meant, in the Lynds' words, 'sex adventure' or 'sensational society' films. At one time, four of these films were running simultaneously in Middletown: *The Daring Years* (1923), *Sinners in Silk* (1924), *Women Who Give* (1924) and *The Price She Paid* (1924). On another occasion, the city's movie-goers had a choice of three: *Name the Man* ('a story of betrayed womanhood', 1924), *Rouged Lips* (1923), and *The Queen of Sin* (1924).[46]

In most of the films of this type, women were the main characters. It was widely believed that such films had a special appeal to female spectators, who were inscribed into the mode of address of much of the publicity surrounding them. 'Girls!', a large illustrated ad promised the potential viewers of one film, 'You will learn how to handle 'em!' One 'well-thumbed' copy of the *Motion Picture Magazine* in 'Middletown's' public library had an article on 'movie kisses' that was clearly addressed soleiy to women. 'Do you recognize your little friend, Mae Busch?', one caption enquired,

> She's had lots of kisses, but never seems to grow blasé. At least, you'll agree that she's giving a good imitation of a person enjoying this one, and if someone should catch you beneath the mistletoe and hold you there like this, what would you do? Struggle? But making love divinely is one of the best things Monte Blue does. Can't you just hear Marie Prevost's heart going pitty-pat?[47]

If films did not have sufficient romance in them to appeal to female movie-goers in

'Middletown', they apparently had little chance of attracting large audiences. *Down to the Sea in Ships* (1927), an expensive spectacular about whaling, failed at the town's leading theatre, its exhibitor asserted, because the whale was the real hero in the film and consequently 'there wasn't enough "heart interest" for the women'.[48]

The second study of Muncie, a decade later, found that movie advertisements 'were interchangeable with those of 1925'. Many captions were still designed to appeal primarily to girls ('You Can't Love a Married Man' or 'What's a Baby between Sweethearts – More or Less?'). One change since 1925 had been the introduction of Saturday matinées showing a special programme for children of both sexes.[49] In terms of specifically female cinema-going practices, the Lynds found that in Muncie, 'especially in the better-class houses, adult females predominate heavily in the audiences and, as one producer remarked, "set the type of picture that will 'go' " ' They buttressed this claim about Muncie (which they thought was 'probably representative of other localities') with an estimate from the owner of one of Muncie's 'better theatres' that his audiences 'consisted of 60 per cent women over sixteen, 30 per cent males over sixteen, and 10 per cent children'.[50]

The Lynds, in their second investigation, found a community characterised by tensions and conflicts. Some – notably those revolving around generational conflict and changes in the way gendered roles were constructed – had been considerably sharpened by the economic depression.[51] But they were also more certain than they had been in *Middletown* that movies were crucially affecting patterns of life. Everywhere in Muncie in 1935 they found 'a sense of sharp, free behavior between the sexes [patterned on the movies]'. They found adolescents modelling themselves on the manner and appearance of their favourite stars. Joan Crawford, they asserted, 'has her amateur counterparts in the high-school girls who stroll with brittle confidence in and out of "Barney's" soft-drink parlour, "clicking" with the "drugstore cowboys" at the tables'. Interestingly, the Lynds saw the girls imitating Crawford on screen as assertive and confident, in contrast to 'tongue-tied' young males.[52] The desire on the part of girls to resemble their movie idols now began at a very early age: even occasional third-graders, the Lynds noted, were using rouge, brightly colouring their fingernails and adopting 'Shirley Temple permanent waves'. It also produced conflicts with parents: 'The age at which one get's one's first "permanent" ', the Lynds noted, 'has become a standard subject of family controversy in Middletown homes'.[53]

The Blumer Study

Detailed information on movie-going habits and tastes, apart from that contained in episodic local surveys, was generally sparse until the early 1930s. Between 1933 and 1935, however, a series of eleven studies financed by the Payne Fund was published. The studies themselves, as Robert Sklar has pointed out, were suspect from the very beginning since their initiator, William H. Short of the National Committee for Study of Social Values in Motion Pictures, was pro-censorship and consequently moulded the project 'from the beginning by his special needs and goals: to get the goods on the movies, to nail them to the wall'.[54] Yet not all the heads of the studies had precisely the same ideas as Short. One in particular, Herbert Blumer of the University of Chicago, believed censorship was far *less* effective in dictating attitudes to the movies than countervailing influences, such as parents, teachers and peer group pressure.[55] One of the two studies Blumer did for the Payne Fund (and the only one he conducted on his own) was dedicated to advancing this proposition. Blumer later claimed to have circulated to a sample of nearly 2,000 people – mostly college and high school students – an invitation to write movie 'autobiographies' of the films they had seen and their responses to them. Extracts from over 300 of these autobiographies, as well as what he regarded as 'typical' examples of a number of complete autobiographies, were published in the book *Movies and Conduct* (1933). While the form used to tell people what to write about in most of the autobiographies and the final selection of material was obviously heavily conditioned by the argument Blumer wanted to make, and – as Kathryn Fuller has observed – he consistently altered biographical data when using multiple extracts from the seven autobiographies he published in full, there are still several reasons why this material ought to be of interest to students of female (and male) audiences and reception.[56]

In the first place, Blumer developed a reputation as a rigorous sociologist. After studying under George Herbert Meade and Robert Park, he taught sociology at Chicago from 1928 to 1939, when he moved to the University of California at Berkeley. In 1955, he became president of the American Sociological Society.[57] Whatever the reasons for his altering the biographical data in the survey (and they may have been as simple as the desire to further protect the anonymity of his respondents), when Blumer claimed, as he did, that the segments he printed were 'typical' of the material gathered, there is no especial reason to doubt him.[58] In the second place, the sex of the people who wrote the extracts is usually fairly easy to establish from their content. Thirdly, the material actually published by Blumer – together with additional, recently discovered material from his survey – is rich and extensive enough to permit interrogation from a number of perspectives that are radically different from those of Blumer himself or his team.[59]

Almost all the scholars who have so far addressed the issue of female spectatorship have done so in one of two ways. They have interpreted it as a concept implicated in the operations of filmic texts by various modes of signification that are themselves analysable from semiotic or psychoanalytical standpoints. Or they have seen it as the object of Hollywood's (and business's) attempts to sell products associated with particular stars or certain movies. Very few scholars have as yet examined what women movie-goers really made of the films they attended or how they responded to the discourse of consumerism that accompanied such films. The Blumer 'autobiographies' and excerpts offer a means of beginning to do these things for the 1920s (the survey, while its findings were not published until 1933, effectively ended in 1930 and almost all the evidence it contains is for the period up to 1929). They offer considerable evidence on how a number of real (albeit mainly upper middle-class and well-educated) female movie-goers created meanings out of the films they saw, and of the extent to which they were influenced by those films to adopt certain styles of dress and patterns of behaviour.

The Blumer survey included a good deal of information on fantasies that women had developed in response to the movies. Much of this presented an image of women as passively positioned and responding in predictable ways to fantasies generated for them by the male-dominated institution of Hollywood. One common fantasy was for women to imagine themselves as the actress being made love to by the male star (Blumer himself found this tendency to fantasise about playing the romantic lead in a film to be twice as common among women than men).[60] Women, reacting to the discourse surrounding stardom found in the popular media as well as to movies themselves, also often reported imagining that they would become a Hollywood star or at least the wife of a star.[61] A number of women, however, seem to have produced fantasies that, by selecting particular elements from the films they saw, allowed them to play around with (and consequently to challenge?) historically-produced ideas of gender roles and appropriate female behaviour. Some rejected, for example, the notion of the passive, suffering heroine present in many films that were primarily intended to appeal to a female audience. 'The role of the fragile, persecuted woman never appealed to me', one respondent asserted; 'it was always as ... the woman who had power that I saw myself.'[62] Fantasies of mastery and female empowerment were paralleled by fantasies of female activism which may well have had their origin in the serial melodramas, starring 'action' heroines such as Pearl White, that many women recalled watching when they were children.[63] One female respondent, for example, frequently day-dreamed of being actively involved in war. 'The excitment – shall I say glamour? – of the war', she confessed, 'has always appealed to me from the screen. Often I have pictured myself as a truck driver, nurse, HEROINE!'[64]

While many women in the Blumer survey identified with female stars to the extent of wanting to copy their appearance, hair-styles, clothes, jewels and personal mannerisms, such identification was often a complicated process. In the first place, women had a social identity: imitating screen stars, at times, needed considerable personal courage. During the 1920s, many parts of the American population disapproved of anything linked to 'flapperolatry', which they associated with women who wore short skirts, used too much make-up, smoked, and liked dancing modern dances (one religious periodical described dances of this kind as an 'indulgence in fleshly lust').[65] Under these circumstances, to copy fashions, modes of beautification, habits and mannerisms associated with the stars frequently involved a complex negotiation between what women wanted and what families and communities were prepared to allow. One of Blumer's respondents noted that her new hair style 'went over' quite well with her family but confessed that 'when I attempted to wear an ankle bracelet one evening, I learned that certain adornments in the "reel" world are not always appreciated in the real world'.[66]

In the second place, women reacted in a variety of complicated and mediated ways to what they saw on the screen. They had to be sure that what they decided to imitate would fit their own appearance and personality. This becomes evident, for example, in how women in the Blumer autobiographies responded to the clothes worn by stars on the screen. For some, this was a fairly straightforward matter: they observed a favourite star wearing a particular item they thought might suit them and set off to buy, or persuade their mothers to buy, an imitation of it from a local department store or cinema shop.[67] For many others, however, it was much more complicated. Instead of attempting to imitate a favourite actress when it came to buying clothes, they borrowed eclectically from several, negotiating between the images presented in movies and their own individual sense of what would 'go'. As one girl explained, the 'styles, colors, accessories, combinations, lines and general effects' seen in the movies were so varied that it was

> simple to pick out the [clothes] ... they most closely resemble, and thus learn to bring out my best points. I have a little two-piece sweater suit suggested by something I saw on Colleen Moore; Norma Talmadge was the inspiration for my dignified dinner dress; my next formal is going to be a reproduction of something that was bewitching on Nita Naldi.[68]

Many women of the 1920s, moreover, still either made or altered their own clothes. While they were unlikely to attempt to copy a whole outfit, they adapted various features seen on screen for their own use. 'Most dresses worn in movies are too striking or too elaborate for me to copy', one girl declared, 'but where there is shown a different collar, a pretty cuff, or a novel trimming, it is certain to crop out in some dress.'[69]

Neither the personality nor the tastes of women, moreover, stayed constant. There is evidence from the Blumer survey that, especially during adolescence, many girls imitated the on-screen conduct and mannerisms of movie actresses. This form of identification doubtless made its contribution to the forming of adult identities. However, it was a process characterised by great complexity and much ongoing negotiation. Firstly, mannerisms were selected from those used by particular stars in particular films. While some girls apparently identified with just one star and imitated her, it was more common to embrace mannerisms from a variety of stars.[70] Secondly, girls practised the movements and gestures concerned in front of the mirror to see if they suited them and would 'go'.[71] Thirdly, since the point of such mannerisms was to enhance the girl concerned's popularity and increase her attractiveness and sense of self-esteem, the next step was to try them out in public to see what effect they had. Those that prompted unfavourable responses were rapidly jettisoned. One girl, trying to copy the wide-eyed look of Mabel Normand, soon realised her friends believed 'there was something wrong with my eyes'. A second, after endeavouring to imitate Garbo's characteristic walk, found people inquiring 'if my knees are weak'.[72]

When it came to the ways in which they identified and copied female stars – and to a lesser extent in how they indulged in cinematically-inspired fantasies – women respondents to the Blumer survey revealed themselves as active rather than passive spectators. This is an important point in the context of the relationship between cinema and American feminine ideals in the 1920s. During that decade, traditionalist critics were convinced that they were seeing a radical undermining of those ideals. Often, they connected this development with the influence of the movies. (Blumer would later agree, describing the emotional impact of 'love pictures' as 'an attack on the mores of our contemporary life'.[73]) One movie cited by many traditionalists as symbolising the evil effects of the cinema was *Our Dancing Daughters* (1928).

In this originally silent film (to which MGM added, at the last moment, a dialogue scene and what one reviewer referred to as 'several love songs, stentorian cheering and ... a chorus of shrieks'), Joan Crawford played Diana Medford, a good-time flapper devoted to dancing and hip flasks, who falls in love with the son of a millionaire.[74] She is soon disappointed, as the millionaire is pushed into marriage with a hard-drinking

Our Dancing Daughters (Harry Beaumont, 1928).

blonde (Anita Page) by her greedy mother. But the new wife falls downstairs and is killed, leaving the millionaire free to find solace with Diana.

Many contemporary critics condemned *Our Dancing Daughters* for its apparent endorsement of freer relations between the sexes, petting, drinking, dancing and smoking. Yet while some of Blumer's respondents saw the film as an encouragement to wilder or freer behaviour, others read very different meanings into it.[75] To them, the film's narrative was essentially a moral one. The Crawford character, according to one girl, always 'played fair'. She even lost her man but remained 'sport enough to play fair'. In the eyes of another girl, the film underlined the message that daughters ought to trust and confide in their mothers more.[76] Some of the meanings attributed to the film by Blumer's correspondents, therefore, at least suggest the possibility that flapperdom was less of a challenge to existing standards of morality and behaviour than many of its conservative critics believed.

Conclusion

During the 1920s and early 30s, a substantial body of evidence suggested that women dominated American movie audiences – either numerically or because, by nature of their influence on their menfolk and children, they effectively decided which films would be most successful. Hollywood responded to this accumulation of evidence in a variety of ways, including producing films that women were known to like (for example, the distinctive genre of the 'women's film' which appeared in the early 30s) and promoting them by means of a discursive apparatus (including fan magazines and a consumerist discourse) that was aimed mainly at women. Yet, despite the priority accorded them by Hollywood itself, with all the consequences this had for the movie industry in general, women audiences of this period have been practically ignored by scholars writing film history.

One reason for this disregard may have been the lack of direct evidence from women movie-goers themselves. Much of what we do know about female cinema-going, as Judith Mayne notes, 'comes from reports of exhibitors, managers, and producers; occasionally from critics; rarely from viewers themselves'.[77] This is particularly true of the 1920s and early 30s – a period that is too distant in time for the effective use of 'ethnographic' techniques and also precedes the introduction of 'scientific' audience research of the kind discussed by Susan Ohmer in the following chapter. A way round the problem of missing primary materials, however, is to re-examine a number of social science surveys for the period concerned to determine what they have to tell us about women's experience of, and reactions to, the movies. This chapter has examined four such sources: those carried out under the auspices of the Chicago sociology department by Alice Miller Mitchell and Herbert Blumer, and the two 'anthropological' studies of Muncie, Indiana, both supervised by Robert and Helen Lynd.

Mitchell and the Lynds shed a good deal of light on women's movie preferences and viewing practices (with the Lynds, in their second survey, citing evidence emphasising the continuing centrality of the female audience). The Lynds also discussed the issue of the influence of the movies on women's appearance and behaviour. These matters were also addressed during the late 20s in a Payne Fund study conducted by Herbert Blumer. There have, in recent years, been two principal approaches to the question of female spectatorship. Both film theorists and analysts of how Hollywood addressed women as consumers have tended to see women spectators in essence as passive subjects. Scholars using ethnographic techniques, by contrast, paralleling work on how women respond to other forms of popular culture,[78] have presented them as actively involved in constructing a variety of meanings through the interaction between their own social and cultural identities and textual and extratextual cinematic practices. The Blumer material suggests that, while women were to a degree positioned by the cinematic apparatus, they also responded in an active way to the films they viewed and constructed a variety of meanings (some of them empowering) from them. Far from what he intended, therefore, the Blumer 'autobiographies' can be read against the grain to suggest that female spectatorship was fundamentally 'active' in constructing meanings from the filmic experience, even if the actual meanings created were at times markedly less radical than many conservative critics of 'Roaring Twenties' women believed – or feared.

Notes

1 Mary Ann Doane, untitled article, *Camera Obscura*, 20/21 (1989), pp. 142–3.

2 See, for example, Charles Eckert, 'The Carole Lombard in Macy's window', *Quarterly Review of Film Studies* 3:1 (Winter 1978), pp. 1–21; Maureen Turim, 'Designing women: the emergence of the new sweetheart line', *Wide Angle* 6:2 (1984), pp. 4–11; Diane Waldman, 'From midnight shows to marriage vows: women, exploitation and exhibition', *Wide Angle* 6:2 (1984), pp. 40–9; Charlotte Herzog and Jane Marie Gaines,

' "Puffed sleeves before tea-time": Joan Crawford, Adrian and women audiences', *Wide Angle* 6:4 (1985), pp. 24–33; Maria La Place, 'Bette Davis and the ideal of consumption: a look at *Now Voyager*', *Wide Angle* 6:4 (1985), pp. 34–43; 'Female representation and consumer culture', *Quarterly Review of Film and Video* 11:1 (1989), special issue, Jane Gaines and Michael Renov (eds); Jane Gaines, 'The Queen Christina tie-ins: convergence of show window and screen', *Quarterley Review of Film and Video* 11:4 (1989), pp. 45–60; Susan Ohmer, 'Female spectatorship and women's magazines: Hollywood, *Good Housekeeping* and World War II', *Velvet Light Trap* no. 25 (1990), pp. 53–68; Charlotte Herzog ' "Powder puff" promotion: the fashion show-in-the-film', in Jane Gaines and Charlotte Herzog, *Fabrications: Costume and the Female Body* (New York: Routledge, 1990), pp. 134–59. On constructions of femininity in fan magazines, see Jane Gaines, 'War, women and lipstick: fan mags in the forties', in *Heresies* 18 (1986), pp. 42–7.

3 See Elizabeth Ewen, 'City lights: immigrant women and the rise of the movies', *Signs: A Journal of Women in Culture and Society* 5: 3 (Spring 1980), pp. 45–66.

4 Jacqueline Bobo, '*The Color Purple*: black women as cultural readers', in E. Deidre Pribram (ed.), *Female Spectators: looking at film and television* (London: Verso, 1988); Helen Taylor, *Scarlett's Women: 'Gone With the Wind' and Its Female Fans* (London: Virago, 1989); Jackie Stacey, *Star Gazing: Hollywood cinema and female spectatorship* (London: Routledge, 1994). The work of several contributors to this volume, including Martin Barker and Kate Brooks, Brigid Cherry, Annette Hill and Annette Kuhn draws on ethnographic research that sheds light on female spectatorship.

5 Garth S. Jowett, 'Giving them what they want: movie audience research before 1950', in Bruce A. Austin (ed.), *Current Research in Film: Audiences, Economics and Law, Vol. 1* (Norwood, N.J.: Ablex, 1985), p. 30.

6 Leo A. Handel, *Hollywood Looks At Its Audience: A report of film audience research* (Urbana, Ill.: University of Illinois Press, 1950), pp. 99–101.

7 Jowett, 'Giving them what they want', p. 30.

8 Handel, *Hollywood Looks At Its Audience*, p. 99.

9 W. Stephen Bush, 'Scenarios by the bushel', *New York Times*, 5 December 1920, cited in Richard Koszarski, *An Evening's Entertainment: the age of the silent feature picture 1915–1928* (Berkeley: University of California Press, 1990), p. 30.

10 Frederick James Smith, 'Does decency help or hinder?', *Photoplay* 26 (November 1924), p. 36; Beth Brown, 'Making movies for women', *Moving Picture World*, 26 March 1927, p. 34. These estimates are cited in Gaylyn Studlar, 'The perils of pleasure? Fan magazine discourse as women's commodified culture in the 1920s', in Richard Abel (ed.), *Silent Film* (London: Athlone, 1996), p. 263.

11 Koszarski, *An Evening's Entertainment*, pp. 28–9.

12 Quoted in Charlotte Herzog, ' "Powder puff" promotion', *Fabrications*, p. 157.

13 Molly Haskell, *From Reverence to Rape: the treatment of women in the movies* (Chicago: University of Chicago Press, 1987), p. 49.

14 Andrea S. Walsh, *The Women's Film and the Female Experience* (New York: Praeger, 1984), p. 30. On women scriptwriters, see Melissa Sue Kort, 'Shadows of the substance: women screenwriters in the 1930s', in Janet Todd (ed.), *Women and Film, Women and Literature*, new series, 4 (New York and London: Holmes and Meier, 1988), pp. 169–85;

Lizzie Francke, *Script Girls: Women Screenwriters in Hollywood* (London: BFI, 1994); Cari Beauchamp, *Without Lying Down: Frances Marion and the Powerful Women of Early Hollywood* (New York: Lisa Drew/Scribner, 1997).

15 Dorothy M. Brown, *Setting a Course: American Women in the 1920s* (Boston: Twayne, 1987), p. 213. Although not all of these women were located in Hollywood, a large number of them were.

16 Haskell, *From Reverence to Rape*, pp. 153–88; Walsh, *The Women's Film and Female Experience*, pp. 23–48; idem., 'The women's film', in Gary Crowdus (ed.), *The Political Companion to American Film* (Chicago: Lakeview Press, 1994), pp. 483–95; Tino Balio, *Grand Design: Hollywood as a Modern Business Enterprise 1930–1939* (New York: Scribner, 1993), pp. 235–55.

17 Ibid., p. 235.

18 Arthur Mayer, *Merely Colossal* (New York: Simon and Schuster, 1953), p. 178.

19 Kathryn H. Fuller, *At the Picture Show: Small-town Audiences and the Creation of Movie Fan Culture* (Washington, D.C.: Smithsonian Institution, 1996), pp. 133, 143, 148.

20 Eckert, 'The Carole Lombard in Macy's window', p. 19.

21 Ibid., pp. 2–3, 6–17, 19–20.

22 Haskell, *From Reverence to Rape*, p. 187.

23 Jeanne Allen, 'The film viewer as consumer', *Quarterly Review of Film Studies* 5:4 (Fall 1980), p. 486.

24 In the previous chapter of this book, Richard Maltby contends that Hollywood's belief in a dominant female audience was actually based on a considerable body of impressionistic and anecdotal evidence, some of it systematically gathered.

25 Robert Sklar relates the growing interest in social science to the diminishing influence of what he terms 'the traditional cultural elite'. This was in turn linked to (and may itself have been defined by) the declining authority of 'literary' judgements made on moral and social questions by 'professors, clergymen, essayists and other cultural figures'. 'Social-science methods', writes Sklar, 'may have been no less subjective, opinionated and classbound than the explanatory modes of lay and ethical essayists, but in the 1920s their aura of modest self-confidence, precision and careful procedure seemed to offer a clarity and persuasiveness that all competing forms of social explanation lacked.' Sklar, *Movie-Made America: A Cultural History of American Movies* (New York: Vintage, 1994), p. 134.

26 Garth Jowett, 'Giving them what they want', pp. 23–6.

27 Harold Ellis Jones and Herbert S. Conrad, 'Rural preferences in motion pictures', *Journal of Social Psychology* 1 (1930), pp. 419–23.

28 Koszarski, *An Evening's Entertainment*, p. 28. These general preferences were repeated in the study of Evansville school-children cited above. Ibid.

29 Alice Miller Mitchell, *Children and Movies* (Chicago: University of Chicago Press, 1929), p. 127.

30 Ibid., pp. 21, 46, 18, 20, 42–5, 29, 31–2, 34–5, 58–62.

31 Ibid., pp. 104–5.

32 Ibid., pp. 109–10.

33 Ibid., p. 113.

34 Ibid., pp. 98–9.

35 Ibid., p. 22.

36 The Scouts were especially 'sporty' in their tastes, being the only group amongst the girls to express a preference (by 53.8 per cent) for baseball over the movies (29.6 per cent). All other female groups voted decisively for the movies. Ibid., pp. 164, 163.

37 Ibid., pp. 164, 166, 165, 167. Interestingly, the preferences for hiking and auto-riding over the cinema were shared by the equivalent groups of boys in roughly equal proportions. While the boy Scouts voted even more decisively than the girls for parties over movies, differences appeared in the much lower majorities for parties on the part of the (less sociable?) high school and grade school boys and the preference for movies in place of reading on the part of all the boys' groups. Ibid.

38 Ibid., pp. 120, 125–6. Frustratingly, there is insufficient evidence in Mitchell's book to explore whether girls actually identified with the character Bow (described by Molly Haskell as a 'working-class flapper') was playing in the film. Sara Evans also points out that Bow was one of the actresses who, in her films 'demonstrated the proper use of new products and clothes'. Haskell, *From Reverence to Rape*, pp. 79–80; Sara M. Evans, *Born for Liberty: A History of Women in America* (New York: Free Press, 1989), p. 179.

39 Mitchell, *Children and Movies*, pp. 124–5.

40 Interestingly, she suggested that some mothers were using the neighbourhood movie 'as a day nursery', leaving small children there 'while they run to the dressmaker or to the dentist'. Ibid., p. 72.

41 Robert S. Lynd and Helen Merrell Lynd, *Middletown: A Study in American Culture* (New York: Harcourt, Brace and Company, 1929), pp. 257, 264–5.

42 Ibid., pp. 268–9.

43 Ibid., pp. 361, 265.

44 One working-class woman with six children was invited, by a female friend with a reputation for teasing men, to accompany her to the movies. She agreed, convinced it was only a joke. When they actually did go, with the friend paying for her transport and admission, she was 'never so surprised in my life'. Her surprise suggests that such outings were not a common part of the movie-going culture, at least of working-class women. As the woman herself sadly observed, the experience had been two years earlier and 'I haven't been anywhere since'. Ibid., p. 264.

45 Ibid., p. 266.

46 Ibid., pp. 242, 266.

47 Ibid., pp. 267, 242.

48 Ibid., p. 267.

49 Robert S. Lynd and Helen Merrell Lynd, *Middletown in Transition: a Study in Cultural Conflicts* (New York: Harcourt, Brace and Company, 1937), pp. 261–2.

50 Ibid., p. 261.

51 'It is our impression', wrote the Lynds, 'that no two generations of Americans have ever faced each other across as wide a gap in their customary attitudes and behavior as have American parents and children since the World War. And this disjunction, we believe, has been increased by the depression.' Lynds, ibid., p. 168. For a very perceptive discussion of gender roles, see ibid., pp. 176–9.

52 Ibid., pp. 170, 262.

53 Ibid., pp. 170–1.

54 Sklar, *Movie-Made America*, p. 134. Sklar's view of the Payne Fund Studies reflects the critique of them by Raymond Moley and the Motion Picture Producers and Distributors Association. This was itself politically motivated. For a recent, balanced assessment of the Studies, see Garth S. Jowett, Ian C. Jarvie, and Kathryn H. Fuller, *Children and the Movies: Media Influence and the Payne Fund Controversy* (New York: Cambridge University Press, 1996). For an assessment of their place in the history of audience studies, see Shearon A. Lowery and Melvin L. DeFleur, *Milestones in Mass Communications Research: Media Effects* (New York and London: Longman, 1995), Chapter 2.

55 See, for example, Herbert Blumer, *Movies and Conduct* (New York: Macmillan, 1933), p. 140.

56 Ibid., pp. 203–7; Jowett *et al.*, *Children and the Movies*, p. 238.

57 Tamotsu Shibutani (ed.), *Human Nature and Collective Behavior: Papers in Honor of Herbert Blumer* (Englewood Cliffs, NJ: Prentice-Hall, 1970), pp. v–vii; Jowett *et al.*, *Children and the Movies*, p. xv.

58 Blumer, *Movies and Conduct*, p. xi.

59 See Jowett *et al.*, *Children and the Movies*, pp. 242–301.

60 Blumer, *Movies and Conduct*, pp. 65, 66, 67, 68, 71, 215, 223, 251; Jowett *et al.*, *Children and the Movies*, pp. 243, 250, 258, 276, 288, 295.

61 Blumer, *Movies and Conduct*, pp. 62, 63, 66, 136, 169; Jowett *et al.*, *Children and the Movies*, pp. 260, 270, 275.

62 Blumer, *Movies and Conduct*, p. 66.

63 'I admired Miss [Pearl] White for her daring and courage', remarked one Blumer respondent. Jowett *et al.*, *Children and Movies*, p. 243. Also see ibid., pp. 246, 251, 276 and Blumer, *Movies and Conduct*, pp. 238–9. On the genre in general, see Ben Singer, 'Female Power in the Serial-Queen Melodrama: the etiology of an anomaly', *Camera Obscura* 22 (January 1990), pp. 91–129.

64 Blumer, *Movies and Conduct*, p. 63.

65 See Brown, *Setting a Course*, especially pp. 182–3.

66 Blumer, *Movies and Conduct*, p. 32.

67 Blumer, *Movies and Conduct*, p. 32. The dresses available in stores, Charlotte Herzog and Jane Gaines point out, were never *exactly* the same in design as the one's worn by stars in the movies. Herzog and Gaines, ' "Puffed sleeves before tea-time" ', p. 25. Nevertheless, Macy's sold half a million imitations of the dress Joan Crawford wore in *Letty Lynton* (1932). Ibid.

68 Blumer, *Movies and Conduct*, p. 31.

69 Ibid. Also on this point, see Herzog and Gaines, ' "Puffed sleeves before tea-time" ', pp. 28, 31. The gap between the fashions seen on screen or in magazines and the clothes women actually wore, according to these writers, represents 'unexplored cultural space'. Ibid., p. 31.

70 Blumer, *Movies and Conduct*, pp. 40–3, 242, 250; Jowett *et al.*, *Children and Movies*, pp. 260, 270, 296.

71 Blumer, *Movies and Conduct*, pp. 34, 37, 40, 43; Jowett *et al.*, *Children and Movies*, pp. 256, 272.

72 Blumer, *Movies and Conduct*, pp. 37–8.

73 See Paula S. Fass, *The Damned and the Beautiful: American Youth in the 1920s* (New

York: Oxford University Press, 1979), especially pp. 21–5, 309; Blumer, *Movies and Conduct*, p. 116. On this point generally, also see another Payne Fund study: Charles C. Peters, *Motion Pictures and Standards of Morality* (New York: Macmillan, 1933).

74 Alexander Walker, *The Shattered Silents: how the talkies came to stay* (London: Elm Tree, 1978), p. 82.

75 Blumer, *Movies and Conduct*, pp. 152–4; Jowett *et al.*, *Children and Movies*, pp. 244–5.

76 Ibid., pp. 184–5.

77 Judith Mayne, 'The female audience and the feminist critic', in Todd (ed.), *Women and Film*, p. 29.

78 See, for example, Janice Radway, *Reading the Romance: Women, Patriarchy and Popular Culture* (Chapel Hill: University of North Carolina Press, 1984), and Ien Ang, *Watching Dallas: Soap Opera and the Melodramatic Imagination* (London: Methuen, 1985).

3   The Science of Pleasure: George Gallup and audience research in Hollywood

Susan Ohmer

At the turn of the century Adolph Zukor opened a luxury motion picture theatre in New York. Wanting to learn more about his customers, Zukor decided to study their reactions. In his autobiography *The Public Is Never Wrong*, he described his research: 'It was my custom to take a seat about six rows from the front ... I spent a good deal of time watching the faces of the audience, even turning around to do so ... With a little experience I could see, hear and 'feel' the reaction to each melodrama and comedy.'[1] From the nickelodeon period to the present day, the film industry has been driven by the question 'What do audiences want?' The primary motivation for studying audience reactions remains the same as it was for Zukor: to develop more popular, and therefore more profitable, movies. How the industry studies these reactions has, however, changed dramatically over time. While Zukor relied on general impressions created by personal contact, modern researchers use surveys to collect information on the specific elements of a movie that are believed to influence ticket purchases. Contemporary research also singles out features of the audience: viewers whom Zukor saw as a mass are now categorised in socio-economic terms.

The contrast between Zukor's era and our own may suggest that audience research has developed smoothly from impressionistic commentary to more objective, scientific methods, but the history of audience research in Hollywood suggests otherwise. Within the trajectory formed by Zukor's on-the-spot observations and the structured questionnaires of today, the 1940s mark a critical juncture. It was during this decade that the film industry began to employ what were considered 'scientific' studies of viewer response, based on carefully constructed questionnaires and population samples. Most of the market research techniques used today, including cast and story tests and demographic surveys, crystallised during this period. Although there were some informal surveys in the 1920s and 1930s, it was not until the 1940s that the film industry adopted systematic, empirical methods for studying its customers.[2]

Understanding how and why the film industry made this shift forms the basis for this essay. To do so, I want to examine the work of a key figure in this process, George Gallup. The name 'Gallup' has, of course, become synonymous with public opinion polling throughout the world. Although he is best known for his political surveys, Gallup spent most of his career in advertising. In 1939, after his political poll had become solidly established, and while he continued to carry out surveys of print and broadcasting media, Gallup founded the Audience Research Institute (ARI), with the goal of adapting techniques used in these other fields to the study of film viewing. During the 1940s, ARI conducted literally thousands of surveys for more than a dozen studios and independent producers. In its scope and comprehensiveness, ARI represented the first full-scale effort at empirical research in Hollywood.

Gallup's career allows us to see the processes by which concepts of public opinion are constructed. His early work on human psychology illustrates how researchers in this field used scientific techniques as a marker of truth, and as the basis for a claim to expertise. Gallup's advertising studies led him to develop a view of media texts as bundles of components that could be manipulated to change audiences' reactions. The political polls that made him famous also became the vehicle through which he studied the demographic characteristics of film audiences. And Gallup's national reputation as a pollster enhanced his status among Hollywood producers.

Yet if we analyse how Gallup came to work in Hollywood, and how the industry responded to his research, it becomes clear that scientific research is shaped by institutional and economic pressures. During the 1940s, the vertically integrated studio system which had existed since the 1910s began to come apart, under the pressure of anti-trust investigations and unionisation. Audience research became one of the grounds on which battles for control over film production were fought. Studio executives felt that ARI's work gave them a measure of control over the film process. To writers and actors, it was a means of manipulation. The studies carried out by the Audience Research Institute are not to be taken at face value, but need to be examined for the assumptions, influences and ideologies that infuse them. Instead of reading off the information ARI developed, it is important to consider how its findings were interpreted and deployed. Audience research, despite its claims to be objective, does not report 'facts'; rather, it constructs a discourse of spectatorship, an interpretative framework that attempts to describe and explain our responses to film texts. By tracing the assumptions that motivated Gallup's work in Hollywood during the 1940s, we can more clearly understand the cultural and ideological forces involved in studies of film spectatorship.

An Edifice of Rational Procedures

Gallup's career in public opinion began when he studied psychology at what is now the University of Iowa. During the 1920s, psychology expanded greatly as a discipline: the number of doctorates in the field doubled during the decade. Many graduates subsequently found work in corporations, where they drew on psychological concepts and techniques to solve everyday business problems.[3] Under the influence of Frederick W. Taylor's theories of scientific management, businesses in the 1920s began to streamline their operations to make manufacturing more efficient. One aspect of this process involved reducing the uncertainties involved in hiring workers.

Gallup's early research illustrates these trends. His first scholarly publication, an analysis of the 'Traits of successful retail salespeople', sought not only to define those traits but also to develop a consistent method for measuring them.[4] His study assumed that human behaviour could be described in terms of specific qualities, which could be categorised and measured with objective tests. During the 1920s, quantitative measurements displaced personal impressions and intuition as a marker of professionalism in the social sciences. It often happened, indeed, that psychologists did not have first-hand knowledge of the fields they researched, but their findings were endowed with an aura of truthfulness because they used statistics.

Gallup's first foray into social science research established a pattern that continued throughout his career: his research into human behaviour was undertaken at the behest of business, not employees or consumers. He and other practitioners in the emerging field of 'applied' psychology were in no sense ideologically neutral. Instead, they became what Donald Napoli has termed 'architects of adjustment', facilitating the adjustment of workers to the demands of expanding industry.[5] The techniques he developed aimed to translate the messy imprecision of human behaviour into numbers that seemed objective, and which could then serve as standards and benchmarks by which business executives could supervise and regulate production.

Although psychology during the 1920s clearly valorised rationality, it was also aware of the importance of unconscious desires. This realm of human behaviour became the focus of Gallup's dissertation. Funded by the publisher of the Des Moines Register, it was entitled 'An objective method for determining reader interest in the content of a newspaper'. In it, Gallup criticised the impressionistic strategies and 'guesswork' that newspaper editors used to determine what readers liked, and detailed an alternative, 'scientific' method, in which interviewers visited people in their homes and went through a copy of the paper with them, page by page, asking them to point out absolutely everything they had read.[6]

The results of these interviews turned accepted wisdom on its head. The survey found that hardly anyone read the news. The most popular feature proved to be the picture page, followed closely by the comics. Sports columns, advice to the lovelorn, and even obituaries received more attention than social and political analysis. Gallup also detected significant gender and class differences in readers' responses.[7]

From the perspective of newspaper editors and publishers, the most important finding to emerge from Gallup's research was that 70 per cent of the population read the comics. In May 1931, General Foods began using comic strip advertising for Grape Nuts cereal. The campaign generated tremendous sales, and its impact on advertisers was equally dramatic. Within six years, the annual national expenditure on comic strip advertising jumped from less than $1,000 to $16.5 million.[8] Market research textbooks for the next ten years cited the Grape Nuts campaign as a model.[9] Gallup's research was understood to have revealed previously inaccessible desires among readers, and to have suggested how advertisers could reach this deeper level of consciousness by using imagery instead of words.[10]

Over the next two years, Gallup's research shifted to focus almost exclusively on advertising. In the spring of 1932, Young & Rubicam, the agency that had developed the Grape Nuts campaign, offered him a position as Director of Research. This was very much a period during which agencies were beginning to hire people with scientific training to provide a more systematic basis for their work in part as a way of countering criticism from the Federal Trade Commission and consumer groups that advertising was deceitful and manipulative.[11] Gallup's research at Young & Rubicam incorporated many of the assumptions about the subconscious and the power of suggestion that governed his earlier studies, yet it also involved much more detailed analysis of media texts. Gallup and his colleagues believed that it was possible to define, down to the smallest unit, what aspects of a text produced an audience's feelings of enjoyment, and to use this knowledge to design other texts that would evoke similar feelings. Operating from the assumption that viewers had to be seduced into reading, and using Walter Dill Scott's theories on the effect of design elements in advertising, they believed that texts could be scientifically manipulated in order to influence audiences.[12] Their research led to changes in the graphic style and placement of the agency's print advertising. Gallup and his colleagues at Young & Rubicam followed a similar strategy for radio advertising, looking for ways to make commercials less obtrusive by embedding them in the programme.[13] Gallup's research offered support for the belief that people were less resistant to commercials when they were 'woven into the fabric' of the entertainment, sounding like the rest of the non-advertising text.

The overriding aim of Gallup's activity at Young & Rubicam was to show his clients how to manipulate texts and audiences in order to maximise profits. Gallup and his staff presented their findings in quantitative form, using percentages, charts and graphs. For example, information about what percentage of an advertisement people read was used to develop average 'noting and reading' scores for ads of comparable size and colour. These average scores then became benchmarks to measure the success of new ads, to determine whether they performed above or below 'par' values. In its radio research, the agency counted the number of radio sets in use, and the number of people listening to each set, for every fifteen-minute period, and computed a 'cost per listener reached' figure to provide an exact measure of sales effectiveness. It was this 'edifice of rational procedures', as historian Donald Hurwitz describes it, that Gallup imported to Hollywood in the 1940s: the use of scientific methods to dissect texts into crucial components that could be varied to change audiences' responses.[14]

As Elmo Roper, another market-researcher-turned-political-pollster, observed, 'public opinion research came out of marketing research – absolutely directly'.[15] Gallup founded the American Institute of Public Opinion (AIPO) in 1936 to apply techniques from advertising to poll Americans for their views on major issues of the day. Like Roper and others, he used a new technique that entered survey research during the 1930s, sampling, which measures the attitudes of a large population by examining a carefully chosen subset that reflects key characteristics of the larger group, such as age, gender, income and education. Other pollsters of the time, including Roper, used sampling, but what distinguished Gallup's surveys was the special effort he made to reach people from lower income groups, rural and small-town Americans, and young adults who had become old enough to vote.[16] Gallup publicised his new poll by announcing that it would compete with the reigning survey of the time, the *Literary Digest*'s, which based its conclusions on ballots that were mailed to millions of people. Although Gallup's poll covering the 1936 presidential election actually underestimated the extent of Roosevelt's victory by 7 per cent, he did accurately predict that FDR would win, while the *Digest* forecast a defeat. Gallup's brazen challenge to the *Digest*, and his promotion of the idea of sampling, brought him overnight fame and provided him with a platform from which to popularise the idea of scientific polling as a reliable indicator of public opinion.[17]

When Gallup shifted his attention to Hollywood, he imported the research techniques and assumptions about public opinion he had developed in his earlier work. In the same way that his previous successes had depended on publishers and advertisers accepting that an outsider using scientific methods could uncover useful information, his success in Hollywood relied on his finding executives who could perceive the value of his work for their companies. Gallup's cultural status as an expert on opinion polling, together with his rigorous techniques and statistical methods, promoted an image of his work as 'objective', but the reception of his research in Hollywood revealed the extent to which 'objective' research was affected by economic and institutional needs.

What the Public Wants

Gallup began thinking about doing research on film in 1934–5, after he had solidified his position at Young & Rubicam, and while he was establishing his political polls. He became interested in film research in part because of the methodological challenges it posed, describing it as 'a researcher's dream that no one had ever thought through'.[18] 'The people we ran into', he recalled, 'said ... "you can research politics and products and advertisements and all these other things, but ... research has no place in the field of motion pictures". So that was sort of a challenge.'[19] Gallup was also attracted to the subject through the same populist conviction that had inspired his political polls. He felt that people in Hollywood were out of touch with Americans' interests:

> They always thought that they could determine what the public wanted out in
> Hollywood. ... here is an industry which never gave a damn about the local theater or
> the managers ... they've never learned to pay attention to what their local audiences
> want, the prices they're willing to pay, the kind of pictures that certain people would
> come to see.[20]

As with his political polls, Gallup saw opinion research as a way to make these voices heard, to represent 'the public' to the people who produced their entertainment.

Gallup's film research 'piggybacked' on his other interests and associations.[21] While he insisted that the American Institute of Public Opinion (AIPO) and ARI were separate organisations, he often reminded his film clients of his political work.[22] Before ARI even existed, Gallup used AIPO polls to obtain information about Americans' interest in cinema, asking questions about a wide range of film-related topics. Young & Rubicam executives promoted Gallup's company to the studios they dealt with, and Gallup hired his film staff, most notably his chief assistant for film research, David Ogilvy, from his contacts at Young & Rubicam.

Gallup made his first formal overtures to the film industry in the spring and summer of 1939. Although both Darryl F. Zanuck and Louis B. Mayer expressed initial interest in his research, neither signed a contract with ARI. According to Gallup, the established moguls who headed financially secure companies were like the newspaper editors he had once complained about:

> in every field ... when it goes from an art to a science, the old boys always hate to make
> the change, hate to accept the new, hate to admit that they don't have all the answers ...
> we could never get along with some of the old boys, the Schencks and the Skourases

and Louis Mayer and Warner Bros. – couldn't communicate with them at all; to them this was some kind of black magic.[23]

Instead, the first people to express interest in Gallup's work were independent producers (David O. Selznick and Samuel Goldwyn) and RKO, which was emerging from bankruptcy in 1939. ARI's research provided Selznick and Goldwyn with evidence to bolster their own strongly held opinions and strengthen their positions as independents in the studio system. For RKO, hiring Gallup was a demonstration of its commitment to produce money-making pictures that audiences would enjoy and thus improve its balance sheets. Later in the decade, other independent producers and small studios, including Walt Disney and Columbia Pictures, also commissioned research from Gallup for the same reasons.

Although Gallup began preliminary research on film in late 1936, he did not make his work public until January 1939, when he released the results of a national survey on *Gone With the Wind*, which had been commissioned by several newspaper publishers, including the *Atlanta Constitution*.[24] Although Selznick had not commissioned the poll, he used its report that the picture had a potential audience of 55 million people – the largest ever indicated for a picture – in his negotiations with the film's distributor, MGM.[25] In order to secure the services of Clark Gable, Selznick had been forced to give MGM distribution rights to the picture and pay MGM 50 per cent of the gross profits.[26] To recoup its investment quickly, MGM wanted to open the picture nationally at ticket prices of 50 cents to one dollar and run continuous screenings.[27] Selznick felt that this exhibition policy did not do justice to a picture that deserved to be handled 'like no other picture to date except *Birth of a Nation*'. Instead, he urged MGM to show the film in roadshow format, at ticket prices between $1.50 and $2.00, and at fixed times.[28] Selznick told MGM that even if Gallup was only half right about its potential audience, at 60 cents a ticket the picture would take in $17 million. Furthermore, if 55 million people wanted to see it, they would pay for reserved seats at set times.[29] In Selznick's mind, this huge potential audience meant that MGM could afford to charge higher ticket prices and arrange longer playoff times, and still recover its investment.

The compromise reached involved a double exhibition format. After its debut in Atlanta, the picture opened in a few key cities in a modified roadshow format. In some cities – New York, Los Angeles, and Boston – it played in two theatres simultaneously. At one theatre, the picture ran twice a day, at set times, with ticket prices ranging from 75 cents to $2.20, the format that Selznick desired. The other theatre in these cities screened the film in MGM's preferred format: three times a day, continuously, with ticket prices from 75 cents to $1.10.[30]

Selznick also used AIPO's findings to negotiate the picture's advertising campaign. Under the terms of their agreement, MGM was to handle all advertising and exploitation for the picture. Since Gallup found that so many people knew about the picture, Selznick argued that MGM would not have to spend much money to publicise it. They could just publish a 'dignified announcement' in local papers that the movie was in town. He also argued that, since the book was so well known, the colour and typeface of the ad should match that of the book's jacket to capitalise on its familiarity.[31] Ads for the picture that appeared in *Variety* did, in fact, imitate the typeface of the book jacket.[32]

Selznick's use of AIPO surveys in his disputes with MGM indicates how audience research became embroiled within the power structure of Hollywood during the studio era. Matthew Bernstein has argued that independent producers in Hollywood during the 1930s were only 'semi-independent': because they had to distribute their films through the majors and earn a profit for them, their decisions could be challenged at every step.[33] For Selznick, Gallup's research provided 'scientific' evidence that he could use in his dispute with MGM. AIPO's survey 'proved' his belief that *Gone With the Wind* would be a major cultural phenomenon. In contrast to his own subjective opinion, however, AIPO's numbers and percentages appeared impartial, and could therefore be used to bolster his position within the Hollywood hierarchy.

Titles, Casts and Stories

In March 1940, Gallup established the Audience Research Institute as a separate polling organisation, and signed a contract to provide market research for RKO Radio Pictures. What was initially a one-year agreement led to a decade-long working relationship, in which ARI prepared over a thousand reports, involving nearly every picture RKO produced and many that did not make it into production. Gallup was hired at the instigation of RKO president George Schaefer and his backer on the board of directors, Nelson Rockefeller, as part of a larger strategy to return RKO to profitability after the studio emerged from bankruptcy in January 1940. Schaefer announced the decision to hire Gallup at the studio's annual sales convention in May 1940, telling the assembly of sales managers and affiliated theatre owners that Gallup would carry out 'a scientific study of the motion picture public and the tastes, habits, and interests of picture patrons'.[34] The repeated references to ARI's 'scientific' approach implied that RKO had discovered a sure-fire way to develop successful pictures that matched the public's interests, and Gallup's credentials were presented as if they were guarantees of success.

In order to determine what the public wanted in their pictures, it was first necessary to determine who the film-going public was. Before 1940, producers who wanted to learn about audiences' likes and dislikes relied on such sources as exhibitor reports, fan mail and columns in the trade papers.[35] Gallup criticised these procedures as 'haphazard' and 'inaccurate', since their sources did not necessarily reflect the views of the majority of film-goers. Nearly 90 per cent of the fan mail studios received, for example, came from girls under twenty-one, while exhibitor reports often expressed the personal biases of theatre owners, rather than the opinions of their patrons.[36] Gallup proposed to apply the sampling method used in his political polls and examine the views of a scientifically-selected portion of the population.

When Gallup started his political polls, he was able to draw on voter rolls and census data from local and national government offices to develop a profile of the voting population. When he began his film research, there were no comparable sources of information about Americans' cinema-going habits. Hollywood kept records about average ticket prices and box office grosses, but these numbers were proprietary and known to be untrustworthy. Beginning in 1936, and continuing into the late 1940s, Gallup and his staff asked the nationwide cross-section of people who responded to his political polls about their film-going habits. Gallup's first film research was, therefore,

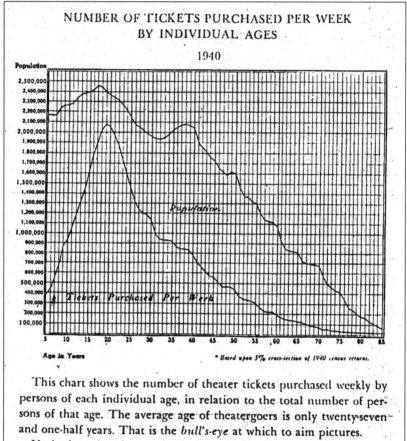

NUMBER OF TICKETS PURCHASED PER WEEK BY INDIVIDUAL AGES

1940

This chart shows the number of theater tickets purchased weekly by persons of each individual age, in relation to the total number of persons of that age. The average age of theatergoers is only twenty-seven and one-half years. That is the *bull's-eye* at which to aim pictures.

Notice how sharply attendance drops away after age nineteen.

Chart showing age distribution of weekly cinema ticket sales in 1940, against population.

literally embedded in his political polls. These methods enabled ARI to develop a detailed statistical analysis of American film-goers in terms of age, gender and class. In the hands of David Ogilvy, whose acerbic opinions flavoured most of the reports for RKO, this demographic data formed the basis for massive generalisations about Americans' tastes.

The Institute's most striking finding concerned the age of the film-going population. In 1941, ARI provided the first statistical evidence that teenagers were the dominant force at the box office. According to its surveys, nearly one-third of all film tickets were purchased by people who were less than twenty years old.[37] This led the company to praise highly any RKO project that promised to appeal to teens. When research for *The Band Played On* (released as *Syncopation* in 1942) indicated that the subject was popular among teens, Ogilvy recommended that the story be slanted 'at this mass market of entertainment-seeking kids' and that RKO eliminate any plot elements teenagers would not like, such as 'the historical aspect and the grim hard struggles' of the musicians it portrayed.[38]

ARI's emphasis on youth also led the company to suggest that RKO should develop more actors and actresses who were under twenty-five. Since less than one quarter of 'A' actors and actresses were under twenty-five, 'this suggests that there are not nearly enough adolescent stars to satisfy the demand'.[39] Several months later, *Film Daily* reported that RKO was grooming younger stars, many of whom ARI had mentioned in its reports.[40] ARI's attention to teenage audiences also hurt the standing of older stars. When RKO asked the company to study public interest in Gloria Swanson before she returned to the screen in *Father Takes a Wife* (1941), Ogilvy told the studio that contemporary audiences would not enjoy her:

> the picture audience is not a standing army – *it is a moving parade*. Miss Swanson made her last picture in 1934. In the intervening years a majority of her admirers have grown out of going to the movies. Their places at the box-office have been taken by a generation which has never set eyes on Miss Swanson. [emphasis in original][41]

In addition to accentuating the differences between teen audiences and older adults, ARI emphasised differences in the reactions of men and women, providing statistical evidence to support the common belief that men liked action films and women liked romance.[42] Its surveys found that the audience for Hitchcock's *Rebecca* (1940) was 71 per cent female while viewers of *The Fighting 69th* (1940) were 62 per cent male.[43] Rather than suggesting that RKO make different films for each audience, ARI reports insisted that the interests of both groups had to be represented. When ARI tested public reactions to *Kitty Foyle* (1940), Ogilvy argued that its popularity with women would not be enough to compensate for a lack of appeal among men. He suggested that RKO should not just rely on the love story element, but should add some other factor to appeal to men.[44]

Ogilvy's discussions of gender differences were picked up by other commentators and circulated within the industry and beyond its borders. In April 1944, William Lydgate, a Gallup Poll staffer, published an article in the business magazine *Sales Management*, later condensed for *Reader's Digest*, in which he used ARI's research to develop a broader argument about gender and the imagination. Women, he argued,

> could identify themselves with the ambitious girl hunting a job in the big city, but not with a woman pilot ... The closer the situation is to the average woman's experience, the better women like it. Men, on the other hand, are interested in stories portraying not only familiar situations, but lives they would like to lead. Their preference is for swift-moving dramas that show them new experiences and fire the imagination. They are less interested than women in emotion on the screen. They want to know what happened, not how people felt about it.[45]

Critics have discussed how the films produced during World War II challenged prevailing gender conventions and privileged female desire.[46] Ogilvy and Lydgate's remarks, however, illustrate how ARI's findings about women and film could be used to reinforce conventional stereotypes.

As he had in his political polls, Gallup's film research drew attention to people from low-income groups. ARI found that poor people (defined as earning less than $15 a week) and people on relief were responsible for 25 per cent of all box office revenues. Film-goers from the lower middle class (defined as earning $25–35 a week) accounted for 22 per cent of the box office gross. These three groups accounted for almost half of Hollywood's total ticket sales. Middle-income groups accounted for 38 per cent, while upper middle and upper income patrons brought in the remaining 15 per cent. According to ARI, the great majority of all movie tickets purchased in United States were bought by people whose family incomes were less than $50 per week.[47]

This information would have allowed studios to target pictures to particular classes if they had wanted to, because ARI told them which segments of the population liked different kinds of pictures. ARI, however, assumed that studios wanted to reach the largest number of people possible, so it offered suggestions about refashioning projects to appeal to 'the majority' of film-goers. As Ogilvy argued, 'When films cost fortunes and distribution has only a few main channels, it is imperative that every feature should appeal to the largest possible number of theatergoers. At present there is no room for pictures which appeal to minorities.'[48] Appealing to the 'majority' meant producing more 'lowbrow' pictures with stars who appealed to the masses. ARI tested several projects for Paul Muni, then under contract to RKO, and found only three that attracted much interest.[49] According to Ogilvy, Muni had 'a problem on his hands':

> His concentration on highbrow and foreign properties has deprived him of marquee value among two important segments of the population – the young and the poor. All indications are that if he persists in this policy he will progressively alienate more and more ordinary theatergoers, to a point where his pictures will become the esoteric taste of a few connoisseurs.[50]

In Ogilvy's opinion, RKO should not produce pictures aimed at a 'highbrow' audience because this would alienate those segments of the population who bought a quarter of the tickets: poor people and those on relief. Yet in none of ARI's reports to RKO in the early 1940s did Ogilvy recommend that the studio make a picture simply because poor people would enjoy it. ARI's main concern about class was that RKO should be sure that low-income audiences know when a picture would appeal to them. In discussing advertising and distribution strategies for a proposed picture called *Battle Stations*, Ogilvy suggested that since the story appealed to men, teens and low-income groups, RKO should slant its advertising to them and open the picture at a theatre 'where low-income patrons predominate'.[51]

In addition to analysing the demographic composition of film audiences, Gallup used factor analysis to divide up films into their individual components. As he had in his print and broadcasting research, Gallup assumed that there were specific characteristics about a picture that viewers responded to. Most industry executives used box-office income to measure a picture's popularity. In ARI's opinion, a picture's general success did not indicate which particular features audiences enjoyed, and thus was not

a reliable guide for future productions.[52] To replace this *ad hoc* approach, Gallup proposed to isolate and evaluate all the factors that contributed to a picture's success or failure. In the early 1940s, he singled out three areas which he believed could be examined
through research: titles, stories and casts. In the postwar period, he added publicity and
marketing campaigns to this list.[53]

In its early studies for RKO, ARI determined that one-quarter of the public bought
tickets on the basis of a picture's title.[54] This made it 'of paramount importance to
insure that every picture carries the strongest possible title ... the fact remains that a
weak title always impairs box office performance, and a strong title always helps it'. In
addition to enhancing the value of a picture, title tests could also discover information
that could be used to promote it. To determine the most successful title for a project,
ARI tested as many as forty choices, usually in groups of four. The tests produced a
simple numerical measurement which seemed to guarantee their accuracy, and executives often made decisions purely on this basis. During pre-production for *Mr. Lucky*
(1943), for example, RKO changed the title six times, as each new survey discovered a
more popular name.[55] A title that tested well was often advertised, as if this achievement
in itself were significant.

According to ARI, titles should serve as an accurate reflection of a picture's content, guiding audiences into the narrative in the same way that newspaper headlines
led readers into a feature story.[56] Through testing, studios discovered what associations a title produced and could judge whether they matched the actual subject of
the picture. They could then adjust the title to target particular segments of the audience, while advertising and sales departments could develop promotional strategies
directed to them. During the late 1940s, for instance, the Disney studio wanted to
expand its audience beyond the traditional juvenile one to include adults. It used
ARI's research to determine whether a title evoked too many reminders of childhood,
and what changes could be made to enhance their pictures' attraction for older viewers. For this reason, *Song of the South* was chosen over *Uncle Remus* as the title of the
studio's 1946 live-action/animated feature, because its popularity was strong among
older viewers.[57]

ARI's agreement with RKO specified that it would furnish the studio with 'certified'
story ideas 'that have been tested for their interest value with the motion picture public'.[58] ARI recommended that RKO use best-selling novels and recently published magazine serials because they had a built-in audience.[59] Adaptations of already classic texts
also had to take audience preference into account. ARI complained that RKO's proposed
treatment of *Little Men*, for example, departed too much from the original. Ogilvy wrote
that: '[T]he audience appeal of *Little Men* derived in large measure from the affection
with which its many readers remember it ... the picture must adhere faithfully to the
original book, if it [is] to capitalize fully on this ready-made market.'[60] Once the public
had passed judgement on a project, Hollywood should not tamper with it, if they
wanted to keep audiences' loyalty. Story tests, usually in the form of sixty-word synopses, presented different combinations of features to determine which aroused the
most interest. ARI recommended that whatever formula earned the best response
should become the basis for a picture's advertising.[61] Story tests for Columbia's *The
Jolson Story* (1946) found little interest among that core group, nineteen-year-olds. After

ARI revised the synopses to emphasise the film's music, teenagers became interested. To attract the attention of this key group, posters and ads listed each of the film's songs.[62]

As Richard Jewell has documented, during the 1940s RKO failed to develop a long-term strategy for creating stars out of contract players.[63] As a result, the studio had few major stars under contract and relied on performers borrowed from other studios. Of the fifteen surveys ARI carried out during the first three months of its contract with RKO, almost half asked about stars. In 1940, the studio's contract with its biggest star, Ginger Rogers, was about to expire. Her last picture with Fred Astaire had not been as successful as their earlier movies, and she wanted to move away from musicals into dramatic roles. Wanting to make the most profitable use of her talents, RKO asked ARI to investigate whether the public preferred seeing her in dramatic roles, such as the ones she played in *Bachelor Mother* and *Fifth Avenue Girl*, or whether they wanted her to appear in another picture with Fred Astaire.[64] Though they liked her dramatic performances, audiences voted for the musicals.[65]

Two months later, ARI decided to find out whether the box office failure of *Broadway Melody* (1940), Astaire's picture with Eleanor Powell, was due to a decline in Astaire's popularity or to negative reactions to Powell. The survey found that people who went to see the movie did so principally because Fred Astaire was in it. The findings from these two surveys led ARI to conclude that Astaire was not washed up, and that 'the public wants to see Ginger Rogers in another dancing picture with Fred Astaire'.[66] Even though RKO had dropped Astaire in 1939, the studio signed another contract with him in July 1940 and announced that he would be reunited with Rogers in 1941. Newspapers reported that RKO made the decision on the basis of this survey.[67] Like the 'certified story ideas' ARI offered, these star studies provided empirical evidence that actors should remain within their established personae.

The conservative effects of these star studies were most striking in ARI's research on Orson Welles. The Institute conducted three surveys about public perceptions of Welles during the summer of 1940, asking which of three projects people wanted him to make: *Smiler with a Knife* or *Heart of Darkness*, which Welles himself had proposed, or a film adaptation of *Invasion from Mars*, which ARI seems to have thought of. As one might expect, ARI found that the public wanted to see Welles in an adaptation of his radio broadcast, and argued that the broadcast's notoriety created a built-in audience for the picture.[68] Although Welles did not adapt his radio programme for the screen, ARI's suggestion that the public wanted to see actors in familiar roles acted as a conservative force within RKO, giving producers evidence to support studio tradition and established practice.

In the summer of 1940, ARI also initiated a quarterly survey it called a 'continuing audit of marquee values', asking respondents whether seeing a star's name on a theatre marquee would in itself induce them to buy a ticket. Announcing this new service, *Variety* declared that its method of 'plotting the ebb and flow of a performer's reception by Joe and Jane America is precisely the same as the familiar barometer of President Roosevelt done by Gallup's American Institute of Public Opinion'.[69] At first, survey results were presented as graphs charting actors' ups and downs as a series of peaks and valleys. Later the charts analysed each star's appeal to different demographic groups. RKO considered this information on stars' recent popularity to be very valuable, and

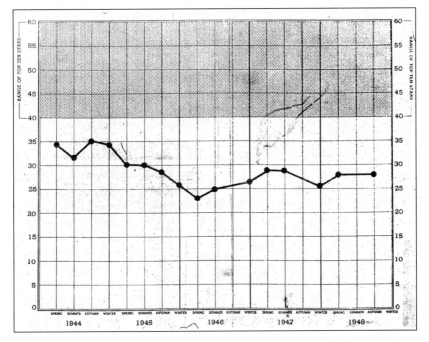

ARI chart showing reception scores for Bud Abbott and Lou Costello for the years 1944 to 1948. The grey area above 40 indicates the range of scores for the 'top ten stars'.

used these findings to evaluate its producers' casting recommendations.[70] ARI also conducted what it called a 'Dark Horse' survey to predict which actors and actresses were likely to gain popularity in the next few years. These measured the intensity of a star's following, on the theory that fans who felt strongly about the actor or actress would make them a star. ARI's predictions – for instance, that Ingrid Bergman would emerge among the top seven stars for 1943 – were often surprisingly accurate.[71]

As well as indicating RKO's uncertainty about how best to use its stars, the existence of these 'audits of marquee values' and the 'Dark Horse' poll testifies to the effort to manage and control stars within the studio system during the 1940s. During World War II, changes in the taxation system prompted many stars to work less. ARI concluded that a star's marquee value declined unless he or she made at least three pictures a year, ammunition that bolstered studios' efforts to keep stars busy.[72] The obvious pro-management implications of this report were not lost on the *New York Times*, which pointed out how convenient it was to have support for the studios' position 'set forth by attractive statistics'.[73]

Preview Profiles and Publicity

Though title, story and cast tests provided early indications of a picture's potential, they did not measure its overall effect. As Gallup himself admitted, pre-production tests could not evaluate the impact of an inventive script, witty dialogue or imaginative direction.[74] ARI began conducting preview screenings with carefully selected audiences early in 1944. Before the 1940s, most previews took place in theatres around Los Angeles, before audiences that included many industry insiders.[75] ARI argued that they could not reflect the interests of the average film-goer, and instead used cross-section sampling to select 'a replica in miniature of the movie masses'.[76] The Institute tracked viewers' responses during a screening with a Hopkins 'Televoting' Machine, a device originally developed for radio research. The Televoting Machine featured a luminous dial that offered respondents five choices: the switch could be turned to positions marked 'very dull, dull, neutral, like, like very much'. Individual responses were combined to produce a chart that provided a second-by-second account of audience reaction, which studios used as a guide in editing sequences that failed to reach a particular level of response.[77] These 'preview profiles' could also reveal areas of confusion in a picture. At a preview for *Gilda*, for example, audiences became confused when the character's husband returned after having been apparently lost at sea. Based on ARI's profile, Columbia filmed an additional sequence showing that he had been rescued after his accident.[78] Studios used these charts to prove the popularity of their pictures to exhibitors: *Gilda*'s impressive graph formed the basis for an advertisement.

The information obtained from pre-production surveys and preview profiles influenced the size of a picture's advertising budget and the type of release it received. In planning publicity campaigns, ARI urged studios to start at least six months in advance, using gossip, background articles and other pieces of news to build audience awareness. Early publicity for a picture established a 'mental rallying point that can be built up and reinforced repeatedly by the release date'.[79] To reach the largest possible audience, the company recommended that studios tailor campaigns to particular markets, rather than use one type of promotion. ARI measured the impact of these marketing campaigns through tests of 'publicity penetration'. Interviewers asked people whether they had heard of a picture, and whether they knew something about it. If they were able to identify its cast or some element of the story, they were said to have been 'penetrated' by the publicity.[80] Penetration tests allowed studios to gauge the effectiveness of different forms of advertising and to determine whether there was sufficient audience interest in a picture. At Disney, advertising executive Card Walker constructed elaborate charts to track changes in audience penetration after ads appeared in national magazines and local newspapers, enabling the studio to co-ordinate promotional campaigns with releases in different cities.[81]

After several years of research, ARI announced that it could use penetration studies and pre-production research to estimate the box office return of a picture. Through a complicated formula computing 'want-to-see', the marquee value of a cast, and penetration research, the company developed charts that allowed producers to determine the level of awareness a picture had to achieve in order to earn a given amount of money. With this information, David Selznick delayed releasing *Duel in the Sun* for six months in order to build its penetration to a level where he could recoup the picture's expenses.[82]

Audience Research Blues

During the 1940s, audience research functioned primarily as a tool for managerial control. Producers commissioned most studies, and they strictly regulated the circulation

of survey data, limiting access mainly to other executives. Within the vertically integrated majors, these studies became a way for executives to maintain authority at a time
when their hegemony was challenged by anti-trust legislation and unionisation. For
independent producers, audience research provided support for their work that bolstered their standing with distributors and exhibitors. During this period, critics,
writers and actors challenged the hegemony of the studio system. Audience research
became one of the battlegrounds for their disputes about control and authority. In
speaking of the audience, producers, writers and actors attempted to assert their authority over film production and reception. Debates about film audiences became a
means to define, understand and manage change and uncertainty within the industry
as a whole.

In July 1947, art critic Ernest Bornemann launched a scathing attack on viewer surveys and the executives who used them in the widely respected magazine *Harper's*.
Bornemann charged that Hollywood's 'utter dependence' on Gallup's polls had turned
film production into 'a sterile, glutted and intractable thing'. The slavish devotion to
empirical research made producers less willing to take risks, he asserted, since it was
easier to create pictures that satisfied a pre-established demand than to experiment with
new approaches. Surveys allowed no room for variations among viewers, and failed to
recognise that films are complex works of art, not industrial products.[83]

Further attacks came from members of the Screen Writers' Guild. Dudley Nichols
deplored the inhibitions that such tests placed on screenwriters who had to develop
characters and narratives to match predetermined patterns. Particular scorn was
reserved for the Televoting machine. Ranald MacDougall, screenwriter for *Mildred
Pierce*, noticed that many people forgot to move the dial when they became absorbed in
a picture, thus registering their reaction as indifference. Audiences also showed a slight
delay in reacting, so that 'a moving scene will register nothing and slightly afterwards a
dissolve from a door opening to a door closing will appear on the graph as one of the
finest pieces of acting yet this year'. Others complained about ARI's focus on 'gum-
chewing bobby soxers'. 'We *know* what junior wants, and he gets it,' MacDougall argued.
'Why not find out *what senior wants*?'[84] In the opinion of these writers, audience
research perpetuated mediocrity in films, by gearing characters and narratives to satisfy
the lowest common denominator among audiences.

Actors and actresses also complained that executives used audience research to control them and limit their creativity. In an article entitled 'Audience Research Blues',
Variety noted that 'columns of statistical surveys' were beginning to play a 'deadly decisive' role in actors' careers. Stars described walking into a producer's office and watching
him 'open that secret drawer, look down on a column of figures, and say, "Sorry, you're
not the type"'. Paulette Goddard and Burgess Meredith expressed fear that somewhere
there was 'a machine-made estimate of us all'.[85] In his analysis of ARI procedures used
to measure actors' popularity, historian Gorham Kindem has suggested that they grossly
underestimated the earning power of Hollywood stars.[86] Even the production executives who were ARI's clients resented its intrusion into production decisions. They
found it difficult to reconcile the rapid pace of film production with the longer time
required for survey research. The results of such hurried studies were not always accurate, and weakened ARI's reputation.

Gallup's incorrect prediction that Thomas Dewey would defeat Harry Truman in the 1948 election damaged the public image of opinion polling and dealt the final blow to the Audience Research Institute. The associations that Gallup had successfully fostered between his political work and his film research now hurt him. Both RKO and Disney, who had been negotiating contract renewals with the company, cut back to a few studies. Though Gallup tried for several years to drum up interest in advertising research, after 1948 studios largely turned away from his techniques.

Although Gallup's formal contacts with Hollywood studios ended in the late 1940s, many of ARI's techniques have been assimilated into industry practice. Film companies today measure responses to titles and proposed casts, screen rough cuts for preview audiences and test the effectiveness of advertising strategies.[87] By recovering the debates that accompanied Gallup's work, we can understand the issues at stake in the use of this research. Polls, argues political scientist Susan Herbst 'give the illusion that the public has already spoken in a definitive manner', effectively supplanting other forms of political and social discourse. In translating the multiplicity and diversity of opinions into percentages and graphs, polls redefine the subject of which they speak. ARI promised executives advance information about the most unpredictable element of film economics, audience reaction. Its surveys seemed to provide an element of control over the risks and uncertainty of film manufacture.

The scientific aura surrounding Gallup's research was due, in part, to its effort to provide a totalising view of film spectatorship. ARI's battery of techniques worked to isolate and define key elements influencing viewer response, from title and cast through to advertising. The fact that ARI continually reworked its methodology suggests, however, that 'scientific' research could never offer a final word on audience preferences. Although market research deploys the authority of science in an effort to control, it also to an extent recognises the power of individuals to resist prediction.

Notes

1 Adolph Zukor, with Dale Kramer, *The Public is Never Wrong* (New York: G. P. Putnam's Sons, 1953), p. 42.

2 Garth S. Jowett, 'Giving them what they want: movie audience research before 1950', in Bruce Austin (ed.), *Current Research in Film: Audiences, Economics and Law, Vol. 1*, (Norwood, N. J.: Ablex, 1985), pp. 19–21.

3 Loren Baritz, *Servants of Power* (Middletown, Conn.: Wesleyan University Press, 1960), pp. 32–4.

4 George Gallup, 'Traits of successful retail salespeople', *Journal of Personnel Research* 4 (April 1926), pp. 474–82.

5 Donald Napoli, *Architects of Adjustment: The History of the Psychological Profession in the United States* (Port Washington, New York: Kennikat Press, 1981), pp. 34–48.

6 George Gallup, 'An objective method for determining reader interest in the content of a newspaper' (Ph.D. dissertation, University of Iowa, August 1928), pp. 17–19 and pp. 36–8.

7 Gallup, 'An objective method', pp. 42–4; George Gallup, 'Guesswork eliminated in new method for determining reader interest', *Editor & Publisher*, 8 February 1930, pp. 5, 55.

8 Otis Pease, *The Responsibilities of American Advertising* (New Haven: Yale University Press, 1958), pp. 185–6; 'Competitive Comics', *Tide* (June 1932), p. 14.

9 See, for example, George Burton Hotchkiss, *An Outline of Advertising: Its Philosophy, Science, Art and Strategy* (New York: Macmillan, 1940), pp. 170–1.

10 T. J. Jackson Lears, 'From salvation to self-realization: advertising and the therapeutic roots of consumer culture, 1880–1930', in Richard Wightman Fox and T. J. Jackson Lears (eds) *The Culture of Consumption: Critical Essays in American History, 1880–1980*, (New York: Pantheon, 1983), pp. 17–8.

11 Stephen Fox, *The Mirror Makers: A History of American Advertising and Its Creators* (New York: William Morrow, 1984), pp. 120–4.

12 David P. Kuna, 'The concept of suggestion in the early history of advertising psychology', *Journal of the History of the Behavioral Sciences* 12 (1976), pp. 347–50; and Edmund C. Lynch, 'Walter Dill Scott: pioneer industrial psychologist', *Business History Review* 42:2 (Summer 1968), pp. 150–2.

13 Information on Gallup's work at Young & Rubicam is drawn from the corporate archive of the Young & Rubicam agency, New York City, NY.

14 Donald Hurwitz, 'Market research and the study of the U.S. radio audience', *Communication* 10 (1988), pp. 237–8.

15 Quoted in Jean Converse, *Survey Research in the United States: Roots and Emergence 1890–1960* (Berkeley: University of California Press, 1987), p. 113.

16 George Gallup and Saul Forbes Rae, *The Pulse of Democracy: the Public Opinion Poll and How it Works* (New York: Greenwood Press, 1968), pp. 79–80.

17 The stand-off between the Gallup Poll and the *Literary Digest* during the 1936 election is one of the most famous dramas in survey history. For an account of the issues involved, see Peverill Squire, 'Why the 1936 *Literary Digest* poll failed', *Public Opinion Quarterly* 52 (Spring 1988), pp. 125–33; and Daniel Katz and Hadley Cantril, 'Public opinion polls', *Sociometry* 1 (July 1937 – April 1938), pp. 158–9.

18 George Gallup, interview by Frank Rounds, Princeton, New Jersey, March–October, 1962, transcript, Columbia University Oral History Collection, New York, p. 126.

19 George Gallup, interview by Paul Sheatsley, Princeton, New Jersey, 22 March 1978, transcript, Columbia University Oral History Collection, New York, p. 14.

20 George Gallup, interview by Thomas Simonet, Princeton, New Jersey, 21 September 1977, transcript.

21 Don Cahalan, interview by author, 20 February 1992, tape recording, Berkeley, California.

22 Gallup, letter to David O. Selznick, 20 August 1943, 'Gallup Poll 1943' file, Box 4443, David O. Selznick Papers, Harry Ransom Humanities Research Center, University of Texas-Austin (hereafter: Selznick Papers).

23 Gallup, interview by Frank Rounds, pp. 144–5.

24 David Ogilvy, letter to Ruth Inglis, 26 March 1942, 'Gallup Poll 1939–1941–1942' file, Box 4443, Selznick Papers.

25 Questions on *Gone With the Wind* appeared in the Gallup survey for the week of 27 January – 1 February 1939. Respondents were also asked whether they were 'satisfied' with the choice of Vivien Leigh. Despite a massive national publicity campaign, nearly one third said they did not know Selznick had signed her. AIPO Ballot 146A and B, 27

January–1 February 1939, Roper Center for Public Opinion Research, University of Connecticut at Storrs. See also 'Surveying Scarlett O'Hara', *New York Times*, 19 February 1939, IX, p. 4.

26 'Agreement regarding *Gone With the Wind*', 12 August 1938, 'MGM–*Gone With the Wind*, including Whitney correspondence' file, Box 159, Selznick Papers. Also Leo C. Rosten, *Hollywood: The Movie Colony, The Movie Makers* (New York: Harcourt, Brace, 1941), p. 331.

27 David O. Selznick, letter to Jock Whitney, 28 June 1939, 'Gallup Poll 1939–1941–1942' file, Box 4443, Selznick Papers.

28 David O. Selznick, memo to Lowell Calvert, 5 April 1939, 'Gallup Poll 1939–1941–1942' file, Box 4443, Selznick Papers.

29 David O. Selznick, letter to Al Lichtman [MGM's head of distribution], 28 June 1939, 'Gallup Poll 1939-1941-1942' file, Box 4443, Selznick Papers.

30 W. R. Wilkerson, 'Trade views', *Hollywood Reporter*, 3 January 1940, pp. 1–2; 'Listen, "The Wind!" ', *New York Times*, 26 November 1939, IX, p. 4; ' "Wind" riding in with "streamlined" sales and merchandising setup', *Motion Picture Herald*, 2 December 1939, pp. 17–8; 'Setting final policies on "Wind" ', *Motion Picture Herald*, 9 December 1939, pp. 14–15.

31 David O. Selznick, letter to John Hay Whitney, 28 June 1939, 'Gallup Poll 1939–1941–1942' file, Box 4443, Selznick Papers.

32 *Gone With the Wind* ad, *Variety*, 15 April 1942, p. 24. Chester B. Bahn, 'Metro turns the trick', *Film Daily*, 12 December 1939, p. 6.

33 Matthew Bernstein, 'Hollywood's Semi-Independent Production', *Cinema Journal* 32:3 (Spring 1993), pp. 41–54.

34 '53 feature films scheduled by RKO', *New York Times*, 28 May 1940, p. 28.

35 Leo Handel, *Hollywood Looks at Its Audience* (Urbana, Ill.: University of Illinois Press, 1950; rpt New York: Arno, 1976), pp. 6–11.

36 Leo Rosten, *Hollywood: The Movie Colony and the Movie-Makers* (New York: Harcourt, Brace, 1941), p. 490.

37 ARI Report XCIII, 'Sue Barton II', in *Gallup Looks at the Movies: Audience Research Reports 1940–1950*, Princeton, New Jersey: American Institute of Public Opinion; Wilmington, Delaware: Scholarly Resources, 1979. This four-reel microfilm set contains the 196 reports that ARI carried out for RKO in the early 1940s, as well as the studies of stars it conducted throughout the decade. It is the most readily available source for Gallup's film research.

38 ARI Report XLVI, '*The Band Played On*', 12 February 1941, *Gallup Looks at the Movies*.

39 'Increasing profits through continuous audience research', *Gallup Looks at the Movies*, p. 14.

40 ' "All Out" effort to groom new stars', *Film Daily*, 2 June 1941, pp. 1, 7.

41 'Increasing profits', *Gallup Looks at the Movies*, p. 36.

42 'Boy meets facts', *Time*, 21 July 1941, p. 73.

43 ARI Report XIX, 'Variations in the composition of audiences', *Gallup Looks at the Movies*.

44 ARI Report XXXII, '*Kitty Foyle*', *Gallup Looks at the Movies*.

45 William A. Lydgate, 'Hollywood listens to the audience', *Reader's Digest*, April 1944, p. 84.

46 See M. Joyce Baker, *Images of Women in Film: The War Years, 1941–1945* (Ann Arbor, Mich.: UMI Research Press, 1980); and Michael Renov, *Hollywood's Wartime Woman: Representation and Ideology* (Ann Arbor, Mich.: UMI Research Press, 1988).

47 'Composition of the motion picture audience, 1940–1941', *Gallup Looks at the Movies*.

48 'Increasing profits through continuous audience research', *Gallup Looks at the Movies*, p. 69.

49 David Ogilvy, letter to George Schaefer, 21 November 1940, 'ARI General Correspondence File No. 1', RKO files, Turner Entertainment, Culver City, California (hereafter: RKO Archive), p. 3.

50 ARI Report, 'The Devil and Daniel Webster', 5 October 1940, *Gallup Looks at the Movies*.

51 ARI Report 148, '*Battle Stations* or pay to learn', 23 March 1942, *Gallup Looks at the Movies*.

52 'Increasing profits', *Gallup Looks at the Movies*, p. 3.

53 'Scientific research as applied to the motion picture public', 28 September 1939, 'Agreement' file, RKO Archive.

54 'A.P. and want-to-see', *Time*, 22 July 1946, pp. 94–6.

55 William Weaver, 'Audience research answers the question of what's in a name', *Motion Picture Herald*, 27 July 1946, p. 39.

56 Paul Perry, 'Marketing and attitude research applied to motion pictures', Paper presented at the International Gallup Conference, New Delhi, India, 26 March 1968, p. 5.

57 Brundage, 'Dr. Gallup polls public so Hollywood can film the "perfect" picture', *Wall Street Journal*, 23 October 1946, p. 1.

58 ARI Report No. XXXVIII, 'Parachute Invasion', 12 December 1940, *Gallup Looks at the Movies*.

59 See, for example, ARI Report XXII, 'An American Doctor's Odyssey', 19 August 1940, and Report XXIII, 'For the Record', 27 August 1940, *Gallup Looks at the Movies*.

60 ARI Report XXXVII, '*Little Men* II', 11 December 1940, *Gallup Looks at the Movies*.

61 'How Gallup Poll samples public opinion', *Business Week*, 19 June 1948, pp. 39–53.

62 *ARI Case Histories, Vol. 1: The Jolson Story,* The Margaret Herrick Library, Motion Picture Academy of Arts and Sciences, Los Angeles, California.

63 Richard B. Jewell, 'A history of RKO Radio Pictures Incorporated 1928–1942' (PhD dissertation, University of Southern California, 1978), pp. 476–84, 546–51.

64 J. R. McDonough, letter to George Gallup, 23 February 1940, 'ARI General Correspondence File No. 1', RKO Archive.

65 ARI Report I, 'Ginger Rogers', 21 March 1940, *Gallup Looks at the Movies*.

66 David Ogilvy, letter to George Schaefer, 21 November 1940, 'ARI General Correspondence File No. 1', RKO Archive, p. 4.

67 Harold Heffernan, 'Films hunt 25,000,000 missing fans with poll', unidentified newspaper clipping, 'ARI General Correspondence File No. 1', RKO Archive.

68 ARI Report XII, '*Smiler with a Knife, Heart of Darkness,* or *Invasion from Mars?*', 15 May 1940, *Gallup Looks at the Movies*.

69 'Gallup rating pix stars', *Variety*, 18 September 1940, p. 1.

70 J. R. McDonough, memo to George Schaefer, 20 January 1941, 'ARI General Correspondence File No. 1', RKO Archive.

71 ARI Report XX, 'Dark Horses', 14 August 1940, *Gallup Looks at the Movies*.

72 'Stars told to make 3 per year', *Hollywood Reporter*, 23 July 1941, pp. 1, 4; 'High salaries prove boomerang to stars', *Los Angeles Times*, 24 July 1941, I, p. 8.

73 'After more than a year', *New York Times*, 3 August 1941, IX, p. 3.

74 Shaw, 'A package deal in film options', *The Screen Writer* 2 (March 1947), p. 33.

75 Handel, *Hollywood Looks at Its Audience*, pp. 8–10.

76 William Weaver, 'Studios use audience research', *Motion Picture Herald*, 20 July 1946, p. 37; Harold Wolff, 'Pre-testing movies', *Science Illustrated*, February 1947, p. 115; William Lydgate, 'Audience pre-testing heads off flops, forecasts hits, for movie producers', *Sales Management*, 15 March 1944, p. 98.

77 'Electric movie "reviewers" record reaction to film', *Popular Mechanics*, May 1947, p. 149; Harold Wolff, 'Pre-testing movies', *Science Illustrated*, February 1947, pp. 44–5, 115.

78 'Gallup Poll finds how to sell a movie', *Look*, 26 October 1948, pp. 53–5.

79 'Goldwyn wants ad agency near studio', *Variety*, 19 June 1946, p. 7.

80 Brundage, 'Dr. Gallup polls public', p. 4; Red Kann, 'On the march: (Audience Research Institute)', *Motion Picture Herald*, 29 July 1944, p. 12; 'How Gallup Poll samples public opinion', *Business Week*, 19 June 1948, p. 49.

81 For example, see the files concernng *Make Mine Music* (1946), Box 14, ARI files, Walt Disney Studio Archive, Burbank, California.

82 Gallup, interview by Thomas Simonet, 21 September 1977, transcript, p. 5.

83 Ernest Bornemann, 'The public opinion myth', *Harper's*, July 1947, pp. 30–3.

84 Ranald Macdougall, 'Reactions to audience research', *The Screen Writer* 2 (April 1947), p. 30.

85 'Audience research blues', *Variety*, 8 May 1946, p. 5.

86 Gorham Kindem, 'Hollywood's movie star system during the studio era', *Film Reader* 6 (1985), p. 18.

87 Olen J. Earnest, '*Star Wars*: a case study of motion picture marketing', *Current Research in Film*, pp. 1–18; Thomas Simonet, 'Market research: beyond the fanny of the Cohn', *Film Comment*, January–February 1980, pp. 66–9.

4 'The Lost Audience': 1950s spectatorship and historical reception studies

Robert Sklar

The post-World War II era poses a challenge to historical reception studies on American cinema. Leaving aside the temporary, Depression-induced setbacks of the early 1930s, it is the only period of major, sustained audience decline in United States film history. Between 1946 and 1960 the average weekly attendance at US motion picture theatres declined from 82 to 30 million patrons, and fell further in subsequent years to stabilise at around 20 million over the following quarter century.[1]

These figures are universally acknowledged and frequently discussed in studies on post-World War II American cinema, and there is widespread agreement on their extrinsic causes. Former movie spectators developed new priorities for their leisure hours. They started families, moved to suburbs, bought automobiles, played outdoors. Then along came television to satisfy their entertainment needs. The new medium did not become generally available until after the drop in motion picture attendance had already begun, but, of course, it soon became the object of a major shift in spectatorial allegiance.

What has been largely missing from accounts of this dramatic transformation is any exploration of its possible intrinsic aspects, stemming from the link between films and their spectators. Did movies themselves change in subject or in style from earlier eras in a manner that alienated former patrons? Were spectatorial interests and desires transformed in ways that film-makers were unable to acknowledge, or to which they could not shape an adequate response? What differences in age, gender, social class, educational attainment or other more subtle yet more salient characteristics were there between those who remained loyal movie fans and those who abandoned the medium?

The focus in historical reception studies on the contexts of spectator/film interaction offers an apt approach to these questions, and several works have begun to examine issues of postwar spectatorship. In *Interpreting Films*, Janet Staiger discusses the development of art cinema exhibition and reception in the post-war period in relation to the motion picture industry's recognition of niche audiences.[2] In *Melodrama and Meaning*, Barbara Klinger considers how a variety of meanings have been constructed for Douglas Sirk's 1950s melodramas through the discourses of industry publicity and promotion, contemporary reviewing and later academic critiques.[3] Some fundamental questions about the period, however, remain largely unaddressed, particularly in light of the precipitous decline in attendance. My purpose in this essay is to investigate schol-

arly writings on film spectatorship from that era and to assess their significance in for-
mulating new approaches to the period in historical reception studies. The existence of
such writing has scarcely been acknowledged in subsequent cinema studies scholarship,
and it has not received a great deal more attention from historians of the social sciences.[4] Perhaps this absence of interest derives from the impression left by several
observers who asserted during the period itself that spectatorship was a neglected subject. Leo A. Handel, the former director of audience research at MGM and author in
1950 of *Hollywood Looks at Its Audience*, wrote in 1953 that 'the movie industry is still
the only major business in the United States which has never made a serious attempt to
study its potential market'.[5] The claim was repeated four years later by Martin Quigley,
Jr., writing in the exhibitor trade paper *Motion Picture Herald*: 'Now in the period of crisis of the motion picture – which may be dated from the end of World War II – there is
much interest and almost no scientific data telling who are the patrons and who are the
members of what some called "the lost audience".'[6]

Despite these viewpoints, a substantial number of scholarly studies on various
aspects of spectatorship were in fact published in the years 1946–60.[7] In surveying this
material and selecting out several major issues and approaches for discussion, my aim
is not to revive authorial reputations or resurrect obsolescent theories and methodologies. It is to open a dialogic relationship with past discourses as an essential step in
framing questions for further historical reception studies of the postwar era. The
period's scholars had three primary concerns: data on audience composition, the effects
of motion pictures, and the function of movie-going.

Data on Audience Composition

Contrary to Martin Quigley, Jr.'s claim, in the years after World War II a considerable
amount of data on movie patrons and the 'lost audience' had been collected. Polling and
social survey organisations reported on such subjects as frequency of movie-going,
attendance by age, income, gender and educational attainment, and even the likes and
dislikes of both film-goers and non-attendees concerning movie subjects and styles.
Much of this material, it is true, was a by-product of research sponsored by other media
in which information about movie attendance was gathered for comparison, or as part
of an overall assessment of media uses. This was, indeed, true of Quigley's own data,
which was drawn from a study of readers of a weekly magazine, *The Saturday Evening
Post*, by Alfred Politz Research, Inc.

Previously published motion picture data had been derived from research conducted by, among others, the Bureau of Applied Social Research at Columbia University,
Elmo Roper for the *Fortune* magazine survey and Leo A. Handel's Motion Picture
Research Bureau. (In addition, George Gallup's Audience Research, Inc. supplied survey
data to motion picture companies and independent producers on a proprietary basis
that was not made publicly available.)[8] The basic assertions about the composition of
the motion picture audience derived from these surveys were summarised by Handel in
his 1950 book, and supported by the data that Quigley cited in 1957:

1. Male and female patrons attend at about equal rates.
2. Younger people attend more frequently than older people.

3. Persons in higher socio-economic brackets attend more frequently than those in lower levels.

4. The more years a person has spent in school, the more frequently he sees motion pictures.[9]

The first, third and fourth of these statements flew in the face of the accepted wisdom about movie audiences. The claims concerning socio-economic status and education were particularly startling. As Quigley later put it, 'It used to be generally held – and some doubtless still believe – that the motion picture's best audience in the United States was composed of those with only a moderate amount of schooling and in the low family income brackets. The figures show the exact opposite.'[10]

The presenters of these data, however, made almost no effort to interpret or analyse them, or do any more than offer them as 'facts'. Rarely did anyone place them in a historical or social context. Was there a transformation in the economic and educational background of the motion picture audience? If so, what were its causes? Such questions were unasked, and therefore unanswered. Since their research was paid for primarily by media organisations, the surveyors may have felt restrained from making qualitative judgements about societies or industries, especially since they were wary of resentment from executives who suspected that pollsters wanted to tell them how to run their business.[11]

Still, the facts did not speak for themselves, as researcher Paul F. Lazarsfeld emphasised. In a 1947 project funded by the magazine publishing firm McFadden, Lazarsfeld co-directed with sociologist C. Wright Mills a survey of women in a small Midwestern city, which he characterised as 'probably the most detailed approach to the movie audience yet undertaken'.[12] Lazarsfeld emphasised the singularity of age as 'the most important personal factor by which the movie audience is characterized'. Income and education, he said, 'mattered little. Studies have been published showing a much higher movie attendance among better-educated people, but this is mainly a spurious result due to the age factor'.[13] His explanation was that the development of the United States educational system meant that the youth who predominated in the movie audience would also show more years of schooling than members of the older generations who attended movies less frequently. However, Lazarsfeld offered no explanation for why he believed income was not a factor. Logically, one might assume that youths of school age or those just beginning their working lives would report lower incomes and thus skew the movie-going data toward lower income groups. In any case, Handel in his book (for which Lazarsfeld wrote the Foreword) referred frequently to Lazarsfeld's 'Audience research' article without engaging any of the issues of its author's dissent from several of his principal findings; he simply stated that 'most studies agree' on the four propositions he put forward as 'facts'.[14]

One author did use survey research data for polemical purposes but, unlike those previously mentioned, he was not a pollster for whom media companies were the primary clients. This was Gilbert Seldes, a pioneering critic of the popular arts, in his 1950 book *The Great Audience*. Seldes had obtained data from Gallup's ARI that detailed the predominance of youth in the movie audience. He interpreted this information to stress the decline in movie-going as persons grow older, and he castigated the movie industry for relying for its revenues on adolescents and allowing the majority of the population 'to vanish from the movie houses'. Seldes cited Eric Johnston, successor to Will Hays as head of the motion picture producers' association, as warning his clients 'that they have not kept pace with the growing intelligence of the public or with the spread of education as represented by the number of high school graduates; he has advised Hollywood to make pictures for adults'.[15] After he established his viewpoint based on survey data, fully a third of Seldes's book consisted of a critique of Hollywood film-making for its lack of 'maturity'.

The Effects of Motion Pictures

Along with research on audience composition, studies into the effects of films on viewers' attitudes and behaviour formed a significant aspect of the discourse on spectatorship in the post-World War II years. These studies were in part a continuation of the enormous effort expended across many disciplines during the war to analyse the nature and function of propaganda and to assess its impact on public opinion. More narrowly, they also responded to a desire on the part of military film-making agencies to gauge the effectiveness of training films and also what they called 'orientation' films, such as the *Why We Fight* series supervised by Frank Capra, which were made with didactic ideological intention. Military units in training also had the advantage of providing testing populations which were relatively stable and definable.

Much of the scholarly writing on effects took on a rather more reflective and ambiguous tone than that on audience composition, which generally aimed for a non-dialogic presentation of data. Awareness of the historical context of movie effects research was a factor in this rhetorical difference. Postwar effects studies in some sense carried the burden of their major predecessor, the Payne Fund Studies published from 1933 to 1935, of which, as effects scholar Franklin Fearing judiciously put it, 'it may be granted that some of the studies were imperfect as judged by rigorous methodological standards and that some of the results were publicized beyond their scientific merit'. The Payne Fund project's general conclusion was that movies did have definite and measurable effects that were 'on the whole bad', Fearing continued, and this view had been rigorously contested.[16] A further source of reflection was the realisation that, as movies rapidly lost their audience in the postwar period, interest in effects studies was shifting away from movies toward television, radio and even comic books.

Some part of this reflexivity may also have derived from the scholarly strategies pursued by Fearing, perhaps the most visible of the effects researchers after World War II. A professor of psychology at UCLA, Fearing was also one of the founders and a member of the editorial board of *Hollywood Quarterly* (later *Quarterly of Film, Radio and Television*), a journal offering media analysis from both professional and scholarly perspectives. Fearing had been a consultant to the wartime Hollywood Writers' Mobilisation, which later came under attack by the California State Un-American Activities Committee as a Communist front organisation. The *Quarterly* also was accused, and Fearing's name appeared on a list of Mobilisation participants whom a source had identified as Communist Party members. Nancy Lynne Schwartz, in her book *The Hollywood Writers' Wars*, characterises Fearing as a liberal who was 'one of the saddest, most bewildered victims' of the committee's attacks, and whose career was among those destroyed because of their associations.[17]

It is unclear in what respects Fearing's career was destroyed, since he remained a UCLA professor and continued his scholarly activities. One may speculate on the effects that his political experiences had on his views of movie effects. Articles with titles such as 'Some sources of confusion' and 'A word of caution for the intelligent consumer of motion pictures' may suggest a wariness related to the costs of political *naïveté*, or, more simply, scholarly prudence.[18] For whatever reason, Fearing's writings show a predisposition to reject sweeping generalisations and large theoretical claims. In 'A word of caution', a published version of a talk to a non-scholarly audience, he conceded that 'research, conducted as carefully as we now know how to conduct it, reveals that the effects of these media – films and radio, especially films – on human attitudes and behavior is unexpectedly slight'. Even where research could identify definite effects among their audience, he continued, as in the case of radio soap operas,

> the relationship between program content and response is not a simple one; it is not an effect in which the ideas that are presented via the program are projected in some direct way on people's minds with direct effects on attitudes and behavior. The effects are selective, and they are dependent on already existing needs. . . . The viewer and listener are dynamic participants in the situation. They react *on* the content presented rather than reacting *to* it.[19]

Fearing also expressed a characteristic scepticism about the production of effects. Several of the effects studies in the postwar period dealt with movies' impact on attitudes toward race. As Fearing described them, these studies demonstrated, firstly, that spectatorial response was conditioned by a viewer's socio-economic background and, secondly, that spectators were capable of restructuring the themes or communication content of a work 'to suit their needs and beliefs'.[20] In the context of such findings, Fearing posed himself the rhetorical question, 'if you could make any kind of a film you wished, with complete control of content and an unlimited budget, and you wished to affect anti-Negro or anti-Semitic attitudes, *what kind of a film would you make?*' Fearing's response was, 'this is an embarrassing question, because we do not know with even approximate precision what it is in the complex *Gestalt* which is the film, that would have the sought-for effect'.[21]

Finally, Fearing's questioning extended to the psychoanalytically oriented discourses on film reception that were emerging in the postwar years. In several commentaries on Siegfried Kracauer's *From Caligari to Hitler*, published in 1947, Fearing conceded the importance of Kracauer's endeavour and found his film analyses 'shrewd' and his insights occasionally useful, but basically he rejected the theories of reception inscribed not only in Kracauer but also in works by J. P. Mayer and Parker Tyler that drew on psychoanalytic or other psychological grounds.[22] Kracauer's study, he wrote,

> is marred by the difficulties implicit in the Freudian method and theory, especially when applied to the interpretation of a cultural manifestation. In the present instance it is necessary to assume that the unconscious forces operating in the minds of the producers result in films containing hidden meanings, which in turn affect the unconscious minds of the mass audience.[23]

When Kracauer found occasion in 1949 to address issues pertaining to the effects discourse, he emphasised one aspect of his argument in *From Caligari to Hitler* that rather contradicts Fearing's formulation in the preceding quote. 'To be sure, American audiences receive what Hollywood wants them to want', he had written at the end of a key section of his theoretical introduction, 'but in the long run public desires determine the nature of Hollywood films'.[24] In an article on 'National types as Hollywood presents them', published in *Public Opinion Quarterly*, he returned to this theme with an emphasis suggesting that the direction of effects went not from movies to spectators but in the opposite direction, from spectators to movies; or perhaps, more precisely, in an unending cycle of mutually interacting effect and effect.[25]

Kracauer rejected as untenable a viewpoint holding that 'Hollywood films more often than not stultify and misdirect a public persuaded into accepting them by its own indolence and by overwhelming publicity.' The film industry, he wrote, 'is forced by its profit interest to divine the nature of actually existing mass trends and to adjust its products to them. That this necessity leaves a margin for cultural initiative on the part of the industry does not alter the situation'. These words were followed by a sentence reiterating his book's argument that public desires determined the nature of Hollywood's films.[26] At the end of his article, he elaborated on this thesis: 'Such desires and tendencies are more or less inarticulate, and they do not materialize unless they are forced out of their pupa state; they must be identified and formulated to come into their own … What matters most in this context, then, is the essential ambiguity of mass dispositions.' Films conform to these wants, yet in doing so they render definite their ambiguity and 'thus determine the nature of the inarticulate from which they emerge'.[27] Kracauer did not attempt in his article to specify the mechanism of interaction, as he did in his book. Nor did he indicate any awareness that, with Hollywood's postwar loss of audience, on one side or the other the mechanism appeared to be breaking down, or shifting to another medium. As Fearing had noted in his critique, Kracauer's work also contained no acknowledgement of audience data and effects research which suggested that segmentation and differentiation were core aspects of group and individual spectatorial responses to the medium.

The Function of Movie-going

Sociologists David Riesman and Evelyn T. Riesman opened their 1952 article on 'Movies and audiences' for *American Quarterly*, the journal of the recently formed American Studies Association, with an eye-catching gambit. They began by citing Gilbert Seldes's view, noted above, 'that older people stay away from movies because the latter are not sufficiently adult and mature'. They then suggested that the facts may be just the reverse: 'films are too mature, move too fast, for older people to catch on to and catch up with'. Young people, they continued, have learned the conventions and emotional vocabularies of the media 'as a mother tongue', and the possibility that the old have to learn these new media languages is one of the ambiguities of communication that are 'related to the tension between the generations, between the social classes, and between character types'.[28]

Nothing in the remainder of the article quite equals the refreshing jolt this counterpunch provides, but it does slightly expand the point in the framework of David

Riesman's then-new and widely influential thesis concerning American character in his 1950 book, *The Lonely Crowd*.[29] The Reismans drew attention to what they described as 'the revolutionary or insubordinate role of the media', and suggested that this role was changing. Twenty years earlier the subjects whom the Payne Fund researchers studied had gone to the movies to see the sex and splendour, the settings and etiquette, which were remote from their own experience. But with rising standards of living and education, splendour, etiquette and 'social know-how generally' were less remote from 1950s movie-going youth.

> Though the evidence is tantalizingly little [they wrote], we have the impression that young people of, let us say, sixth grade level and up resort to the movies today, not so much to have a look at an exotic and make-believe world . . ., but increasingly to understand complex networks of interpersonal relations. This change in audience use of films is connected with a change in American character, from what in *The Lonely Crowd* is termed 'inner-direction' to what is called 'other-direction', and this change in turn is connected with large-scale developments in the conditions of modern metropolitan life.[30]

The Riesmans' perspective was linked in a significant way with a facet of Paul F. Lazarsfeld's findings in his 1947 article 'Audience research in the movie field'. Lazarsfeld concluded his article by noting 'one aspect of the movie audience which deserves special attention': the phenomenon of the movie 'opinion leader' to whom others look for advice on what movies to see. 'In an overwhelming number of cases', Lazarsfeld wrote, 'they are young people, many of them below twenty-five years of age. This is a very remarkable result. One general notion is that the young learn from the old. In the movie field, advice and acceptance of advice definitely flow in the opposite direction.'[31]

The Riesmans might have argued that not enough of this inter-generational advice-giving was going on; but while they were concerned with how the 'inner-directed' old were going to catch on to the new, their interest in 'other-directed' youth was in peer-group interaction, and the one social science researcher they cited on this subject was the sociologist Eliot Friedson, who happened to be finishing a dissertation in David Riesman's department at the University of Chicago at the time when the Riesmans' article appeared. Friedson's unpublished dissertation, completed in 1952, was called 'An audience and its taste: a study of 79 children'. In the next few years he published several articles related to this research.

Friedson interviewed 'a group of 79 third-generation, Polish-Catholic, upper-lower class public school boys from the kindergarten, second, fourth and sixth grades . . . with a view to finding out what relevance the social situation of contacting mass media has to audiences responses'.[32] His conclusion was that the social situation of contact was indeed relevant to the study of spectator response, which in his view rendered 'mere study of the relation of content to the demographic attributes of an audience – i.e., age, sex, education, socio-economic status' inadequate for explaining 'why the spectator responds as he does'.[33] Specifically, Friedson found that the children he studied watched television with their families, read comic books alone and went to the movies with their peer group. As they grew older (through the elementary school grades) the movies took on greater importance as a setting where they could be away from their family and 'alone' with their friends. 'One would expect this trend to continue as adolescent courtship begins', he added in a footnote.[34]

The Riesmans cited Friedson's work because it accorded with their view of the movies as a privileged site for the acting out of other-directedness. It happened that Friedson's subjects did not quite fulfil the Riesman's notion that 'the films are a place to show sophistication'.[35] His sixth-graders typically attended matinees at which few adults were present.

> Although the movie situation permits the child to select the type of content he wishes [Friedson observed], his opportunity to concentrate attention on the content is limited by an audience that is shouting, running up and down the aisles, and fighting. The context of neighborhood-theater matinees interferes with attention and seems to diffuse effects that may be potential in the content itself.[36]

As a consequence of the age range of his subjects, Friedson did not confront the possibility that once adolescent courtship begins, sophistication awaits.

Friedson used his research as the basis for a theoretical paper, 'Communications research and the concept of the mass', in which he critiqued the view, argued in a 1936 paper by sociologist Herbert Blumer, one of the key Payne Fund authors, that the movie audience could be characterised as a mass audience.[37] In Friedson's account, Blumer had held that the movie audience possessed the characteristics of mass behaviour because its members were anonymous, heterogeneous, unorganised and spatially separated, and the content of the movies was concerned with something that lay outside the local lives of the spectators. Friedson countered this position with his own thesis that the movie audience consisted not of discrete individual spectators engaged in collective behaviour, but of participants whose experience of movie-going is social and related to local life.

> An adequate concept of the audience [he wrote], must include some idea of its social character, some idea that being a member of a local audience is a social activity in which interaction with others before, during and after any single occasion of spectatorship has created definite shared expectations and predisposing definitions.[38]

It is worth noting that Friedson drew on Handel's *Hollywood Looks at Its Audience* for evidence to support his argument, which included the concept of the 'opinion leader' previously articulated by Lazarsfeld.[39]

Historical Reception Studies

Historical reception studies on post-World War II American cinema have so far derived more from a primary concern with films rather than with spectators. In the past quarter century of academic film studies, scholars have developed new names and identities for several important postwar genres – most significantly, film noir and the family melodrama – that were described differently by contemporary reviewers and in movie industry discourse. In the light of new critical and historiographical interpretations of these genres, historical reception scholars have grown interested in the discourses that formed the contexts of spectatorship in that era.

Historical spectators, to be sure, can only be apprehended in their contemporary setting by what was said to and about them. In her study on the reception of Sirk's films, Barbara Klinger's use of studio publicity discourses and journalistic reviews enables her to construe 'some of the historical conditions at work in a significant moment of a film's reception'.[40] My study on the scholarly spectatorship studies from that era also suggests that they can be used to 'lengthen the questionnaire' (in Paul Veyne's term) of historical reception studies and reframe the spectator/film relationship in ways that also shed light on the interpretation of films.

The implied debate between Gilbert Seldes and David and Evelyn T. Riesman (inscribed in the latter's' article 'Movies and audiences') would be one productive place to start. Seldes had argued that the crisis of 'the lost audience' in the postwar era had come about because movies were not mature enough, particularly in view of the public's growing educational attainments. The Riesmans had countered that, conversely, movies were too mature for older audiences of the period. These contrasting viewpoints could be juxtaposed, for example, with such later scholarly studies as Thomas Doherty's *Teenagers and Teenpics: The Juvenilization of American Movies in the 1950s*, to reassess not only the segment of movie audiences in the period, but also the social and cultural discourses of the 'teenpic' genre.[41] Did films addressed to the teenage audience, in short, inscribe the lack of maturity that Seldes lamented, or were the 'complex networks of interpersonal relations' that the Riesmans claimed represented in postwar cinema at a pace and level of maturity that older movie-goers were not prepared to accept? More broadly, the questions of changing audience expectations and social relations of which both Seldes and the Riesmans spoke could be linked with an exploration of cinematic transformations in the postwar years. With the exception of the genre studies noted above, cinema studies scholars, perhaps overly wedded to synchronic notions of a 'classical' Hollywood cinema that stretched from the 1920s to the 1960s, have given insufficient attention to evidence and arguments that point to significant changes in movie-making styles within the so-called classical era. The critic Manny Farber posited such changes in a provocatively titled 1952 *Commentary* magazine article, 'Movies aren't movies any more'.[42]

'A revolution [has] taken place in Hollywood', Farber declared. 'If the significance of the New Movie is understood, it may well be that Hollywood will never be able to go home again.'[43] 'Home' for Farber was the pre-war movies, which 'rested on the assumption that their function was to present some intelligible, structured image of reality – on the simplest level, to tell a story and to entertain, but, more generally, to extend the spectator's meaningful experience, to offer him a window on the real world'.[44] Postwar Hollywood had abandoned 'the old flowing naturalistic film' and replaced it with 'new mannerist' works that were 'surrealistic fun-houses' or 'expressionistic shotguns', betraying what the spectator is looking for when he or she buys 'a simple ninety-cent seat in a simple mansion of leisure-time art and entertainment'.[45]

Farber's polemic about changing postwar cinematic styles stands alongside Seldes's argument that spectatorial expectations had changed and the Riesmans' view that American character and modern life had changed. A critique and elaboration of these assertions could lay the groundwork for a more wide-ranging historicisation of the relation between spectators and films in the postwar era than has been offered by historical reception studies up until now.

Notes

Acknowledgements: The author would like to thank Adrienne Harris and Barbara Klinger for their helpful criticisms of an earlier version of this essay.

1 Joel W. Finler, *The Hollywood Story* (New York: Crown, 1988), 'General film industry and TV statistics', p. 288.

2 Janet Staiger, *Interpreting Films: Studies in the Historical Reception of American Cinema* (Princeton: Princeton University Press, 1992), pp. 178–95.

3 Barbara Klinger, *Melodrama and Meaning: History, Culture, and the Films of Douglas Sirk* (Bloomington: Indiana University Press, 1994).

4 I discuss post-World War II motion picture audience research in the chapter 'The disappearing audience and the television crisis', in Robert Sklar, *Movie-Made America: A Cultural History of American Movies* (New York: Vintage, 1975, revised and updated 1994), pp. 269–85, as does Garth Jowett in his chapter, 'The decline of an institution', in *Film: The Democratic Art* (Boston: Little, Brown, 1976), pp. 333–63. Of the authors cited in this article, only Paul Lazarsfeld is mentioned in the historical survey by Shearon Lowery and Melvin L. De Fleur, *Milestones in Mass Communication Research: Media Effects* (New York: Longman, 1983), for his studies on the role of personal influence in the flow of mass communications. For the 1950s, Lowery and De Fleur give principal attention to the research and controversies over the effects on children of comic books and television.

5 Leo A. Handel. 'Hollywood market research', *Quarterly of Film, Radio and Television* vol. 7, Spring 1953, p. 308.

6 Martin Quigley, Jr., 'Who goes to the movies', *Motion Picture Herald*, 10 August 1957, p. 21.

7 In choosing the writings I have discussed, I consulted all available references from the period listed in Bruce A. Austin's indispensable bibliographic compilation *The Film Audience: An International Bibliography of Research* (Metuchen, N.J., and London: Scarecrow Press, 1983). I thank Daisuke Miyao for assistance in gathering this material.

8 See, respectively, Paul F. Lazarsfeld, 'Audience research in the movie field', *Annals of the American Academy of Political and Social Science* vol. 254, November 1947, pp. 160–8; '*Fortune* survey: the people's taste in movies, books, and radio', *Fortune* vol. 39, March 1949, pp. 39–40, 43–4 (also published as 'The quarter's polls: moving pictures', *Public Opinion Quarterly* vol. 13, Summer 1949, pp. 359–60); and Leo A. Handel, *Hollywood Looks at Its Audience* (Urbana, Ill.: University of Illinois Press, 1950). With reference to Gallup, a survey conducted for the Motion Picture Association of America by Opinion Research Corp., another branch of the Gallup organisation, was publicised in 1958; see 'MPAA survey seeks answer to biz decline; TV still chief villain', *Variety*, 22 January 1958, p. 10.

9 Handel, *Hollywood Looks at Its Audience*, p. 99.

10 Quigley, 'Who goes to the movies', p. 22.

11 A point made by Handel in 'Hollywood market research', pp. 304–5.

12 Lazarsfeld, 'Audience research', p. 160, note 1.

13 Lazarsfeld, 'Audience research', p. 163.

14 Handel, *Hollywood Looks at Its Audience*, p. 99.

15 Gilbert Seldes, *The Great Audience* (New York: Viking, 1950), pp. 12, 22.

16 Franklin Fearing, 'Influence of the movies on attitudes and behavior', *Annals of the American Academy of Political and Social Science* vol. 254, November 1947, p. 73. No less than Fearing himself, the Payne Fund Studies were generally neglected in the scholarship of later decades,with the exception of such works as the cultural and social histories respectively by Sklar and Jowett, cited in note 4. They received highly favourable notice, however, in Lowery and De Fleur's *Milestones in Mass Communication Research: Media Effects*, which praises them as 'one of the most significant milestones in the development of mass communication as a scientific field of study' (p. 55); devoting a full chapter to the Studies, the authors do not mention the controversies over their sponsorship and public promotion that Fearing alluded to in his remarks. More recently, an outstanding work of archival research and historical analysis by Garth S. Jowett, Ian C. Jarvie and Kathryn H. Fuller, *Children and the Movies: Media Influence and the Payne Fund Controversy* (Cambridge, Eng.: Cambridge University Press, 1996), provides a thorough and judicious account of the Payne Fund Studies' origins, preparation and reception.

17 Nancy Lynne Schwartz, completed by Sheila Schwartz, *The Hollywood Writers' Wars* (New York: Knopf, 1982), pp. 234–5, 287. Ms Schwartz's book was uncompleted at her untimely death, and some caution should be exercised by readers toward material that the author might have modified or revised had she been able to complete the work.

18 Franklin Fearing, 'Some sources of confusion', *Journal of Social Issues* vol. 3, Summer 1947, pp. 2–7, and 'A word of caution for the intelligent consumer of motion pictures', *Quarterly of Film, Radio and Television* vol. 6, 1952, pp. 129–42.

19 Fearing, 'Word of caution', pp. 131–2, 138–9.

20 Fearing, 'Word of caution', pp. 134–7, commenting, respectively, on Mildred J. Wiese and Stewart G. Cole, 'A study of children's attitudes and the influence of a commercial motion picture', *Journal of Psychology* vol. 21, January 1946, pp. 151–71; and Daniel M. Wilner, 'Attitude as a determinant of perception in the mass media of communication: reactions to the motion picture *Home of the Brave*', unpublished PhD dissertation, University of California, Los Angeles, 1951.

21 Fearing, 'Influence of the movies', p. 78.

22 Franklin Fearing, *Motion Pictures as a Medium of Instruction and Communication: An Experimental Analysis of the Effects of Two Films* (Berkeley and Los Angeles: University of California Press, 1950), p. 107, and Fearing, 'Influence of the movies', pp. 76–8; works cited are Siegfried Kracauer, *From Caligari to Hitler: A Psychological History of the German Film* (Princeton: Princeton University Press, 1947), J. P. Mayer, *Sociology of the Film* (London: Faber & Faber, 1946), and Parker Tyler, *Magic and Myth of the Movies* (New York: Holt, 1947). See also Franklin Fearing, 'Films as history', *Hollywood Quarterly* vol. 2, 1947, pp. 422–7.

23 Fearing, *Motion Pictures*, p. 107.

24 Kracauer, *From Caligari to Hitler*, p. 6.

25 Siegfried Kracauer, 'National types as Hollywood presents them', *Public Opinion Quarterly* vol. 13, Spring 1949, pp. 53–72.

26 Kracauer, 'National types', p. 56.

27 Kracauer, 'National types', pp. 71–2.

28 David and Evelyn T. Riesman, 'Movies and audiences', *American Quarterly* vol. 4, 1952, pp. 195–202, quotation p. 195.

29 David Riesman, with the collaboration of Reuel Denney and Nathan Glazer, *The Lonely Crowd: A Study of the Changing American Character* (New Haven, Conn.: Yale University Press, 1950).

30 Riesman and Riesman, 'Movies and audiences', pp. 195–6.

31 Lazarsfeld, 'Audience research', pp. 166–7.

32 Eliot Friedson, 'The relation of the social situation of contact to the media in mass communication', *Public Opinion Quarterly* vol. 17, Summer 1953, pp. 230–8, quotation p. 231.

33 Friedson, 'The relation', p. 238.

34 Eliot Friedson, 'Consumption of mass media by Polish-American children', *Quarterly Review of Film, Radio and Television* vol. 9, 1954–5, pp. 92–101, quotation p. 96, note 4.

35 Riesman and Riesman, 'Movies and audiences', p. 197.

36 Friedson, 'Consumption', p. 97.

37 Eliot Friedson, 'Communications research and the concept of the mass', *American Sociological Review* vol. 18, June 1953, pp. 313–7. Herbert Blumer's paper was 'The moulding of mass behavior through the motion picture', *Publications of the American Sociological Society* vol. 29, 1936, pp. 115–27.

38 Friedson, 'Communications research', p. 317.

39 Handel, *Hollywood Looks at Its Audience*, pp. 88–90.

40 Klinger, *Melodrama and Meaning*, p. 68.

41 Thomas Doherty, *Teenagers and Teenpics: the Juvenilization of American Movies in the 1950s* (Boston: Unwin Hyman, 1988).

42 Manny Farber, 'Movies aren't movies any more', was reprinted in Chandler Brossard (ed.), *The Scene Before You: A New Approach to American Culture* (New York: Rinehart, 1955), pp. 3–15. Farber changed the title to 'The gimp' when he included the article in his collection *Negative Space: Manny Farber on the Movies* (New York: Praeger, 1971), pp. 71–83.

43 Farber, *Negative Space*, p. 82.

44 Ibid., p. 72.

45 Ibid., pp. 71, 72, 82.

5   A Powerful Cinema-going Force? Hollywood and Female Audiences since the 1960s

Peter Krämer

According to received wisdom shared by much of the film industry trade press, magazine and newspaper journalists, and academic critics, Hollywood, an industry dominated by men, has been catering primarily to a young male audience since the 1960s. Yet in its 1995 'Box Office Review' of the American market, the British trade journal *Screen International* observed: 'After children, women are the second most powerful cinema-going force. The all-female ensemble picture and the revamped romantic comedy/melodrama were probably the year's steadiest performers.'[1] The article also pointed out that 'action pictures' performed best when they 'attracted equal numbers of female and male viewers, thanks to female-friendly stars' such as Pierce Brosnan and Brad Pitt. A similar emphasis on female audiences characterised statements made by leading Hollywood executives in 1995. During a Directors' Guild workshop, for example, Laura Ziskin, president of Fox 2000 (News Corp's adult-oriented film production subsidiary) and formerly a producer whose filmography includes *Pretty Woman* (1990), stated that she intended to make films for mature women, for both economic and personal reasons (it was the audience segment she felt closest to).[2] As a consequence of demographic trends, she pointed out, women over twenty-five currently make up an increasing share of Hollywood's potential audience, and they are also presumed to be the ones who pick the film when going to the movies with their male partners. Quoting Ziskin, a later article in the *New York Times*, suggestively entitled 'What do women want? – Movies', noted a fundamental change of direction in mid-1990s Hollywood: 'After years of making action and adventure films for boys of all ages studio executives are concluding that a new audience has emerged that is changing all the rules. Women.'[3] The article noted that Hollywood's increased output of films appealing specifically to women resulted partly from 'the growing number of female studio executives with the power to give the green light to a movie'.[4]

There are obvious problems with such claims concerning the feminisation of American cinema in the mid-1990s. Firstly, Hollywood's decision-makers continue to be predominantly male. In *Premiere* magazine's 1996 list of 'The 100 Most Powerful People in Hollywood' the first woman (Viacom/Paramount executive Sherry Lansing) appeared at number 15, the next (Julia Roberts) at 45, and there were only twelve women on the entire list.[5] Secondly, the major Hollywood studios continue to spend much more money on the production and marketing of what are traditionally perceived as male genre films (such as action-adventure and science fiction) than on what may be called 'female' genres (romantic comedy, musicals, melodrama/weepies, costume drama). In 1995, for example, female-oriented films made on comparatively low budgets of $15–25 million, were often substantial hits, grossing $50–80 million at the North American box office (*Clueless, Waiting to Exhale,* and *While You Were Sleeping,* for example), yet Hollywood's overall output during that year was dominated by big budget action-adventure and Science Fiction films, costing anywhere between $60 million and an astonishing $180 million (*Waterworld*).[6] Thirdly, while it is true that several of these big-budget films performed poorly in the United States, they often redeemed themselves at foreign box offices. Moreover, in *Die Hard With a Vengeance,* this group of male-oriented big budget movies gave rise to the biggest international hit of the year, grossing $354 million worldwide, or about twice the international gross of the most successful female-oriented film of that year, *While You Were Sleeping.*[7] The situation was similar in 1996, with modestly budgeted female-oriented hits being completely overshadowed by expensive male-oriented blockbusters such as *Independence Day* (international gross $780 million) and *The Rock* ($330 million).[8]

Thus, on closer examination, mid-1990s Hollywood was far from undergoing a reorientation driven by female executives and audiences. Only rarely were women directly and specifically addressed as an audience. When they did go to the cinema on their own behalf – rather than accompanying their partners or children – they were responsible for a few modest hits in a steady stream of modestly budgeted films. Such films were unable to compete with the success of male- or family-oriented movies. This state of affairs prompts a number of questions: What is actually known about the female audience and its cinema-going habits and preferences in recent decades? Why have female movie-goers and female-oriented movies become marginal in Hollywood since the 1960s? And are there any reliable indications that this marginalisation could be prevented?

What Do Women Want?

An audience survey conducted in 1982 found that comedy was by far the most popular genre with both sexes, irrespective of age.[9] When asked about the types of films they intended to see in the coming year or about their favourite genre, in addition to comedy, women (especially older ones) most often listed drama and musicals, whereas men were more likely to tick the categories SF, adventure/war and Western. Thus, women appeared to be primarily interested in characters and emotions, whereas men demanded violent action and excitement. Rather than catering for all of its potential audience, Hollywood's output has clearly been biased towards men. The favourite genres of Hollywood's potential audience (male and female) were (in this order): comedy (favoured by 33.5 per cent of all respondents), drama (17.8 per cent), SF (12.4 per cent), musical (10.1 per cent), and only then adventure/war (6.8 per cent). The levels of interest in viewing certain types of films in the coming year were: 80 per cent for comedy, 59 per cent for drama, 44 per cent for musical, with SF and adventure/war further down the list. Potential movie-goers, then, preferred medium-budget comedies and dramas, often oriented toward female viewers, to those male-oriented genres for which contemporary Hollywood reserves its biggest budgets (SF, adventure).

Furthermore, when asked which types of films respondents had actually seen during the preceding year, comedy and SF came out on top (seen by about 50 per cent of respondents), followed by drama (with 43.8 per cent). Adventure/war was far behind with 24 per cent and the musical category was hardly mentioned at all. Firstly, these figures show that the audience for comedy and drama was spread fairly widely across the spectrum of respondents, whereas adventure films had only been seen by about a quarter of respondents, most of them young men. The high figure for SF was largely the result of one universally popular movie, *E.T.* If this film is taken out of the equation, the reach of the SF genre was as limited as that of adventure films. Hollywood's big releases are indeed servicing a minority audience. Secondly, it is clear from the above figures that the film industry's output of musicals, and to a lesser extent of comedies and dramas, was insufficient to meet the great demand, especially on the part of female cinema-goers. Women definitely did not get what they wanted in cinemas. Yet they still went almost as frequently as men – mostly, it seems, to accompany their male partners or children. In fact, children's films, which few adults declared to be their favourites, had nevertheless been seen by about a fifth of all respondents (mostly women over twenty-five, who had probably gone with their children). The survey also showed that, as a consequence of the film industry's failure to cater to their specific needs in movie theatres, women, who were generally more avid film-viewers than men, preferred to watch films, both old and new, on the small screen at home. This applied especially to older women.

These results confirmed research carried out in previous decades. A 1973 survey, for example, found that women were just as likely as men to go to the movies at least once a year (59 per cent of respondents did), yet they tended to go less frequently.[10] This perhaps suggests that women were basically willing cinema-goers, yet were much less likely than men to find films attractive enough to justify a trip to the movie theatre. While single people went to the cinema much more often than married ones, married people with children were much more likely to go to the cinema than couples without children, which again suggests that many women went to the cinema to accompany their children.[11] The list of preferred genres of all respondents in this 1973 survey was again headed by comedy, followed for female respondents by love stories, drama and musicals, and for men by Westerns, drama and suspense. When asked about their least preferred type of movie, X-rated films came out on top for both sexes, followed by horror films. Yet many more women than men objected to these genres and, for women, the list continued with war films, SF and Westerns, whereas for men it continued with musicals, love stories and animated features. What men objected to most, it seems, were sentimentality and the blatant display of emotions, whereas women objected most strongly to sex and violence. Such insights into gender-specific movie-going habits and preferences in fact go back at least to the 1940s, when the film industry first conducted systematic audience research.[12] It is quite surprising, therefore, that Hollywood would choose to ignore the well-known and apparently stable likes and dislikes of its female audience.

Who Cares What Women Want?

Already in 1972, *Variety* observed that the 'Recent box-office boom in violent pix has underscored the lessening commercial impact of femme-slated features.' In the past, the article went on, Hollywood had considered women as one of the 'most steadfast and reliable markets' and the strong presence of female characters, able to appeal to this audience, had been deemed crucial for a film's commercial success. However, more recently, television had serviced this 'heretofore captive audience' and movie outings 'became increasingly dominated by the male breadwinner's choice of screen fare. Result is that most b[ox] o[ffice] hits of recent times barely feature women in supporting roles.'[13] The article reflected the assumptions informing Hollywood's operations at the time: women prefer television to the cinema; men pick the film when going to the cinema with women; men are interested primarily in stories about men. These assumptions were in sharp contrast to the beliefs which had underpinned Hollywood's output and marketing strategies in earlier decades, when the major companies saw women, especially mature women in charge of regular cinema-outings with their husbands and children, as the key audience for movie theatres.[14] As recently as the mid-1960s, Hollywood had catered to this traditionally conceived audience with big budget female-centred superhits such as the costume drama *Cleopatra* (1963), and the musicals *Mary Poppins* (1964) and *The Sound of Music* (1965), which were amongst the highest-grossing films of all time up to this point and had turned Elizabeth Taylor and Julie Andrews into the highest-paid and most popular of all Hollywood stars.[15]

By 1972, however, there were numerous indications that Hollywood had re-oriented itself towards a new target audience of men, especially young men. *The Godfather* (1972), an epic gangster movie concerned primarily with the familial relationships and violent interaction of groups of men, was well on its way to replacing *The Sound of Music* as the highest-grossing film of all time. In Hollywood's production schedules and in the annual box-office charts of the late 1960s and early 1970s, there was a predominance of genres which women were known to dislike, and which were now given a particularly violent inflection as well as a particularly strong focus on male relationships. Amongst the top hits of the period were successful cycles of war films, including *The Dirty Dozen* (1967) and *M*A*S*H* (1970), science-fiction films, including *2001: A Space Odyssey* (1968) and the *Planet of the Apes* series starting in 1968, and Westerns, including *Butch Cassidy and the Sundance Kid* (1969) and *Little Big Man* (1971). There was also a successful run of extremely violent crime and police films from *Bonnie and Clyde* (1967) to *Dirty Harry* (1971), as well as adventure films such as the James Bond series, a top box-office attraction from 1964 onwards, and the beginning of the hugely expensive cycle of top-grossing disaster movies with *Airport* (1970) and *The Poseidon Adventure* (1972). The male-centredness of these films and of the industry as a whole was reflected in the stars whom American film exhibitors considered to be box-office attractions. After many years in which women were consistently featured in the top three positions in the annual polls, they disappeared from these places in 1969 and from then on had a hard time making it into the top ten. At the same time, in sharp contrast to the previous run of female-oriented multiple-Oscar winners such as *West Side Story* (1961), *My Fair Lady* (1964) and *The Sound of Music*, the Academy Awards went primarily to male-oriented films such as *Midnight Cowboy* (1969), *Patton* (1970), *The French Connection* (1971) and *The Godfather* (1972).[16]

Apart from the fact that women were notably absent from many critically and commercially successful films, female audiences were also affected by the replacement of the Production Code with a ratings system in 1968. Through the Production Code, the major studios had regulated the content of their films in such a way as to ensure that they were unlikely to cause offence to any segment of the audience. In particular, Hollywood had tried to avoid offending women. The introduction of a ratings system regulating access to individual films according to the age of the movie-goer signalled the industry's willingness to abandon the notion of inoffensive entertainment for everybody, and instead to appeal strongly and specifically to some audience segments, especially young males, even if that meant excluding other segments such as women and children.[17] The X-rated *Midnight Cowboy* (1969) and the horror film *Rosemary's Baby* (1968) indicated to women that perhaps it was not safe for them to go to the movie theatre anymore.[18] This impression was certainly enhanced by the dilapidated, insanitary state of many mainstream movie houses and, in big urban centres, their frequent proximity to porn cinemas.[19]

During this period, the production of musicals, romantic comedies and melodramas continued, with major box-office hits such as *Oliver!* and *Funny Girl* (both 1968), *Love Story* and *Hello, Dolly!* (both 1970), *Fiddler on the Roof* (1971) and *What's Up, Doc?* (1972). However, at this point budgets for major musicals had become so inflated that, despite high box-office grosses, films such as *Hello, Dolly!* were reported to have lost millions of dollars. These losses, together with the ruinous performance of films such as *Dr. Dolittle* (1967) and *Star!* (1968) encouraged the studios to invest more heavily in other, male-oriented genres, especially disaster movies.[20] Yet the enormous success of re-releases of classic, female-oriented films such as *Gone With the Wind* (in 1967/68), *The Sound of Music*, and *Mary Poppins* (both 1973) indicates that the studios gave up too quickly on their traditional core audience of women, who had a continuing predilection for big-budget spectacles dealing with the trials and tribulations of female characters.

So why was Hollywood so eager to focus on the young male audience? According to Thomas Doherty, this re-orientation was the industry's belated response to audience research conducted in the 1940s, which showed that teenagers and young adults were the most frequent movie-goers.[21] This research was confirmed in subsequent decades: a 1968 survey, for example, found that 16–24-year-olds bought almost half of all cinema tickets, with 16–20-year-olds being the most frequent movie-goers.[22] Doherty argues that rather than continuing its attempts to win back or at least maintain its mature audience over twenty-five (the majority of the population, which rarely went to the cinema), Hollywood focused ever more exclusively on teenagers and young adults under twenty-five, a minority which constituted the group of regular movie-goers. In so doing, it adopted the doctrine known as 'The Peter Pan Syndrome', which had underpinned the successful marketing strategy developed by American International Pictures for exploitation cinema in the 1950s: since younger children will watch what an older child is interested in, and girls will watch what boys are interested in, 'to catch your greatest audience you zero in on the 19-year-old male'.[23]

In the mid-1970s, *Variety* criticised Hollywood for its fixation on youth, examining the impact of the post-war baby boom.[24] The baby-boomers, most of whom had entered their prime movie-going age (16–24) in the late 1960s and early 1970s, constituted the bulk of the cinema audience in this period, but by about 1980 most of them would be about to move into the 25–34 age group. *Variety* argued that this age group should, therefore, become a key target audience for Hollywood. Since the ageing baby-boomers were 'bearing fewer children, and often at more advanced ages than their parents', if appropriate measures were taken by the industry, 'the traditional drop off in filmgoing [after the age of twenty-five] ... may become less drastic'. *Variety* also urged Hollywood to drop its conception of cinema and television as separate markets for young people and older people. With the rapid spread of pay-TV services, in particular movie channels such as HBO, in future there would be considerable overlap between the theatrical audience and the home audience. *Variety* itself expressed the hope that 'films may again be made for a truly mass audience – a paying audience both in theatres and in homes.'[25]

This new mass movie audience did come into existence in subsequent years, but only for special occasions. Beginning with the extraordinary success of *Star Wars* (1977) and its first sequel, *The Empire Strikes Back* (1980), Hollywood has consistently managed to bring a cross-section of the American population, including the majority of infrequent movie-goers who may never see any other films at the cinema, back into the movie theatre for one or two family-oriented adventure movies a year, released in time for a long run during the summer holidays or the Christmas season, and destined for an equally successful performance in the video and pay-TV markets.[26] Apart from these exceptional hits, however, the film industry largely continued its previous practice of investing most heavily in films addressed primarily, and often exclusively, to young movie-goers, especially young males. The wide release of *Jaws* in June 1975 (with an unprecedented 500 prints), for example, provided the model for future action-adventure movies. Released mostly during the summer, these films focus on the violent actions of their male heroes and are driven by stunts and special effects, drawing a lot of attention to their record-breaking opening weekend box-office figures and to their ever-escalating budgets, including multi-million-dollar salaries and profit-participation deals for their male stars.[27] This production trend has given rise to many of the top-grossing movies of the last two decades, including Sylvester Stallone's string of hits with the *Rocky* and *Rambo* series from 1976 onwards; Burt Reynolds's action comedies, starting with *Smokey and the Bandit* (1976); the continuing series of James Bond movies (for example, *The Spy Who Loved Me*, 1977); rogue cop movies featuring Clint Eastwood (*The Enforcer*, 1976), Eddie Murphy (starting with *48 HRS*, 1982), Mel Gibson (most notably the *Lethal Weapon* series, starting in 1987), or Bruce Willis (starting with *Die Hard* in 1988); combat movies (most notably *Platoon* and *Top Gun*, both in 1986); and Arnold Schwarzenegger's 'serious' action films such as *Total Recall* (1990). Also included are more family-oriented films, most notably Schwarzenegger's comedies (starting with *Twins*, 1988), the *Superman* (first instalment, 1979) and *Batman* (1989) series, the *Star Wars* (1977), *Indiana Jones* (1981) and *Back to the Future* (1985) trilogies, as well as the *Karate Kid* (1984) series and horror comedies (starting with *Gremlins* in 1984).[28] These and other action-oriented films made up about half of all films in the annual lists of the ten biggest box-office hits from 1976 onwards, often holding the top positions.

During the same period, women made a moderate comeback in American cinema, in comparison to the rather disastrous decade for female genres and stars from 1966 to 1976. In 1977, the romantic comedy *Annie Hall* was a considerable hit which established Diane Keaton as a top box-office attraction, the Jane Fonda vehicle *Julia* won most of the major Academy Awards, and the release of *Saturday Night Fever* led to a revival of the musical genre.[29] Melodramas/weepies also made a comeback, albeit often with a focus on the social and emotional trials and tribulations of male rather than female characters, generating a string of multiple Academy Award winners. Many of these films were also massive box-office hits, starting with *Kramer vs Kramer* (1979) and *Ordinary People* (1980).[30] Throughout the 1980s, the annual lists of top ten box-office hits usually included three to five female-oriented (yet quite regularly male-centred) films: musicals such as *Flashdance* and *Staying Alive* (both 1983); romantic comedies such as *Tootsie* (1982) and *Moonstruck* (1987); melodramas such as *Terms of Endearment* (1983) and *Rainman* (1988); female ensemble comedies such as *9 to 5* (1980) and female ensemble dramas such as *The Color Purple* (1985).[31] With few exceptions, these films could normally be found in the bottom half of the top ten lists and, even at their best, they tended to gross only about half as much as their male- or family-oriented competitors.

In 1989, for example, the top three positions in the end-of-year box-office chart were held by male- or family-oriented action films: *Batman*, *Indiana Jones and the Last Crusade*, and *Lethal Weapon 2* – with *Ghostbusters II* and *Back to the Future II* featured further down the list.[32] All but the last of these films had been released between the end of May and the beginning of July. Budgeted in a range between $25 million and $42 million, each film played in 1800 to 2400 movie theatres, earning opening weekend grosses of between $20 million and $37 million, and total grosses going as high as $250 million.[33] In sharp contrast, female-oriented films such as the romantic comedies *When Harry Met Sally* and *Look Who's Talking*, the comedy drama *Parenthood*, and the melodrama *Dead Poets Society* all hit an earnings ceiling around $100 million.[34] Budgeted at under $20 million (on average $10 million less than the action-oriented top grossers) and opening in fewer than 800 cinemas (less than half the number of theatres as action films), they had opening weekend grosses of around $10 million (again less than half of the figure for action films).[35]

In the 1980s, then, films specifically targeted at women had regained a secure place in Hollywood's overall scheme of things, yet in comparison with male- or family-oriented films, Hollywood's output of female-oriented films remained marginal and failed to satisfy the considerable demand for comedies, dramas and musicals that audience surveys had identified. At the same time, earlier predictions of an ageing movie audience became a reality. By 1989, the share of 16–24-year-olds had dropped to 33 per cent (from about 50 per cent in 1968) and that of 16–20-year-olds to 19 per cent (from 30 per cent in 1972), and the 25–49 age group had gained a larger share of overall paid admissions (46 per cent) than the 12–24 age group (44 per cent).[36] The commercial implications of these changes in audience composition were highlighted by the unexpected performance of two women's films in 1990.

Sometimes Women Do Get What They Want!

When *Pretty Woman* was released on 23 March 1990, the surrounding publicity highlighted those aspects of the film which were expected to appeal specifically to women.

Pretty Woman (Garry Marshall, 1990).

For example, Buena Vista's press book quoted the film's leading lady Julia Roberts saying the film 'is about finding love in unexpected places', and director Garry Marshall asserting that it was 'a unique love story'.[37] In an interview with the *New York Times*, Marshall declared his rather 'unmanly' intentions with this film: 'I like to do very romantic, sentimental type of work. . . . It's a dirty job, but somebody has to do it.'[38] In order to put this 'dirty' work into a respectable tradition, he pointed out that the film had 'elements of *Pygmalion*, *My Fair Lady* and Holly Golightly', thus alluding both to myth and theatre as well as the great romances and female stars (especially Audrey Hepburn) of the Hollywood of an earlier era.[39]

Reviewers were sharply divided in their evaluation of the film, many objecting vociferously to its unrealistic portrayal of prostitution, its emphasis on money and shopping, its unconvincing characterisations, and the dubious sexual politics of the central couple's relationship.[40] Yet even detractors of this kind rarely failed to mention the venerated tradition within which the publicity had situated the film. Similarly, for the film's supporters, *Pretty Woman* appeared first and foremost as a welcome return to the themes and style of the Hollywood of the past. John Simon, for example, wrote in *New York* that the film 'takes us back to Hollywood's softly beguiling entertainments of the fifties', pointing out that it is not an 'erotic fantasy' but a 'straight romantic comedy'.[41] Vincent Canby declared in the *New York Times* that *Pretty Woman* was 'the most satisfying romantic comedy in years'.[42] Like other critics, he highlighted the film's female lead, linking her to a glamorous and, by now, near-mythical tradition of female Hollywood stars, declaring that Julia Roberts had produced 'the most invigorating debut performance since Audrey Hepburn's in *Roman Holiday*'. Andrew Sarris published 'a professional love letter' to Roberts in the *New York Observer*, while Janet Maslin wrote in the *New York Times* that 'Ms Roberts ... is a complete knockout, and this performance will make her a major star.'[43] Most reviewers, then, related *Pretty Woman* to older traditions of storytelling and popular entertainment, comparing it to classic works. *Pretty Woman* was seen both by detractors and by supporters as standing out from contemporary Hollywood's regular output in an attempt to revive the lost art of romantic story-telling focused on a captivating leading lady.

A few months after the initial flurry of reviews and articles, the film's extraordinary success gave rise to further reflections in the press. In July, the *New York Times* noted with astonishment that *Pretty Woman* was still performing strongly at the box-office. Indeed, very unusually, even in its 17th week, the film still played in 1,200 theatres, as compared to 1,300 in the first week and 1,800 at the point of the film's widest release in the 9th week.[44] The film was now competing directly with the big summer releases which, the article reminded the reader, 'tend to be either action movies or films for young audiences'. As 'an adult Cinderella story', 'a traditional tale updated with modern psyches and settings', *Pretty Woman* had succeeded in finding an audience rarely catered for in the summer: 'Magazine and newspaper articles indicate that the movie has proved particularly appealing to women.' Thus, the film was seen to provide a welcome alternative for all those who were dissatisfied with Hollywood's usual summer fare.[45]

When this article appeared, *Ghost* had just been released. Unlike *Pretty Woman*, *Ghost* was not marketed exclusively as a female-oriented 'love story', but was described by Paramount's press book as both a 'suspense thriller' and 'a startling love story'.[46] However, the nod towards the male following of thrillers was overshadowed by the marketing campaign's heavy emphasis on love, passion and spirituality. The poster showed Patrick Swayze and Demi Moore in a passionate naked embrace with Swayze kissing her neck. In the press book, Swayze described his character, Sam, as someone who fails to declare his love while he can, and then desperately tries to make up for this failure. Moore said about her character: 'Molly Jensen is given the opportunity to experience a last goodbye from Sam and be reassured that where he's going is a place of love.' And scriptwriter Scott Rudin emphasised the film's spirituality: 'I was intrigued by the idea of capturing the sensations and emotions of a person who suddenly realises they have passed from life into an immaterial world – a new universe.'

The film's review in *Variety* was reasonably optimistic about its box-office prospects, describing it as a 'lightweight romantic fantasy ... purely for escapists', along the lines of Patrick Swayze's previous surprise hit, *Dirty Dancing*.[47] The reviewer expressed a definite sense of unease, though, about this 'odd creation', with its 'unlikely grab bag of styles' and compendium of constantly shifting moods and emotions, barely held together by the film's 'thriller elements' and its 'romantic momentum'. Most reviewers shared this perception and found much to criticise in the film's peculiar mix of incompatible elements, most notably the special effects sequences depicting the demons of the underworld, Whoopi Goldberg's performance and the film's unimaginative view of an afterlife.[48] At the same time, the majority of reviews described it as a highly unusual summer release. *The West Side Spirit*, for example, wrote that '[a]s far as simple summer movies go, *Ghost* is truly a breakthrough movie' because, by subtly mixing genres, it demonstrated that 'in this season of stick-em-up and blow-em-up flicks, a little tenderness can be a wonderful thing'.[49] A generally very critical article in the *Christian Science Monitor* conceded that *Ghost* offered 'a touch of sentiment that isn't present (or is swamped by special effects) in its high-tech cousins'.[50] Ultimately, it was the film's ability to provoke strong emotions in its audience which clearly set it apart. In *Time*, Richard Corliss declared *Ghost* to be 'a bad movie that a lot of people will like' because it 'will touch movie-goers with its heavenly message that love can raise the dead'.[51] Jami Bernard predicted in the *New York Post* that the 'ending can provoke a *Wuthering Heights*-scale cry, depending perhaps on how many unresolved attachments you have.'[52] This reference to a classic women's film and the legitimacy of its ability to make viewers cry indicates that, much like *Pretty Woman*, *Ghost* could best be understood as a return to an older, half-forgotten tradition of powerful storytelling, which combined a strong emotional impact with a clear moral message. Indeed, in *Film Journal*, David Bartholomew explicitly linked *Ghost* to Hollywood's self-regulated film production after the implementation of the Production Code in the early 1930s: 'The movie is as moral as a post-Hays Office woman's picture.'[53]

Ghost's extraordinary success at the box-office led to further reflections on its significance. In November, the *New York Times*, for example, declared *Ghost* to be 'one of the biggest sleeper hits in Hollywood history', and a most unlikely one at that: 'A romantic suspense comedy, shot on a modest budget and without a major box-office star, that flirts with the supernatural.'[54] Sixteen weeks after its release on 13 July, the film was still popular enough to play in 1,750 movie theatres and take in more than $3 million per week.[55] Market research conducted by Paramount indicated that the movie's staying power was partly due to the fact that 'many women, who were the main target audience for both *Ghost* and *Pretty Woman*, have returned to see both movies several times', a rare occurrence in female genres. The article loosely grouped the two films together under

Ghost (Jerry Zucker, 1990).

the label 'romantic comedy' – 'a genre that in recent years had become less appealing to Hollywood studios intent on making blockbuster action-adventure films'. However, now that *Ghost* and *Pretty Woman* had outperformed 'a host of costly action-adventure films that had been expected to dominate the market this year', the major studios were 'planning to increase their production and support for romantic comedies'.

These predictions about a general re-orientation of the film industry were supported by Amy Taubin's article on *Ghost* and *Pretty Woman* in the *Village Voice* a few weeks later: '[T]he big news is that after a decade in which sci-fi, horror and action movies dominated the box-office, romance is back.'[56] Taubin emphasised the low status that films such as *Ghost* and *Pretty Woman* had within the industry and outlined one of their primary cultural functions as 'archetypal dating movies': 'They affirm for couples of all stages that romantic involvement is not some kind of temporary insanity but a state of bliss that can endure longer than six days (*Pretty Woman*) and even transcend the death-do-us-part cutoff point specified in the marriage vow (*Ghost*).' By defining movie-going as an important dating and relationship ritual, Taubin pointed out that romantic films, with their particular appeal to women, who would bring their male partners along, could become the cornerstone of a reconfigured film industry. Box-office statistics supported such speculation. *Ghost* and *Pretty Woman* topped the chart of top grossing movies for 1990.[57] Furthermore, *Pretty Woman* was at number 15 in *Variety*'s list of all-time domestic box-office hits, and *Ghost* was at number 10.[58] By the time they had completed their world-wide release, *Pretty Woman* would be in 5th place on *Variety*'s list of all-time international top grossers, and *Ghost* would be second (behind *E.T.* and ahead of *Star Wars*).[59] The enormity of the films' success did indeed call into question many of the basic assumptions which had guided Hollywood's operations since the late 1960s. Yet, as we have already seen, Hollywood went back to business as usual in the 1990s.

Conclusion

When, at the beginning of 1991, Anne Thompson looked back on the long runs and steady box-office performance of 'films appealing to women' and the rapid drop-off at the box-office of 'male-oriented actioners' in the previous year, she posed a crucial question in *Variety*: 'So why does Hollywood continue to resist movies with strong female appeal that are cheaper to make and more profitable when they are successful?'[60] She received a range of answers from studio executives. Firstly, executives rejected the idea that films appealing primarily to women through strong female protagonists and high-profile female stars were viable, although, as one executive admitted, they once had been viable in 'decades past, when women flocked to films carried almost solely by screen queens like Bette Davis and Joan Crawford'. Now, however, it was understood that female stars 'can't carry a movie', because young men were mainly looking for male identification figures and young women were unlikely to drag their boyfriends along to films without a 'big male star'. It was, therefore, also understood that female-oriented movies were dependent on 'reaching adult audiences and garnering good reviews'. Since executives claimed that the overall number of mature women who actually went to the cinema was simply too small, their conclusion was that 'You can't make movies just for a women's audience anymore.' Secondly, executives still considered the under-25s as

Hollywood's most important audience, since films appealing to this audience segment were seen to have a guaranteed young male audience on the first weekend and in foreign markets. Most significantly, it was believed that young women were more willing to watch boys' movies than young men were to watch women's films, and thus young men were perceived to 'drive the purchase decision' when couples went to the cinema.

Obviously, there are some omissions from these arguments (such as the demographic shift towards older audiences and the influence of women on the film choices of mature couples) and there is also a basic circularity. The industry appeals primarily to the youth audience because older people are reluctant to go to the cinema; yet older people are reluctant to go to the cinema precisely because the films appeal primarily to youth. Similarly, Hollywood films are primarily addressed to young men, because boys' movies can be enjoyed by young women as well; yet young women have accommodated themselves to boys' movies, precisely because there are comparatively few alternatives offered to them and their male partners by Hollywood.

In the end, then, the basic question remains: what lies behind these self-fulfilling prophesies and feedback loops and this avoidance of basic demographic facts? In response to this question, at least one executive pointed the finger at Hollywood's basic sexism: 'Most studio executives are male ... They are more comfortable with male-oriented product.'[61] This answer, however, raises yet further questions: how did the equally male-dominated and much more conservative film industry of the past manage to cater primarily to women? Are there other reasons, apart from demographic shifts, for Hollywood's reorientation towards a young male audience in the late 1960s? Is it conceivable that the film industry will one day take demographic trends and the demand of female audiences into account again and return to its previous conception of a female-led mass audience, and is *Titanic* the film which can make this happen?[62]

Notes

1   Ana Maria Bahiana, '1995 box-office review: nuclear family business', *Screen International*, 26 January 1996, p. 60.

2   Discussion with Laura Ziskin, 9 August 1995, 15th Annual Directors Guild of America Educators Workshop, Los Angeles. See also Ziskin's statements in Bernard Weinraub, 'What do women want? – Movies', *New York Times*, 10 February 1997, pp. C11, 14.

3   Weinraub, 'What do women want?', p. C11.

4   Ibid., p. C14.

5   'The 1996 *Premiere* power list: the 100 most powerful people in Hollywood', *Premiere*, May 1996, pp. 76–90. 'Masters of the universe: the power 100', *Screen International*, 15 December 1995, pp. 12–28.

6   Production costs are given in the annual review of the US theatrical market in the German magazine *steadycam*, which uses figures provided by the American trade press. For the 1995 survey, see 'In Zahlen', *steadycam* no. 31, Spring 1996, pp. 11–12.

7   Ibid., and Leonard Klady, 'B.O. with a vengeance: $9.1 billion worldwide', *Variety*, 19 February 1996, pp. 1, 26.

8   'In Zahlen', *steadycam* no. 33, Spring 1997, pp. 19–21.

9   'Movie Omnibus – Sept. 1982', a survey of the film viewing habits of 1,000 people aged

18 and over, contained in the Audiences Clippings File, Museum of Modern Art, New York. See also Jim Robbins, 'Survey says public likes sci-fi but really loves comedy', *Variety*, 22 September 1982, p. 22.

10 'Movie going and leisure time', *Newspaper Advertising Bureau*, January 1974; results of 769 interviews with people aged eighteen and over conducted in July 1973, contained in file MFL x n.c.2, 101 no.4, Billy Rose Theatre Collection (BRTC), New York Public Library at Lincoln Centre, New York. See also results of 1972 MPAA survey reproduced in Garth Jowett, *Film: The Democratic Art* (Boston: Little, Brown, 1976), p. 486.

11 A 1974 survey of 3,835 female heads of households in metropolitan areas suggested that only 28 per cent of all respondents went to the movies at least once a month; for those living on their own or with another adult, the figures were 16 per cent and 24 per cent respectively, whereas for women with children it was more than 30 per cent. See 'Shoppers on the move: movie-going and movie-goers', *Newspaper Advertising Bureau*, November 1975; contained in file MWEZ + n.c.26,510, BRTC. See also results of MPAA surveys conducted in 1988–90, which are reproduced in 'Industry economic review and audience profile', Jason E. Squire, (ed.), *The Movie Business Book* (New York: Fireside, 2nd ed., 1992), p. 390.

12 See Leo A. Handel, *Hollywood Looks At Its Audience: A Report of Film Audience Research* (Urbana: University of Illinois Press, 1950), pp. 118–27.

13 'Old 4-hanky "women's market" pix, far, far from 1972 "Year of Woman"', *Variety*, 30 August 1972, p. 5.

14 Tino Balio, *Grand Design: Hollywood as a Modern Business Enterprise, 1930–1939* (Berkeley: University of California Press, 1995), pp. 1–12, 179–312; Richard Maltby, *Hollywood Cinema: An Introduction* (Oxford: Blackwell, 1995), pp. 10–11.

15 For information on the box-office performance in the United States of Hollywood's hit movies, see Cobbett S. Steinberg, *Film Facts* (New York: Facts on File Inc., 1980), pp. 17–28, and Joel W. Finler, *The Hollywood Story* (London: Octopus, 1988), pp. 276–8. For the results of the annual polls amongst film exhibitors about the top box-office stars, see Steinberg, pp. 55–61. For information on star salaries see Steinberg, pp. 66–9.

16 Ibid., pp. 233–47.

17 Maltby, *Hollywood*, pp. 10–1, 340–1.

18 The astonishing success of *The Exorcist* (1973), which eventually grossed even more than *The Godfather* and initiated a cycle of successful horror films, would confirm this perception of the movie theatre as an unsafe space. Furthermore, Academy Awards continued to go to male-oriented films – *The Sting* (1973), *The Godfather* Part II (1974), *One Flew Over the Cuckoo's Nest* (1975) and *Rocky* (1976), and the lists of top ten box-office stars featured only one woman per year from 1973 to 1976 (Barbra Streisand in 1973–5, Tatum O'Neal in 1976). See Steinberg, *Film Facts*, pp. 27–8, 61, 248–52

19 Jerry Lewis, 'Children too have film rights', *Variety*, 5 January 1972, p. 32; James Harwood, 'Films gotta cater to "aging" audience', *Variety*, 23 February 1977, p. 7; Judy Klemesrud, 'Family movies making a comeback', *New York Times*, 17 February 1978, p. C10; Douglas Gomery, *Shared Pleasures: A History of Movie Presentation in the United States* (London: BFI, 1992), pp. 93–102.

20 Thomas Schatz, 'The New Hollywood', in Jim Collins, Hilary Radner and Ava Preacher

Collins (eds), *Film Theory Goes to the Movies* (New York: Routledge, 1993), p. 14; Nick Roddick, 'Only the stars survive: disaster movies in the seventies', in David Bradby, Louis James and Bernard Sharratt (eds), *Performance and Politics in Popular Drama*, (Cambridge: Cambridge University Press, 1980), pp. 243–69.

21 Thomas Doherty, *Teenagers and Teenpics: The Juvenilization of American Movies in the 1950s* (Boston: Unwin Hyman, 1988), pp. 62–3, 230–4.

22 'Pix must "broaden market"', *Variety*, 20 March 1968, pp. 1, 78, quoted in Doherty, *Teenagers and Teenpics*, p. 231. Garth Jowett cites a 1972 study, according to which 73 per cent of the audience were between 12 and 29, and 43 per cent were between 12 and 20; 16–24-year-olds had a share of 46 per cent. The most frequent movie-goers were 16–20-year-olds, accounting for 30 per cent of paid admissions. Jowett, *Film*, p. 485.

23 Robin Bean and David Austen, 'U.S.A. confidential', *Films and Filming* no.215, November 1968, pp. 21–2, quoted in Doherty, *Teenagers and Teenpics*, p. 157.

24 A. D. Murphy, 'Audience demographics, film future', *Variety*, 20 August 1975, p. 3. Cf. John Belton, *Widescreen Cinema* (Cambridge: Harvard University Press, 1992), p. 74; Steven Mintz and Susan Kellog, *Domestic Revolutions: A Social History of American Family Life* (New York: The Free Press, 1988), pp. 179, 198; Ben J. Wattenberg (ed.), *The Statistical History of the United States* (New York: Basic Books, 1976), p. 10. See also Robert Allen's discussion of baby boomers in his essay in this volume.

25 See similar comments on the emerging video market in Frank Segers, 'Gallup check *re* likes: theatre, and/or, homes', *Variety*, 25 May 1977, p. 13.

26 Peter Krämer, 'Would you take your child to see this film? The cultural and social work of the family-adventure movie', Steve Neale and Murray Smith (eds), *Contemporary Hollywood Cinema* (London: Routledge, 1998), pp. 294–311.

27 Schatz, 'The new Hollywood', pp. 17–19.

28 These films are taken from the top ten of the annual box-office charts, as listed in Steinberg, *Film Facts*, pp. 27–8; 'The 1980s: a reference guide to motion pictures, television, VCR, and cable', *The Velvet Light Trap* no. 27, Spring 1991, pp. 81–3; and the annual 'In Zahlen' column in *steadycam*.

29 Steinberg, *Film Facts*, pp. 28, 61, 253–4.

30 Ibid., pp. 256–7; 'The 1980s', pp. 81–5.

31 'The 1980s', pp. 81–2.

32 Ibid., p. 81.

33 'In Zahlen', *steadycam* no. 13 (1989), p. 19; no. 14 (1989), p. 9; no. 15 (1990), p. 10.

34 'The 1980s', p. 81. With its extended run into 1990, *Look Who's Talking*, a November 1989 release, eventually earned about $140 million. Due to its magically talking baby and the childish perspective associated with it, this romantic comedy can also be considered as a family movie, which helps to explain its greater success.

35 'In Zahlen', *steadycam* no. 14 (1989), p. 9; no. 15 (1990), p. 10.

36 'Industry economic review and audience profile', p. 389. Cf. Leonard Klady, 'Numbers game at showest', *Variety*, 10 March 1997, pp. 7, 15.

37 Press book contained in file MFL x n.c.3.106 no. 19, BRTC.

38 Lawrence van Gelder, 'At the movies', *New York Times*, 23 March 1990, p. C8.

39 Holly Golightly is the character played by Audrey Hepburn in *Breakfast at Tiffany's* (1961). Hepburn also played Eliza Dolittle in the 1964 film version of the musical *My*

Fair Lady, key scenes of which are restaged in *Pretty Woman*. Hepburn makes an appearance in *Pretty Woman* in a clip from *Charade* (1963), which Vivian watches on televison.

40 Dave Kehr, 'Pretty ugly: a crass movie desecrates a classic song title', *Chicago Tribune*, 23 March 1990, Section 2, p. 6; Gary Giddins, review, *Village Voice*, 27 March 1990, p. 61; Julie Salamon, 'Film: get rich, get happy?', *Wall Street Journal*, 29 March 1990, p. A12; Richard Corliss, 'Sinderella', *Time*, 2 April 1990; Linda Winer, '*Pretty Woman*, ugly message', *Newsday*, 27 April 1990, Part II, p. 2; David Sterritt, '*Pretty Woman*'s ugly message', *Christian Science Monitor*, 27 April 1990, p. 10; Paul Baumann, 'What's left of desire?', *Commonweal*, 4 May 1990, p. 296.

41 John Simon, review, *New York*, 31 April 1990, p. 61; Lewis Archibald, 'Fun – if you don't make many demands', *Downtown*, 28 March 1990, p. 12A.

42 Vincent Canby, *New York Times*, 3 June 1990, Section 2, p. 19. Cf. Roger Ebert, 'Pretty good', *New York Daily News*, 23 March 1990, p. 39.

43 Andrew Sarris, 'Star Roberts: the stuff dreams are made of', *New York Observer*, 16 April 1990, p. 30; Janet Maslin, 'High-rolling boy meets streetwalking girl', *New York Times*, 23 March 1990, p. C20.

44 Geraldine Fabrikant, '*Pretty Woman* finds best friend in profit', *New York Times*, 21 July 1990, p. 29.

45 Cf. Joseph Gelmis, 'A sexy Cinderella, or "My Fair Hooker"', *Newsday*, 19 October 1990, Part II, p. 41.

46 Press book containted in file MFL x n.c.3 108 no. 21, BRTC.

47 *Variety*, 11 July 1990, p. 30.

48 Julie Salamon, review, *Wall Street Journal*, 12 July 1990, p. A8; Terry Kelleher, review, *Newsday*, 13 July 1990, Part II, p. 13; Georgie Brown, review, *Village Voice*, 17 July 1990, p. 63; Terrence Rafferty, review, *New Yorker*, 30 July 1990, p. 80. For a mixed review see, for example, Roger Ebert, *New York Daily News*, 13 July 1990, p. 43.

49 Susan Kittenplan, review, *The West Side Spirit*, 31 July 1990, p. 22.

50 David Sterritt, '*Ghost* provides a second-rate showcase for a first-rate talent: Whoopi Goldberg', *Christian Science Monitor*, 22 August 1990, p. 11.

51 Richard Corliss, review, *Time*, 16 July 1990, pp. 86–7.

52 Jami Bernard, review, *New York Post*, 13 July 1990, p. 27.

53 David Bartholomew, review, *Film Journal*, August 1990, p. 22.

54 Larry Rohter, 'Top movie of the year a sleeper: it's *Ghost*', *New York Times*, 3 November 1990, p. 13. Cf. Joseph McBride, '*Ghost* to top domestic b.o. at year's end', *Variety*, 12 November 1990, p. 3.

55 *Ghost* opened in 1,101 movie theatres, taking in $12.2 million. By contrast, the most expensive summer release, *Total Recall* (reputedly the most expensive film of all time up to this point, with a budget of over $60 million, as opposed to *Ghost*'s $18 million), opened in 2,060 theatres and took in $25.5 million during the first weekend, yet had dropped down to 1,787 theatres and $4.2 million by the 6th weekend, when *Ghost* was still performing very strongly with $8.3 million on 1,766 theatres: 'In Zahlen', *steadycam* no.17, 1990, p. 11. There was enormous demand for *Ghost* from video rental shops, and even at the high price of $100 it performed well in the sell-through market. 'Believers in *Ghost*', *Newsday*, 26 April 1991, p. 78.

56 Amy Taubin, 'Stocks and the bonds that tie', *Village Voice*, 4 December 1990, p. 11.

57 'In Zahlen', *steadycam* no. 18, 1991, p. 11.

58 Leonard Klady, ' "Apollo" launched on all-time b.o. list', *Variety*, 26 February 1996, p. 46.

59 *Variety*, 3 June 1996, p. 70.

60 Anne Thompson, 'Studios stick to their guns over sex appeal of pics', *Variety*, 7 January 1991, pp. 109, 111.

61 Quoted in Thompson, 'Studios stick to their guns', p. 111.

62 See Peter Krämer, 'Women First: *Titanic* (1997), action-adventure films and Hollywood's female audience', *Historical Journal of Film, Radio and Television* vol. 18 no. 4, October 1998, pp. 599–618.

6 Home Alone Together: Hollywood and the 'family film'

Robert C. Allen

The first shot of *Junior* opens on the back of a donnishly dressed Arnold Schwarzenegger, as he walks through the stacks of what appears to be a research library. He and we hear the wails of an infant, which Arnold locates lying alone atop the circulation desk. 'There's a baby here,' he notes with surprise to himself and the audience. 'There must be a mother. Hell, there's a baby.' Seeing no-one else around, Arnold reluctantly picks the baby up, holding it in front of him at arm's length as it were a bomb about to go off. Which it does: relieving itself all over Arnold's jacket and pants. 'Help,' he cries, carrying the baby toward the camera. We switch to a reverse shot which reveals an 'audience' of other babies, sitting in armchairs arrayed theatre-style watching him. We cut to a close-up of Arnold's horrified expression, but as the shot pulls back we see him in pyjamas in his bed. His encounter with babies has been a nightmare.

Behind the opening credits of *Home Alone*, a policeman (Joe Pesci) approaches the front door of a large, upper-middle-class, suburban home, and tries unsuccessfully to gain the attention of a succession of children as they scurry through the foyer, intent on the completion of individual missions. We cut to a bedroom in the house, where Catherine O'Hara's character is simultaneously talking on the phone and packing things into suitcases spread out on the bed. Kevin (Macauley Culkin), a pre-adolescent boy, enters the room to complain that his Uncle Frank will not allow him to join the big kids watching a feature film on video. 'And it is not even rated "R",' he protests. Meanwhile, back at the front door, the policeman (who turns out to be a burglar posing as a policeman) asks one of the hurrying children, 'Are your parents home?'

'Yes', she says, 'but they don't live here.' She darts past him.

He asks another the same question.

'My parents live in Paris – sorry,' is her reply.

'Are your parents home?' he asks a third.

'Yes.'

'Do they live here?'

'No.'

'All kids, no parents,' Pesci's character concludes to himself and the audience. 'Probably a fancy orphanage.'

These two scenes speak in different ways to the conjunction of social, demographic, technological and economic forces that link contemporary popular media to the contemporary family (as both a set of diverse and dynamic social units and as a discursive formation) through what we might call postmodern family entertainment. In *Junior*, the 1980s' most famous slayer and player of monstrous masculinity confronts a 1990s version of the monstrous other, an abandoned baby, who attacks the helpless Arnold before an audience of its peers for their pleasure. In *Home Alone*, Kevin's alienation from his extended family is signalled by his exclusion from the VCR audience for films made for an older generation of viewers. Kevin needs a film that the entire family, including eight-year-old boys like himself, can watch and enjoy – a film precisely like the one he is in! The family home as depicted in *Home Alone* is the site of frantic, uncoordinated activity – children and parents circulating in separate orbits, meeting only when they collide. Home is a place where parents are not and where, if adults are 'home,' they do not live. Family ties are so loose that a child can be abandoned without the parents realising it until they are thousands of miles away.

In this chapter I propose to examine one aspect of postmodern family entertainment: the reorientation of the movie industry toward both its audience and its markets in the last half of the 1980s. This reorientation resulted not only in the creation of a new movie type, the family film; as paradoxical and provocative as it might sound, it brought about nothing less than the death of Hollywood cinema, at least as it had been known and experienced from the 1910s up to that point. Although not 'determined' in any unidirectional sense by them, the emergence of Hollywood's version of postmodern family entertainment is a cultural response to separate – though interlaced – demographic, technological and social phenomena: the 'echo boom,' the VCR and the postmodern family.

Baby Boom, Bust and Echo Boom

Following a half-century of relatively constant birth rates in the US, the period between 1946 and 1964 saw an explosion in live births, which came to be known as the 'baby boom'. By the end of the boom, in 1965, some 76 million boomers had been added to the US population and four out of every ten Americans were under the age of twenty. Then, contrary to the expectations of virtually every demographic expert, the baby boom not only subsided but was immediately followed by an equally, if not more, remarkable implosion of birth rates. The fifteen-year baby 'bust' between 1965 and 1980 saw birth rates in the US fall below replacement level to their lowest levels in American history. As late as 1986, conservative commentators noted the implications of this with alarm: new home construction would plummet, computer sales would drop, industry would be rendered unable to innovate as the number of younger, more imaginative workers declined, and, most frightening of all, with fertility rates in the West below replacement levels but still high in Asia, Africa and Latin America, white American babies would be greatly outnumbered by a tidal wave of black, brown and yellow tots.[1]

Birth rates began rising again in 1977, but it was not until 1989 that live births again topped the 4 million mark for the first time since 1964. Births remained at this level through 1993, and began falling in 1994. 'Echo-boomers' or 'Generation Y' (the 72 million new Americans born between 1977 and 1995 – most of them born in the last decade of that period) represent a demographic bulge almost as large and arguably as socially important as their baby boom parents' generation. By 1995, children eighteen years of age or younger comprised 28 per cent of the overall US population, a cohort roughly equal to baby-boomers aged thirty-one to forty. Despite the fact that birth rates began levelling off in the mid-1990s, the overall size of what some are now calling the Millennium Generation in the US continues to grow, fuelled by immigration as well as birth rates. The total number of Americans under the age of eighteen in 1998 topped 70 million for the first time in US history, surpassing the previous generational record set by the baby boom in 1966.

The political agendas of both major political parties during the Clinton era have been shaped by 'echo boom' issues, including tobacco legislation, education reform and health insurance. Many social observers believe that, over the next twenty years, American culture and politics in large measure will be organised around the relationship between the 'baby boom' and the 'echo boom'. The conflicting economic and political interests of the two groups are already manifest in local debates over school funding and in national debates over the future of social security and Medicare. As *American Demographics* noted in 1995,

> Like the baby boom before them, their huge numbers will profoundly influence markets, attitudes, and society. Their true power will become apparent in the next five years as the oldest members come of age. Their habits will shape America for most of the 21st century.

One immediate effect of the echo boom has been a cultural 'preoccupation with parenting' for the first time since the 1950s. Even GenXers, despite popular stereotypes, have demonstrated a procreative urge more strongly and earlier than their immediately preceding age cohort. Beginning in the 1980s, women in their thirties and forties began having first children at a far greater rate than had ever been the case, and these same women continue childbearing far longer than demographers have predicted.[2]

A New Technology for a New Generation

Just as the baby boom overlaps almost exactly with the diffusion of television technology and the maturation of broadcast television as an institution and cultural form, the echo boom also has its defining technology, the VCR. The diffusion of VCRs began within a few months of the beginning of the echo boom birth-rate rise and reached domestic saturation about the time the echo boom tailed off in the mid-1990s. Sony introduced the Betamax in 1975, but home use of video technology did not move out of the 'videophile' phase and into the mass market until 1984. From then on, the rate of diffusion of the VCR into American households was extraordinary – and perhaps unprecedented. It took seventy years for the telephone to reach 50 per cent penetration of US households, cable television thirty-nine years, and television fifteen years. It took the VCR just twelve years, with 80 per cent of that penetration occurring in less than forty-eight months. In 1983 only 8.3 million US households, less than 10 per cent of the total, owned a VCR; in 1987, 45.8 million households, slightly more than half of all US homes, had them. To put this remarkable rate of adoption into perspective, we should recall that another revolutionary piece of electronic technology, the personal computer, was also introduced in the early 1980s. By the end of 1997, fewer than half of American households owned a computer, while nearly 90 per cent owned a VCR.

1984 is also the year in which the term 'media center' entered the vocabulary of domestic American architecture. The setting aside of space in house plans for a 'media center' in addition to – or instead of – a den, living room, family room or great room signals the reconfiguration of living space in the middle-class home around an expanding array of audio-visual technologies: the VCR, CD player, video-game console, personal computer, satellite receiver and television monitor – only one of which was the television set itself and only one use of which was the viewing of terrestrial broadcasting programmes.

The 4 million babies born at the high water mark of the echo boom in 1987 came home from the hospital to find the VCR already there, warmed up, and ready to use for different purposes than those for which it had initially been marketed. Several factors combined to spur the growth of the pre-recorded tape market in the early 1980s: Hollywood studios' decision to make more films available on video cassette; the establishment of VHS as the dominant video format; a reduction in the price of VCRs from over $2000 to less than $500; and the extension of recording time from two to four hours. In turn, the increase in sales of pre-recorded tapes further accelerated household VCR penetration. Total home video software revenue exceeded $1 billion for the first time in 1983, by which time some 12,000 titles were available, with 200 new video titles being released each month. Rental transactions in 1983 amounted to a total of $800 million.[3]

Once VCR penetration had reached the 50 per cent mark in 1987, the end-user technology base existed to move the principal basis for the VCR's utility beyond 'time-shifting', and to make video rentals a nationally branded, mass-marketed retailing industry. Between 1987 and 1990 – in less time than it took the average undergraduate to accumulate enough hours to graduate with a film studies major – watching a feature film rented from the local video store at home supplanted going to a movie theatre as the most common mode of engagement with 'the movies' for a large portion of the population of North America. By the end of the 1980s, video rentals at more than 25,000 locations in the US reached a total of $8.4 billion, nearly twice as much as was being taken in at movie theatres. A December 1991 poll of 1000 VCR-owning households revealed that watching a movie at home was the preferred leisure activity of nearly 70 per cent of the sample – an increase of 50 per cent in only two years. Going out to the movies was preferred by only 22 per cent, down 38 per cent over the same period. *The Ladies Home Journal* observed that watching movies on video was America's 'new family fix'.[4]

The explosive growth of video rental as a distribution channel for Hollywood films is well illustrated by the growing ascendance of Blockbuster Video as a national force in the industry. Originally a local chain of nineteen rental outlets in Dallas, Texas, Blockbuster built or franchised 1300 locations nationwide between 1987 and 1991. By 1992, Blockbuster stores boasted an annual revenue of $1.1 billion, and in 1994 Chief Executive Officer Wayne Huizinga sold the chain to Viacom for $8.6 billion.[5]

By 1990, it was clear to marketing executives in Hollywood that selling videocassette copies of theatrical films to video rental outlets could produce up to $30 million in profit for a film which had exhausted its potential income from theatrical exhibition six to nine months earlier. Initially, the studios priced feature films on videocassette at roughly $75 wholesale or $100 retail. This was well above the amount most households were willing to pay to own a copy of a particular film, but still low enough for video rental stores to make a profit on thirty rentals per copy. This arrangement effectively placed an upper limit on the number of video copies sold, even of the biggest box office hits, of around 500,000 units – the number required to service video rental outlets in North America.

Between 1985 and 1989, some studios experimented with an even more lucrative way of marketing some films on video: selling copies directly to consumers at a price low enough (less than $30) to tap a mass market. *E.T.*, for example, was priced for 'sell-through' at Christmas 1988, selling 12.5 million copies and giving Steven Spielberg and Universal Studios a $200 million Christmas present. Between 1983 and 1992, the number of feature films priced for sell-through increased at an average annual rate of 52 per cent, from 5.9 million copies to 264 million. In 1992, the retail value of video sell-through exceeded the total US theatrical box office for the first time. In that year, Disney's Buena Vista Home Video division became the largest and most profitable 'film' studio in Hollywood, contributing three-quarters of Disney's 1992 operating profits of $508 million. As the video rental business reached a plateau in the early 1990s (sales of pre-recorded videos to rental dealers actually fell 5 per cent between 1991 and 1994), retail sales of feature films on video continued to grow at an average rate of 20 per cent a year.[6]

The explosive growth of the video sell-through market was remarkable not only because so many people were buying so many films on video, but also because of where they were buying them. Although video rental stores like Blockbuster sold new and 'pre-viewed' copies of videos as a sideline to their core rental business, by 1990 fully one half of the volume of sell-through business was occurring at discount mass retail stores, such as WalMart, Target, and K-Mart. When a rival accused Disney's home video unit of thinking more like a soap company than a film studio, its president Bill Merchant replied, 'We're competing with Rubbermaid.'[7] By 1994, more than half of all 136,000 US grocery stores were stocking videos for sale, adding another 77,500 video retail locations which together accounted for 18 per cent of the $14.7 billion video retail business.[8]

Hollywood and the 'Family Film'

What was referred to in the trade as the 'family film' emerged in the late 1980s and early 1990s as Hollywood's attempt to exploit the profit potential of the video markets, particularly sell-through, as fully as possible. The most frequently cited example of the family film is undoubtedly *Home Alone*, which grossed $285 million at the box office in 1990, and sold 10 million video copies in the following year. 'What *Home Alone* has done', said Tom Sherak, marketing vice president for Fox, 'is [to] show that there is a broad audience out there and you don't have to be afraid of using young people – kids are not taboo.'[9] *Home Alone* inaugurated contemporary Hollywood's full embrace of the cross-generational family film, particularly films that 'can be made cheap and can reap deep[ly]'. At a time of ballooning budgets for R-rated action pictures, *Home Alone* cost only $18.5 million to make.[10]

But what exactly is the 'family film', and what is the 'family' in relation to which it is made? Film industry discourse reveals that the family film has not been constituted as a genre in traditional sense, since it has included realistic comedies (*Three Men and a Baby, Home Alone*), adventure fantasies (*Hook, Honey, I Shrunk/Blew Up the Kid/s*), animated films (*Little Mermaid, Aladdin, The Lion King, Anastasia, Toy Story*, etc.), as well as live action/animation hybrids (*Jurassic Park, Babe, Flubber, Jumanji*). Nor does the term 'family film' necessarily indicate films manifestly about the family (although in a number of notable cases, this was certainly the case). Nor, as the term had suggested in the 1960s and 1970s, does it signify films addressed exclusively at children (although children have constituted an important market segment addressed by these films). Rather, the family film became the discursive marker for a set of narrative, representational and institutional practices designed to maximise marketability and profitability across theatrical, video, licencing and merchandising markets by means of what we might call cross-generational appeal.

At the same time as Hollywood was rediscovering the family audience, the question of what constituted the family was becoming a matter of obsessive speculation in the United States, and the subject of 'family values' a central concern in American politics and public policy. Concluding his 1975 history of the American family, Edward Shorter proclaimed that the era of the modern family had ended, but that it was as yet impossible to predict what reconfigurations of family would supplant the model of the nuclear family. The American family, Shorter noted, was on a historical trajectory so unpredictable that it was as if it had set course for the sun. The adjective he applied to this unprecedented and unstable re-figuration of the contemporary family was 'postmodern'.[11]

Shorter made a useful distinction between 'the families we live with and the families we live by'. In constructing this dichotomy, he acknowledged the differences between the conjugal and kinship relations we experience in our personal histories and the social and cultural ideals against which we measure the success or normality of them. In every age, individuals have been enmeshed in parental, sexual, filial, domestic and kinship relations. These relations are always imperfect, complex and frequently fraught with ambivalence, contradiction, uncertainty and instability. Yet, at every turn, we encounter representations of the family in relation to which we are asked to gauge our own experience. Every day we hear 'the family' invoked as if it were a unitary social 'fact' or a constant element in everyone's life – everyone's, that is, except our own.

In pointing in the direction of the postmodern family, Shorter suggested that the gap between the bewildering variety of family relations we live with and the much more circumscribed idealisations of family life we live by was assuming chasmic proportions. Those relations – sexual, parental, filial, domestic, biological – that fall under the sign of 'family' have in every age and every culture been subject to cultural idealisation and social regulation, so central are they to the very notion of human society itself. The radical collapse of those structures of social authority and sanction in the US and elsewhere in the West that once regulated the formation, organisation, reproduction and dissolution of the family is, however, unprecedented, as is the concomitant extension of the notion of radical individualism to all areas of life choice. With what Zygmunt Bauman calls the 'universal dismantling of power-supported structures' in the postmodern era, the constitution of families is *ad hoc* rather than prescribed; relations among family members are contingent rather than enduring; and the very distinctions – biological, ethical, affective – that mark out the family from other forms of social relations are increasingly blurred. More than ever before in western history, families are products of human choice, and yet these choices are made in the absence of socially authorised sources of approval or arbitration. Instead, both the self and the family are the result of unending processes of self-assembly, and the guidelines for both have been radically privatised. As Bauman expresses it: 'ethics has become a matter of individual discretion, risk-taking, chronic uncertainty and never-placated qualms'.[12]

It is little wonder, then, that politicians of every stripe desperately grasp for some purchase on 'family values', while their constituents turn to the popular media for models of family life, validation for the family life choices they have made, or merely reassurance that everyone's family is dysfunctional in some way. As the New World Order replaced the Cold War in the 1980s, 'the crisis of the family' replaced communism at the centre of political and policy agendas for both major political parties, even if no one seemed quite sure what 'the family' was any more. Relying on the same statistics, feminists and neo-traditionalists alike declared the death of the nuclear family into which the baby-boomers had been born, differing mainly over whether this was an occasion for sack-cloth or party frocks.[13] In short, since the 1980s, family has become the 'black hole' of contemporary American social discourse and popular culture: impossible to identify in its exact characteristics yet exerting inescapable gravitational force.

By the end of the 1980s, Hollywood had come under attack from a number of groups (including, but not limited to, political conservatives and the religious right) for making films that were not suitable for the family, whatever 'the family' was. This criticism grew louder as R-rated films made for adult theatrical audiences were made available for viewing at home on video. A study conducted by the Junior League of New York in the late 1980s found the average 10–11-year-old watched four R-rated videos each month, the equivalent, according to one commentator, 'of fifteen days per year of schooling in sadistic and harmful ways of thinking'.[14]

Conveniently for Hollywood, the very films that were most consistently profitable across the widest range of markets in the late 1980s and early 1990s – films such as *Three Men and a Baby*, *Look Who's Talking*, *Home Alone*, *E.T.*, *Honey I Shrunk the Kids*, and, of course, Disney animated features – also allowed the film industry to claim that it was family-friendly. Although some critics would continue to rail at Hollywood's continuing embrace of the R-rated feature (most conspicuously Bob Dole during the 1996 presidential campaign),[15] others would see the increasing numbers of G, PG and PG-13 releases as evidence that Hollywood had 'grown up', and was, like its adult baby-boomer audience, returning to traditional 'family values'. In 1993, the editor of the Christian Television and Film Commission's guide to films and video applauded Hollywood for realising that it was in the industry's best interest to make films that 'appeal to the broad segment of American society that upholds traditional Judeo-Christian ideals and values'.[16]

The audience for the family film had dissolved into a set of overlapping markets. These were grounded principally in whatever social units were produced by the interpenetration of two expanding demographic groupings: those over the age of thirty and those under the age of eighteen. Furthermore, because the marketing life of a given film now extended over a year or more – from before its actual theatrical release through its release on video for sale and/or rental and in other ancillary venues (cable, pay-per-view, broadcast TV, syndication, etc.) – and because millions of households now owned their own copies of feature films and controlled when they were viewed, there were no fixed temporal boundaries within which the 'audience' for a given film could be contained. As the production and marketing logic behind a substantial fraction of Hollywood films shifted from reaching audiences in movie theatres to exploiting as many markets as possible for as long as possible, and as the nuclear family fractured into increasingly diverse social groupings, it became less and less in Hollywood's interest to align itself with any particular figuration of the family or any unequivocal set of 'family values'. 'Family' for Hollywood basically meant those markets more effectively exploited by films that were not rated R. With boomers taking their kids (or being dragged by them) to the movies, and with kids more likely than any other group to go to the theatre to see a film more than once, by 1991 PG and PG-13-rated films were twice as likely as R-rated ones to earn $60 million and three times more likely to earn $100 million at the box office.[17]

But while there was still a movie audience and a strong video rental market for R-rated films, most R-rated films missed out on the chance to cash in on the video sell-through bonanza. Since 1990, one of the most important marketing decisions a studio makes is whether to price the video version of a given film for rental or sell-through. The rule of thumb is that a film needs to sell at least two million copies priced at less than $30 to net the studio a greater return than would be achieved by pricing that film on video at $75 wholesale. Routinely, viewers at film previews today are asked whether they would purchase a video copy of the film in question. Although some R-rated films have sold well as videos, market dynamics favour family films. In households with children, kids influence or determine 75 per cent of household purchasing decisions. The single largest category of video purchases is parents buying videos for their children. Videos aimed specifically at kids (whether feature films or direct-to-video speciality titles) represent 37 per cent of all video sales. Although it is becoming less so, the video sell-through market is still highly seasonal, with the weeks prior to Christmas representing the most important period of the year for video retailers. Also, regardless of time of year, 30–40 per cent of videos are purchased as gifts. R-rated films are much less likely to be bought as gifts than more 'family-rated' fare. Furthermore, some of the largest mass retail chains like WalMart and Target and many grocery stores, on whom Hollywood now depends for 40–50 per cent of video sales, either refuse to stock R-rated titles or refuse to give them prominent shelf placement. No grocer, said *Supermarket News*, 'wants to antagonise a $100–200 per week customer over a $3 video rental'. Thus, *Lethal Weapon II*, the third highest-grossing box-office hit of 1989 sold only 2.5 million video copies when it was released on video the following year – far fewer than its theatrical box-office appeal might have suggested. By contrast, the family film *Beethoven*, which had taken only $50 million at the box office, sold 3 million video copies. Almost every week's list of top-selling videos since the start of the 1990s has been led by family films or explicitly children's titles. *Beauty and the Beast* has sold more than 20 million video copies to date, producing more than $500 million in revenue for Disney.[18]

Hollywood's Demographic Earthquake

In the 1980s, Hollywood had to reposition itself in relation not so much to its audience (or audiences) as to a shifting, decentred constellation of markets for its products. *Junior* illustrates the strategy that Arnold Schwarzenegger deliberately employed in the early 1990s to reconstruct himself not only for a changing theatrical audience but also for different markets for his films. *Junior, Twins, Kindergarten Cop, Jingle All the Way*, and the appropriately titled *Last Action Hero* were all PG or PG-13 rated family films, and all were priced for video sell-through.

The box office market itself felt the demographic tremors mentioned at the start of this chapter as a kind of audience sinkhole, as the core movie-going audience of the 1970s and early 1980s diminished. Since the late 1960s, if not before, films had been marketed at what Hollywood with empirical reason regarded as its 'primary' box-office audience: young people between the ages of thirteen and twenty-five (particularly white males within that age group). Whereas the 'average' movie-goer in the 1980s went approximately six times a year, this youth audience went to the movies twelve times a year. As long as the baby boom lasted, this age cohort replenished itself every year. The extraordinary popularity of *Star Wars* in 1977 was due, in part at least, to the demographic fact that the audience segment at which the film was pitched – viewers aged between thirteen and twenty-five – had increased 17 per cent since 1967.

The effect of the baby 'bust' that began in 1964 was that, by 1980, the number of young movie-goers was in decline while at the same time the preceding age cohort, the boomers, was ageing out of the prime movie-going group. Between 1980 and 1990, the percentage of the total US population under the age of eighteen fell from 28 per cent to 25 per cent, while the percentage between the ages of thirty-five and sixty-four rose from 31 per cent to 34 per cent, from 70 million to 105 million people. By the early 1990s, these overlapping demographic shifts produced a dilemma for Hollywood: the age cohort of core 'heavy-goers' was shrinking both as a percentage of the total population and of the movie audience, while the age cohort of fringe 'infrequent' movie-goers (four times a year on average) was growing. In 1983, tickets sold to 13–25-year-olds represented 55 per cent of all admissions. By 1992, teenagers and young adults constituted only 38 per cent of the US movie audience, and the percentage of the teen movie audience (aged between sixteen and twenty) had dropped from 24 per cent of the total audience in 1981 to only 15 per cent in 1992. Over the same period, the proportion of the movie audience made up by boomers in their forties rose from 6 per cent to 16 per cent. In 1993, Disney executive Joe Roth complained that Hollywood could not rely upon its young audience any more. Young people, he claimed, had lost the 'tribal rite' of going to the movies every week. Instead they watched videos and played video games at home. The almost century-old American tradition of one generation of young moviegoers being replaced by another of equal or greater size was, he feared, over.[19]

Of course, this is not to say that Hollywood simply ignored what it referred to as the 'adult' audience after *Easy Rider* in 1968: the 1970s and 1980s saw a number of successful films, such as *Kramer vs. Kramer, On Golden Pond*, which were clearly not aimed at a teenage and young adult audience. But these 'story-driven' or 'character-driven' films, as they were typically referred to in industry discourse, were developed and marketed as alternatives to *Animal House* and *Carrie*, and the audience for 'adult appeal' titles was assumed to be distinct from, and not overlapping with, young men under twenty-five.

During the 1980s, the domestic theatrical market was itself shrinking both as a proportion of overall revenue and, more importantly, as a proportion of overall profitability for the studios. The problem that Hollywood confronted in the 1980s was how to reposition itself in relation to a domestic box-office market that was markedly different from what it had been a decade earlier. At the same time, the home video rental and sales industries, having emerged in the mid-1980s, positioned themselves in relation not to the baby-bust generation, as to some extent Hollywood continued to do, but to the two generations on either demographic side: the post-twenties baby-boomers and their 'echo boom' children. These two age cohorts, joined together in the industry's imagination around the glowing (video) hearth of the middle-class home, would emerge as 'the family' audience that would drive the video industry and transform the film business in the early 1990s.

It is important to understand the magnitude and direction of the shift in film-viewing behaviour that has been generated by the conjunction of technological innovation and demographic change. In 1996, the total US domestic film theatrical box office produced takings of approximately $5.9 billion. In the same year, US consumers spent $8.7 billion renting videos and another $7.6 billion buying pre-recorded video tapes. Theatrical distribution of movies accounted for only 23 per cent of domestic studio revenue that year, while video sales represented more than 55 per cent. Each month, between 44 and 53 per cent of all US consumers – some 100 million people in around 45 million households – rent a video at least once. More than 60 per cent of all US households own feature films on video, with the average number of titles in family collections currently standing at forty-one. The core markets for both video rentals and sales are families with children under the age of seventeen. Households with children are more than twice as likely to be frequent renters and heavy buyers of films on video.[20]

The Movie on the Lunchbox

In the early 1990s, the 'family film' was increasingly defined in relation to another huge set of complexly interconnected markets which mined the film for the 'exchange value' it could add to other commodities through product placements, merchandising, licencing and promotional tie-ins with fast-food restaurants, soft drinks and other non-filmic products.[21] *Star Wars* first demonstrated the extraordinary profitability of licencing the use of a film's title, logo, character likenesses, storyline, props and other features in conjunction with the manufacture and marketing of other products. Between its initial release in 1977 and 1992, some $2.6 billion worth of *Star Wars* paraphernalia had been sold. As one studio executive expressed it, for the right film pitched at the right audience, licencing could result in 'almost infinite amounts of cash'.[22]

In 1977 the total retail value of the licenced product market was only $7 billion a year. By 1983, the licenced merchandise industry had doubled in value. Over the last twenty years, it has increased ten-fold and, with a retail value now in excess of $70 billion, it dwarfs the theatrical film business, video rental and sales, and the cable television industry combined. With children's products constituting 65-75 per cent of the licenced product market, the most licenceable film projects are cross-generational 'family films',

especially those specifically targeted at children. When *Home Alone* was released the-
atrically in 1990, it was such a surprise hit that Fox did not have the necessary lead time
to work out extensive tie-in or licencing promotions. John Hughes made sure that the
same thing did not happen with the sequel. Collaborating fully in one of the most sophisticated promotional and licencing arrangements to date, Hughes worked directly with
Tiger Electronics to develop two toys that could be used by Macauley Culkin's character in the film and then sold commercially: the 'Talk Boy' voice-altering cassette
recorder and Monster Sap soap.[23]

The shifts occurring in relation to the family film – from audience to markets, from
film as celluloid experienced in a theatre to film combined with so many other mani-
festations over a longer period of time – not only alters the logics by which films are
made and marketed, but also alters what a film 'is' in an economic sense and, by extension, in both an ontological and epistemological sense as well. For example, in the summer of 1991, McDonald's offered *Batman* action figures as part of its Happy Meal
promotion during the theatrical run of *Batman Returns*, which had been rated PG-13
for its violence and language. McDonald's received considerable criticism for promoting the film to children who, presumably, were barred from seeing it. A McDonald's
executive attempted to explain the problem away by saying that McDonald's 'simply
[wanted] to allow young people to experience the fun associated with the character
Batman and [that the campaign] was not designed to promote attendance at the
movie'.[24]

Beyond the blatant disingenuousness of this remark (which winks at the likelihood
that some children had seen the first *Batman* on video and would see *Batman Returns*
when it came out on video), this public relations débâcle suggests that, as a marketable
commodity and enhancer of value for other, non-filmic commodities, a film is no
longer reducible to the actual experience of seeing it. This, and other similar examples
of the complex relationship between a film and its promotion through other objects,
raise any number of interesting questions about what now, in a phenomenological
sense, constitutes 'the film', and in what relationship it stands to things that are not it
but of it. When my daughter was three years old, a visiting adult friend asked her what
character she wished to be on the next Halloween. 'Batgirl,' she responded. My wife and
I looked at each other quizzically, knowing that Madeline had not to our knowledge
been allowed, in the words of the McDonald's executive, 'to experience the fun associated' with this character. 'Where have you seen Batgirl?' we asked her in unison. 'In the
movie,' she responded. 'In what movie?' we asked. 'You know,' she said, 'the movie on
the lunchbox.' One of her classmates at pre-school, it turned out, had a *Batman Returns*
lunchbox featuring Batgirl.

Licencing complicates what we think of as a given film. It also changes the role of the
movie star in relation to it. Since licencing is such a lucrative proposition for the studios, it becomes increasingly important for them to be able to extract the likeness of a
film's stars in character and to transfer that likeness from the filmic text to licenced
products and tie-in promotions. Studios usually secure the co-operation of big stars in
allowing the use of their character likeness on licenced merchandise by giving them a
piece of the licencing royalties. The 'value' of character likenesses might seem to
emanate from the recognisability of the star as a star; that is, the trans-textual charisma

that is the basis and definition of the classical Hollywood movie star, and is what he or she brings from outside the film to the embodiment of a particular character. But with so much of the licencing and tie-in market directed at children, whose knowledge of or interest in any adult star might be non-existent, the value of a star's character likeness is based much less on star power than on preserving a co-extensive identity between the licensable character in a film and its extra-filmic representation.

In line with this dictum, industry insiders were predicting disappointing returns for the expensive, Spielberg-directed family film *Hook* in 1991 before anyone had seen it, precisely because stars Robin Williams, Dustin Hoffman and Julia Roberts had refused to allow their likenesses to be used on paraphernalia. The *Wall Street Journal* predicted that as a result, children would be confused by three different versions of Peter Pan, Hook and Tinkerbell: those in the film (as embodied in the stars), generic versions produced by the studio, and other generic versions on toys manufactured under licence by Mattel. By 1995, quipped *Variety*, it was clear who the real stars were in Hollywood: McDonald's, Burger King and Pepsi. Executives from these and other companies contemplating tie-in arrangements with particular films now routinely review scripts before they go into production to make sure that the film under consideration is consonant with the image the company wishes to project for its soft drink, fast food or other product line.[25]

Hollywood has developed other ways to get around the problem of overpaid stars who dislike the prospect of their image forming the focus of a merchandising campaign. Hollywood's embrace of fantasy over the past decade has been, in large measure, a result of the fact that fantasy characters are more easily licenced and marketed, so that the studios can keep a larger share of the licencing royalties. Fantasy characters lend themselves to the graphic condensation of the 'visual icon', as one advertising executive put it. In the language of the toy industry trade papers, they are more 'toyetic': they make a better basis for toys than recognisable human figures. Moreover, their identities are often separable from particular human representations. Disney and other animation producers might use stars to provide the voices for their characters, but there are no star rights or royalty issues involved in the marketing of Little Mermaid bathmats or Aladdin toothbrushes. Nor did the sentient pigs, dogs, cats, whales or other creatures who have filled movie screens for the last five years or so demand a cut of the *Babe* underwear licence royalties or the *Free Willy* bathroom slippers. Marketing discourse in the trade press routinely notes the considerable advantage represented by films whose concept is reducible to a graphic sign that can easily be applied to a range of objects, packages and advertising forms. The distinctive *Batman* logo is an excellent example. Conversely, advertising executives frequently complain about the difficulty of exploiting films that are not so reducible. One such executive lamented that so few films planned for the 1992 holiday season would be promoted through tie-ins or licencing. 'I can't see Jimmy Hoffa on a Pizza Hut Collector's Cup,' he moaned.[26]

The step beyond writing toys into film scripts for human characters to use is, of course, making toys themselves into characters, a feat accomplished by Disney with its release of *Toy Story* in 1996. The 3-D effect produced by computer animation rendered characters more convincingly than could have been done through conventional cel animation processes. 'For Mr. Potato Head, we were able to get that pebbly texture that plastic has, which adds a sense of believability to the character', *Toy Story* director, John Lasseter, noted. Fidelity to the audience's experience of a toy has now become the standard of character 'believability' and verisimilitude. The film's logic makes the 'human' characters in the film not the forces that transform toys into characters, but rather the opposite: in the presence of 'human' characters the toys 'freeze into icons of their toy origins', as *Variety* put it so well.[27]

By the 1990s, George Lucas was in the product licencing business as much as he was in the film-making business, with the *Star Wars*™ films functioning as a part of a complex corporate strategy, the goal of which is to keep the licence viable indefinitely as a merchandising asset. Any given *Star Wars*™ film adds value to the brand, in part because of the qualities it possesses as a distinctive *Star Wars*™ experience. By this point in the history of the brand, however, any participating film's value is also what we might call contingent or anaclitic: the experience of film itself leans heavily on the audience's exposure to *Star Wars*™ products, promotions and discourses, which may include, but are not limited to, previous *Star Wars*™ films. Current and new products, promotions, and discourses in turn lean on the experience of new™ films and the hype associated with them. A film becomes the narrative and iconographic field through which old licences are renewed and from which new licences can be harvested – the malleable materials of fantasy from which other fantasies can be fashioned. Trade paper discourse routinely exposes the house-of-cards structure of licencing relationships by rhetorical conflation. A pyjama manufacturer analysed the Spielberg-produced animated film *An American Tale: Fievel Goes West* in these words: 'We think *American Tale* will be strong in sizes 2–7.'[28]

Another force driving both the organisation of film-making around the family film and around the production of films as marketing assets is the consolidation of the entertainment industry since the 1980s. Especially for Disney, the company most identified with the family film, but also for multinational media conglomerates such as Viacom, News Corporation and Time-Warner, what they 'own' as assets are licences or brands and what they control, attempt to control, or leverage is access to the markets where these licences and brands can be exploited. They are no longer in the film business or the television business or, arguably, even the entertainment business, but in the business of 'synergistic brand extension'. As Disney's Michael Eisner put it, 'If you don't have synergy, you have nothing but new products. . . . If you have synergy, it goes on and on.'[29]

The Role of the Post-Hollywood Movie: Size Matters

Have the movies simply become an interchangeable prop for a licensable asset, as what I have been arguing might seem to suggest, or is there something unique that the film as film continues to represent? Clearly, I think, the Hollywood cinema – the institutional, cultural and textual apparatus we have known since the 1910s – is dead. For the eighty years from roughly 1910, when film began separating itself from vaudeville and established 'movie-going' as the activity around which movie theatres would be structured, until the late 1980s, the principal business of the Hollywood film studios was making movies for movie theatres, particularly North American movie theatres. To be sure, films were distributed internationally and, from the mid-1960s onward, television provided a post-theatrical life for feature films, but these and other markets were ancillary to Hollywood's main business. Films were conceived, written, cast, shot, edited and marketed for an imaginary American audience going out to a movie theatre, observing what the industry placed on offer, choosing from among those films currently on release, paying for a ticket, and going home a few hours later. Certainly the nature of the movie experience varied over time, from town to town and neighbourhood to neighbourhood, and the audience for the movies was never unitary or unchanging, but the imagined universe of movie reception was pretty clearly bounded, and the theatrical experience of movie-viewing was clearly at its centre. Furthermore, modern cinema studies, as it has been practised since its emergence in the late 1960s, has conceived itself in relation to a model of reception that places the theatrical experience of movie-going at its centre and largely excludes other modes of engagement with cinematic texts.

And yet, although Hollywood would continue to refer to them as such long after they ceased to be accurately reflected in the term, by 1987 so-called 'ancillary markets' provided fully one-half of studio revenues, and by 1990 studios received $3.2 billion from video sales alone – 50 per cent more than from the box office that year. As late as 1980, the domestic box office represented 80 per cent of studio revenue; by 1992 the box office was good for no more than 25 per cent. Only two films out of ten were making back negative and marketing costs at the domestic box office alone,[30] and Jack Valenti, the film industry's long-time chief cheerleader and lobbyist had started speaking of theatrical exhibition not as the core business of the film industry, but rather as a 'platform to other markets'. Of these 'other markets', video rental and sale were clearly dominant, equalling all other sources of revenue (including theatrical, broadcast television, cable, and pay per view) combined. As the emblematic form of American popular entertainment, as an enterprise devoted to the experience of being engulfed by larger-than-life images on movie screens and economically driven by people buying the right to sit in the dark for two hours in a movie theatre, the Hollywood cinema is no more. This economic shift also reflects a profound change in the manner in which films are experienced by viewers. Most people today in the US watch most films through a VCR, not in a movie theatre. This applies with particular force to American students who over the next few years will emerge as the first generation of 'film' students who have probably encountered films on video long before ever setting foot in a movie theatre.[31]

But the movies are not dead and, to stand Walter Benjamin's argument in 'The work of art in the age of mechanical reproduction' on its head, the movies continue to possess a lingering residue of their connection with the cinema in their promise of the auratic elevation of products, people and experience above the level of the ordinary, the quotidian, the mere commodity. The movies continue to want to claim the ground of authenticity, as the originating site of experience in relation to which licenced products are souvenirs, as the prior body for which the 'Happy Meal' figure is substituted as fetish part. Or, to express this another way, the movies desperately try to retain the power to enchant, to transform human beings into celestial bodies, labour into dream works, multinational corporations into magic factories, the release of run-of-the-mill movies into 'events'. This enchantment is the 'value' added by the embodiment of a licensable asset in a film. It is the cinema, not human beings, that brings the toys in *Toy Story* to life.

Thus, more and more effort has to be expended continually to re-enchant individual movies, to make them, in industry parlance, 'events' that stand above the everyday and command our attention. When Hollywood was in the cinema business and movie-going in the local picture palace was habitual, the release of any new film drew upon the cinema's institutional capacity for enchantment, and individual films were 'promoted' by their participation in the cinema. Today, however, films have to constitute themselves as events on an *ad hoc* basis, and they need as much help as they can get from pro-motional tie-ins to stand tall as movie 'events' at least for a couple of weeks. Thus, the Happy Meal toy our kids demand before the film is released derives its value through its strange metonymic connection (in which the part precedes the whole) to a movie that commands our attention as a cinema event because it has already been prefigured as the inedible part of a Happy Meal.

Many Hollywood executives believe, with some justification, that a film's domestic theatrical release and subsequent two-week run in movie theatres across the country are influential or even determining factors in that film's profitability, overall marketability in other formats, and value as a generator of licences and other ancillary revenue streams. The first two weeks are, quite literally, the most profitable for the film's pro-ducers because box-office revenue during that period is split overwhelmingly in favour of the distributor/producer, with the exhibitor being left with as little as 10 per cent of each box-office dollar. The hype surrounding the film's release (through direct media advertising, coming-attraction 'trailers' shown in theatres in the months preceding, promotional tie-ins, star interviews on television and radio, etc.) is designed to create a 'buzz' about the film, through word-of-mouth communication that this is a film that 'everybody' is seeing in the movie theatre. Hollywood executives, journalists and indus-try pundits talk about 'water cooler' film experiences: films that become the topic of dis-cussion around the figurative office water cooler in the days and weeks following their theatrical debuts. 'Buzz' about a film can help give a film 'legs': sustainability as a the-atrical box office draw, which, in turn, increases the film's stock as a licensable property and marketable asset in video and other markets.

To get audiences into movie theatres these days, Hollywood must sell them not only on the inherent pleasurability of a given film but on the experience of seeing that film in a movie theatre – which is to say, on the distinctive sensory and social qualities of theatre film-viewing. In the first decades of Hollywood's competition with television broadcasting, it could claim that distinctiveness in relation to the range of subject mat-ter that could be represented on movie screens: certain 'mature' themes, glimpses of body parts, and language could be experienced only in the movie theatre and not on television screens. Since the advent of cable television, satellite services and the avail-ability of films themselves on videocassette (including hard-core pornographic films viewable almost exclusively through a television set since the collapse of the theatrical market for movie porn in the 1980s), the distinction between movie and television 'con-tent' no longer works as a marketing ploy. Studios have turned increasingly to selling theatrical film-viewing in terms of physical size, sensory intensity and phenomenal scale. The computerisation of special effects since the 1980s has made it possible for Hollywood films to imagine resurrected dinosaurs, cataclysmic natural disasters, nuclear-mutated monsters, doomed luxury liners, atomic Armageddon and colliding meteors with a verisimilitude and visceral impact on the viewer hitherto unachievable. Interpersonal relationships, social tensions and individual anxieties have been radically externalised and rendered as gigantic epiphenomena of cosmic proportion and import. The movies are still important, Hollywood seems to be saying, because the movies are about such big things, and only the movies can afford to spend the tens of millions of dollars required to render a convincing Los Angeles-inundating tidal wave or bus-crushing monster.[32]

Belying this aesthetic of literal and phenomenal gigantism in contemporary cinema, however, is an unavoidable anxiety over size that arises precisely from the fact that the film and its parts will be experienced in relation to very different relative scales (between 'viewer' and filmic manifestation) in other formats and versions. The same film marketed during its theatrical release as an unprecedented and unreproducibly BIG event is marketed a year later for display on the 'small screen' of the home television monitor. The spacecraft whose massive size eclipses the sun over an entire American city is shrunk to fit in an eight-year-old's pocket when released as an officially licenced toy.

The television advertising campaign supporting the theatrical release of the 1998 film *Godzilla* played quite self-consciously with Hollywood's fascination with, and anxiety over, size and scale. Prior to the theatrical release date of the film (20 May 1998), promotional tie-in advertisements were carefully orchestrated to conceal the full body of the monster from view and to suggest its gargantuan proportions metonymically by displaying only small parts of its body in relation to human figures and artefacts. If you want to see all of the beast, the campaign suggested, you'll have to wait until the big-screen venue was ready to contain him. In the month prior to the film's release, Sony even placed ten-foot-tall computerised displays in 150 key movie theatres depicting a Godzilla-ravaged New York City but not showing the monster himself. The key fast-food tie-in with the film was Taco Bell, whose advertising mascot was a chihuahua, one of the smallest of domestic dog breeds. In one ad, the dog is shown at the Taco Bell drive-through window ordering thousands of tacos and soft drinks for his 'friend' Godzilla, whose enormous shadow we see as he opens his mouth to engulf the food. The joke, of course, derives both from Godzilla being impossibly large and the dog being inappropriately small for his role as the canine embodiment of fast-food consumption. The ad suggests that both Godzilla the creature and *Godzilla* the movie are too big to fit on the TV screen. Furthermore, to the extent that the Taco Bell chihuahua is a creature of television, the ad suggests that television is both the 'friend' of Godzilla and something that could be consumed by the cinematic monster. However, the ad also has a closing tag, displaying the range of *Godzilla* figures offered as premiums with the purchase of Taco Bell kid's meal figures. Both Godzilla and *Godzilla*, it turns out, are protean phenomena in terms of their size and power: they can be larger-than-life devourers of non-cinematic experience and the toy portion of a child's meal.[33]

A further irony, of course, is that the merchandising logic that results in *Batman* collector's cups and *Jurassic Park* soap dishes works to disenchant the cinema as its magic dust is sprinkled over an ever-growing miscellany of products and as those products take their place as parts of the quotidiana of mass culture. Moreover, the marketing logic upon which the studios now depend for their profitability further contributes to its disenchantment, because it encourages as many people as possible to buy a film in a store where it shares shelf space with motor oil and foot powder, and in a medium that subjects the text to the promiscuous manipulation of the viewer – zipping, zapping, glancing, heckling, extracting – in the domestic, unglamorous, over-familiar settings of everyday life, where the messy dynamics of postmodern family life are not left behind but become the social dynamics of reception.

Ambivalence and Indeterminacy in the Post-Hollywood Era

The rise of the post-Hollywood cinema, whose earliest and clearest expression was the family film of the late 1980s and early 1990s,[34] also manifests itself in a number of narrative and representational strategies within films themselves. Ambivalence and indeterminacy are the distinguishing formal qualities of texts that are subject to protean refashioning as commodities. What post-Hollywood films of the 1990s have to 'say' in any coherent moral, ideological or narrative sense is much less important than how they 'play'. I take the notion of ideological play from Joseph Natoli's recent book on popular films in the early 1990s. In accounting for the lack of narrative or moral resolution at the end of a film like *Basic Instinct*, he says:

> The undecidability of the ending makes the whole film undecidable and therefore not able to be funnelled toward a firm ending. We don't end choosing a story; we get caught up in a story we can't end. The story we leave with is not just a story. It's a chart of the way the film plays us, or, how we are brought both with our consent and against our will into the play of the film.

Similarly, in her book about the contemporary family romance, Dana Heller finds some films employing the ideological tactic of 'deniability', whereby films admit of equally plausible but opposing readings. In an essay on the popularity of *Total Recall*, David Bennett argues that the narrative and representational device of virtual reality functions in that film to render undecidable, both for Schwarzennegger's character and the audience alike, the 'reality status of every setting, experience and identity'. Rather than being an initial or complicating factor in the film's narrative logic awaiting eventual resolution, 'ontological indeterminacy, it seems, is precisely the commodity on which the consumer of media spectacles is spending his disposable income'.[35]

The structuring indeterminacy identified in the thriller and action-adventure films of the 1990s operates differently from that in such family films as *Home Alone, Mrs Doubtfire, Jumanji, Matilda, Addams Family Values*, or *Problem Child*. But moral and, by extension, ideological ambivalence is the defining feature of the family film. To be sure, some of these films do express an eventual – if equivocal – nostalgia for the nuclear family, but most are characterised by a profound ambivalence, a tendency toward ideological incoherence, a polyvalence which is not a matter of making room for alternative readings so much as an undecidability about what these would be alternative to.

These features are to be found in both *Junior* and *Home Alone*. For example, in *Junior*, Arnold's character has allowed himself to be impregnated to demonstrate the efficacy of a miscarriage preventative. When it comes time to terminate the clinical trial and hence the foetus, however, Arnold decides to carry the baby to term. 'It's my body

Home Alone (Chris Columbus, 1990).

and my choice,' he says defiantly to the audience. Here is Hollywood's most visible sup-
porter of Republican 'family values' uttering the rallying cry of the abortion rights
movement. But, of course, the narrative context of the utterance stands the meaning of
this motto on its head: the 'choice' Arnold's character fights to exercise is to bear a child,
not to have an abortion.

What everyone remembers from *Home Alone* is, of course, Kevin's infliction of pain
and humiliation upon the two would-be house burglars – a sequence which we tend to
remember as longer than the fifteen minutes of the film it actually occupies. In the scene
immediately prior to the siege, however, Kevin goes to the supermarket. In keeping with
his new identity as the self-sufficient guardian of his home, Kevin does not fill his shopping cart with ice cream and Twinkies™ but with the kinds of things his mother would
buy if she were shopping for the family: bread, milk, detergent and so on. Kevin even
remembers to bring coupons. When his family does return home on Christmas morning (to a spotless house), Kevin does not say a word about his battle with the two burglars. His father breezily asks him what he did while they were away – as if the family
had just gone out to McDonald's and not to Paris and back: 'Oh, I went shopping,' he
replies. 'Shopping?' his brothers and sisters shout. 'Yeah, you know, the things Mom
would get: bread, milk, fabric softener.' His father's response is, 'What a funny guy.'

Kevin is a 'funny guy' because he has learned to be both mother and father to himself. Despite the film's Capraesque allusions and the restoration of the nuclear family in
its final scene, these ideological alliances are undermined by the lesson Kevin seems to
have learned: if being a child in a postmodern family means being alone – whether the
family is physically present or not – then the appropriate coping strategy is to reconstruct the nuclear family within yourself. Kevin's family need never know of Kevin's
valiant defence of their home since the change he has undergone is in relation to him-

self and his house, not in relation to them. While the film appears to maintain that we all need and want families, it also shows that Kevin clearly does not need his.

What the family film lacks in narrative or ideological coherence, it makes up for by providing a collection of other pleasures for its audiences: visual (sight-gags, special effects, visual puns); auditory (the penchant for the use of already popular music for the soundtracks of family films, elaborate sound systems in movie theatres – and increasingly in home theatres – to reproduce 3-D audio effects, the rise to prominence of foley artists as producers of intricate noise tracks for films); narrative; representational (using computer-generated effects to make animals talk, manipulate object size, 'morph' faces and bodies from one state to another, and allow live-act figures to interact with animated creatures and characters from other movies); allusional (building in references to other products, films and cultural phenomena). By staying 'open', by refusing unequivocal ideological alliances, by leaving us with a 'yes, but ...' at the end, the family film increases its stock as a source of meaning in some other place, as some other licenced version of itself, and as a part of someone else's narrative. As a Mattel spokesman put it, 'We found that boys really need a fully developed concept and characters in order to play out their fantasies.'[36] In this way, family films are not just entertainment for the postmodern family but postmodern entertainment for the postmodern family. They are, like postmodern culture generally, characterised, in Zygmunt Bauman's words, by 'pluralism, absence of universally binding authority, leveling up of hierarchies, interpretative polyvalence, ... [and] by the overabundance of meanings, coupled with (or made all the more salient by) the scarcity of adjudicating authorities'.[37]

Finally, the new logics of Hollywood film-making and marketing produced by the confluence of technological, demographic and social change suggest the need to review the ways in which cinema studies is taught and films studied. At the very least, certain features of these films – their indeterminacy and systematic equivocation; their episodic, almost hypertextual syntagmatic organisation; their constant allusion to versions of parts of the films (characters, settings, iconographic motifs) that already exist or might exist outside the text itself; and their marked ideological ambivalence – call into question hermeneutic strategies commonly employed as models in media studies and communication studies. Regardless of the theoretical position that anchors them, close readings of such texts tend to stretch them upon grids designed for the closed, unified and organic texts of modernity. Even cultural studies, which has emphasised the polysemic character of popular texts and the variety of reading positions from which texts can be interpreted, clings for the most part to the notion of a dominant reading, the semiotic and ideological basis for which resides within the text and in relation to which, presumably, alternative readings are discerned.

This chapter has argued that the family film, emblematic of post-Hollywood cinema, undermines our ability to identify its audience at all, except as a set of markets across which a given film and its related, but by no means identical, versions, characters and licenced paraphernalia are exploited. These markets 'open' prior to the actual theatrical release of a given film (in the case of Godzilla fully a year in advance) and operate long after the film's theatrical run is but a dim memory. The physical site of film-viewing in the US is now dispersed across 50 million households, and these 'home theatres' now contain more than 500 million legally reproduced copies of Hollywood films on video alone.

Thus, it is now time to write the last chapter of the history of Hollywood cinema and its audience, a chapter that will also serve as the first chapter of a new history whose object we have yet to identify. But, whatever we call it, this new history will have to account not only for what happens when people sit in dark rooms with concession stands attached to them, but also what they do at Walmart and McDonald's and at the mall, where they go on vacation, and what kinds of pyjamas their children wear.

Notes

1 See Susan Mitchell, 'The next baby boom', *American Demographics*, October 1995; Landon Y. Jones, *Great Expectations: America and the Baby Boom Generation* (New York: Coward, McCann, and Geoghegan, 1980), especially Chapter 2, pp. 19–35; Jerry Hagstrom, 'The West's thinning ranks', *National Journal*, 8 March 1986, p. 584; Stewart Powell, 'Measuring the impact of the "baby bust" on US future', *U.S. News and World Report*, 16 December 1985, p. 66; Ben J. Wattenberg, *What Happens When People in Free Countries Don't Have Enough Babies?* (New York: Pharos, 1987).

2 Mitchell, 'The next baby boom'; 'Tense times for families', *The Public Pulse*, January 1991, p. 1; Dale Russakoff, 'Under-18 population hits record numbers', *Raleigh News and Observer*, 1 July 1998, p. 1-A, 12-A.

3 On the rise of the VCR as a domestic appliance in the 1980s, see, among many articles in the general and trade press: 'VCR's: videocassette recording', *Broadcasting*, 20 August 1984, p. 42; 'As the video craze captures American families', *U.S. News and World Report*, 28 January 1985, p. 58; Don Braungel, 'Is your VCR smarter than you?', *San Diego Union-Tribune*, 13 July 1988, p. D-13; *Communications Daily*, 25 October 1989, p. 9; *Broadcasting and Cable*, 5 December 1994.

4 *Communications Daily*, 22 January 1992; Katherine Barrett, 'Video: the new family fix', *Ladies Home Journal*, February 1990, p. 118.

5 Alan Citron, 'Blockbuster vs. The World', *Los Angeles Times*, 22 June 1990; 'Hurricane Huizenga', *Business Week*, 24 February 1997, pp. 88–93; Andrew E. Serwer, 'Huizenga's third act', *Fortune*, 5 August 1996, p. 73–6.

6 On sell-through, see: Denise Gellene, 'Kids turn on to video', *Los Angeles Times*, 13 February 1989, Part 4, p. 5; Paul Schreiber, 'A picture of volatility', *Newsday*, 20 November 1989, p. 3; Peter Newcomb, 'Can video stores survive?', *Forbes*, 5 February 1990, p. 39; Richard Turner, 'Marketing', *Wall Street Journal*, 6 June 1990, p. B-1; Peter Nichols, 'Pricing videos', *New York Times*, 29 January 1991, p. C-11; Karen Blumenthal, 'Children's tapes help the sales market grow up', *Wall Street Journal*, 24 December 1991, p. B-1; Richard Turner, 'Pretty woman lures new video buyers', *Wall Street Journal*, 9 January 1991, p. B-1; 'Mom and Pop video stores continue to fade', *Hollywood Reporter*, 30 July 1992.

7 Richard Turner, 'Tape transfer', *Wall Street Journal*, 24 December 1992, p. 1.

8 Nancy Brumback, 'Kids' stuff keeps growing', *Supermarket News*, 13 February 1995, p. 3A; 'Supplier roundtable', *Supermarket News*, 24 April 1995, p. S-22; Dan Alaimo, 'A finish with a flourish', *Supermarket News*, 21 August 1995, p. 4A; Joseph Gelmis, 'Love the movie? Then buy it', *Newsday*, 2 October 1994, p. 18; Peter M. Nichols, 'Facing up to the

big screen', *New York Times*, 30 July 1993, p. D-15; Jim McCullaugh, 'Consumers Are sold on sell-through', *Billboard*, 10 July 1993, p. V-4.

9 Brian D. Johnson and Anne Gregor, 'Home for Christmas', *McLean's*, 9 December 1991, p. 54.

10 Richard Corliss, 'Hollywood's summer: just kidding', *Time*, 28 June 1993, p. 62.

11 Edward Shorter, *The Making of the Modern Family* (New York: Basic Books, 1975), pp. 269 – 80.

12 See Zygmunt Bauman, *Intimations of Postmodernity* (London: Routledge, 1992).

13 See, for example, David Popenoe, *Life Without Father* (New York: Free Press, 1996) and Judith Stacey, *In the Name of the Family* (Boston: Beacon Press, 1996).

14 Thomas Radecki, 'Television and film entertainment', *Mothering*, 22 December 1989, p. 54.

15 Hal Hinson, 'In Hollywood, family matters; changing demographics may have made Bob Dole's broadside at movies obsolete', *Washington Post*, 25 June 1995, p. G-4.

16 'Moral of 1993: family films drive box office', *PR Newswire*, 3 March 1994.

17 See Richard Turner, 'Marketing', *Wall Street Journal*, 6 June 1990, p. B-1; 'Pretty woman lures new video buyers', 9 January 1991, B-1; Mary Ann Farley, 'Studios serve hearty helping of family fare', *Video Business*, 27 May 1994, p. 38; Joseph Gelmis, 'Love the movie? Then buy it', *Newsday*, 2 October 1994, p. 18; John Horn, 'Kids boost "Home Alone 2"', *Chicago Tribune*, 4 December 1992, p. B-2. On the theatrical box office success of 'family films' in the early 1990s, see Leonard Klady, 'Kidpower propels nat'l b.o.', *Daily Variety*, 6 April 1993, p. 1; Marshall Fine, 'Family fare on the summer movie plate', *Gannett News Service*, 16 June 1993.

18 Jim McCullaugh, 'Consumers are sold on sell-through', *Billboard*, 10 July 1993, p. V-4; Greg Muirhead, 'The screening process', *Supermarket News*, 25 January 1993; Joseph Gelmis, 'Love the movie? Then buy it', *Newsday*, 2 October 1994, p. 18; Karen Blumenthal, 'Children's tapes . . .', *Wall Street Journal*, 24 December 1991, p. B-1; Richard Corliss, 'Kid power conquers Hollywood', *Time*, 7 January 1991, p. 81.

19 *Los Angeles Times*, 8 June 1993; Fred Pampel, Dan Fost and Sharon O'Malley, 'Marketing the movies', *American Demographics*, March 1994, p. 48.

20 Statistics on video rental and ownership are taken from the websites of the Motion Picture Association and the Video Software Dealers Association. Information is current up to June 1998.

21 On the marketing value of product placement, particularly at a time of ballooning marketing budgets, see Jennifer Pendleton, 'Hollywood shuns the "cheap" shot', *Daily Variety*, 21 August 1992.

22 Nancy Millman, 'Box-office lingo', *Chicago Tribune*, 26 November 1992, p. 1.

23 Millman, 'Box-office lingo'; Jennifer Pendleton, 'Studios rolling out big guns to market Yule pix', *Daily Variety*, 11 November 1992, p. 2; Thomas R. King, 'Marketers' interest dims in movie tie-ins', *Wall Street Journal*, 13 November 1992, p. B-1.

24 McDonald's had a similar problem in the promotion of *Jurassic Park* the following summer, which was also rated PG-13. This time, however, the fast food chain used the film to support a 'value meal' promotion rather than a Happy Meal: the *Jurassic Park* value meal consisted of a triple cheeseburger, 'dino' sized fries, and a 32-ounce drink sold in a collector's cup. The enormous quantity of food represented by this value meal

presumably exceeded the stomach capacity of most children under the age of thirteen. See Millman, 'Box-office lingo'.

25 Joanne Lipman, 'Advertising: holiday films spawn tie-ins, raising stakes', *Wall Street Journal*, 21 October 1991, p. B-1; Anita M. Busch, 'Summer pix get a fast food fix', *Variety*, 20–26 February 1995, p. 1; Thomas R. King, 'Advertising: firms grow choosier about film tie-ins', *Wall Street Journal*, 10 June 1992, p. B-1; Ian Johnson, 'Movies: not just popcorn anymore', *Newsday*, 28 December 1992, p. 25.

26 Elaine Dutka, 'A startling new concept: family films', *Los Angeles Times*, 22 March 1993, p. F-1; Geoff Brown, 'Exploitation with a human face', *The Times* (London), 20 December 1990; Thomas R. King, 'Movies: studios face animated box-office battle', *Wall Street Journal*, 5 November 1991, p. B-1.

27 Gregory Solman, 'Pixar reboots with Disney "Toy Story" ', *Daily Variety*, 7 August 1995; 'A-B(eatles)-C spells success for synergy-minded', *Daily Variety*, 22 November 1995.

28 Danny Biederman, 'Licencing success', *Children's Business*, June 1991, p. 46.

29 'Summer's last stand', *Business Week*, 3 March 1997, pp. 67–74; Jay Carr, 'Do all discussions of summer movies have to begin and end with money?', *Boston Globe*, 16 July 1995, p. B-27; Betsy Streisand, 'It's a divisive world after all', *U.S. News and World Report*, 14 July 1997, pp. 45–6.

30 Richard Natale, 'Less proves more at b.o.', *Daily Variety*, 1 December 1992, p. 1.

31 See Martin Booe, 'Why films are getting younger as boomers get older', *Washington Post*, 27 June 1993, p. G-8; Jessica Seigel, 'Sexy-psycho-killer-bang-em-ups not the ticket, movie honchos say', *Chicago Tribune*, 11 March 1993, p. C-1; 'Marketing the movies', *American Demographics*, March 1994, p. 48.

32 Bruce Orwall, 'Here is how Disney tries to put the "event" into the event film', *Wall Street Journal*, 30 June 1998, p. A-1, A-6.

33 Ronald Grover, 'He's big. He's upset. He's invisible', *Business Week*, 6 April 1998, pp. 123–5.

34 Some commentators see the 'golden age' of the family film waning as early as 1994. That summer, several of the films studios thought would reproduce the success of *Home Alone* (among them *Getting Even with Dad*, *Little Big League* and *Baby's Day Out*) turned out to be flops. Industry observers lay part of the blame on Hollywood's misreading of the success of films, such as *Home Alone*, as evidence of a cultural desire for fantasies of juvenile empowerment. Such a fantasy was not enough to sustain these films or *Blank Check*, in which a Macauley Culkin wanna-be accidentally acquires a million dollars and winds up, as critic David Kehr put it, chasing a girl 'like Frank Sinatra in a 50s movie'. With the echo boom itself ageing, producers became just as wary of a film that aimed itself at too young an audience and thus alienated the pubescent market as one that courted an 'R' rating. By 1997, studios were once again looking at the teen market with new interest, even reprising genres from the 1970s in an attempt to lure both echo-teens and boomer parents. Neo-slasher films such as *Scream*, *Scream 2*, *I Know What You Did Last Summer*, and even a new entry in the *Halloween* series reprising Jamie Lee Curtis (H_2O) hit American movie screens in 1997 and 1998. The summer 1998 release of *Can't Hardly Wait* was regarded by some critics and industry watchers as the first in a new wave of teen comedies (Leonard Klady, ' "Show" takes win; Ford, Heche a hit', *Variety*, 22 – 28 June 1998, p. 8). Also, the baby-boom gener-

ation itself continued to age out of the child-bearing and child-rearing cohort, signalled by the oldest boomers turning fifty in 1996. Hollywood responded to this demographic trend with paranoid fantasies (*Breakdown, Absolute Power, The Edge, The Game, Ransom, Airforce One, A Perfect Murder*) addressing the masculine anxieties of grumpy old(er) men and providing vehicles for its ageing baby-boom male stars, including Clint Eastwood, Harrison Ford, Mel Gibson and Michael Douglas. In some of these films, a middle-aged, white, usually wealthy and powerful man is propelled into a scenario in which he is required to reassert his lost, scarred or diminished masculinity one last time to save himself, his wife, his family and/or his nation. The book and film versions of *The Bridges of Madison County* might be seen as a 'feminine' counterpart of the grumpy old(er) men tendency in post-Hollywood cinema with masochistic melodrama substituted for paranoid action-adventure. On the 'decline' of the family film after 1993, see Richard Natale, 'Family films abound, but successes don't', *Los Angeles Times*, 25 August 1994, p. F-1; Michele Willens, 'So much for the family trend?', *Los Angeles Times*, 21 September 1995, p. F-1; Stephen Galloway, 'Hollywood's focus on kids' films for kids is giving way to movies that teenagers and parents can also enjoy', *Hollywood Reporter*, 24 October 1995.

35 See Joseph Natoli, *Hauntings: Popular Film and American Culture 1990–92* (Albany: State University of New York Press, 1994); Dana Heller, *Family Plots: the De-Oedipalization of Popular Culture* (Philadelphia: University of Pennsylvania Press, 1995), pp. 192–3; David Bennett, 'Hollywood's indeterminacy machine', *Arena* 3 (1994): 23–32.

36 Danny Biederman, 'Licencing success: only in the movies?', *Children's Business*, June 1991, p. 46.

37 Bauman, *Intimations*, p. 31.

PART TWO

7 'That day *did* last me all my life': Cinema memory and enduring fandom

Annette Kuhn

It is the early years of the twentieth century, and in a small New England town a Spring festival is in full swing. Two elderly women are overheard in conversation: 'I was Queen of the May once,' recalls one. Witnessing a tiff between young lovers, another is moved to look back to her own youth, to the night of her glittering debut as a singer 'many, many years ago' in Paris, at the court of Louis Napoleon . . . .

Dizzy with success and too restless to sleep, the young Marcia Mornay ventures out into the night for a drive. By chance she meets a fellow American, Paul Allison, a talented but unambitious baritone. They strike up a brief acquaintance which culminates in a perfect, and perfectly innocent, day at a May fair. But in the duet ('Will You Remember?') in which they declare their mutual love, their parting is already anticipated; and there follows a seven-year separation, during which Marcia enters a loveless marriage with her impresario Nikolai, and scales the heights of operatic fame.

Back in the USA, Marcia and Paul meet again when cast in the leading roles in an opera. Marcia at last resolves to elope with Paul, but it is too late: the jealous Nikolai shoots him. Dying, Paul tells Marcia that their day together in Paris '*did* last me all my life'. As the aged Marcia concludes her story ('I found Paul too late'), the spectral figure of Paul appears before her, and Marcia's young self steps out of her dying body. United in death, the couple walk arm-in-arm into the distance, flanked by cherry trees in bloom.

*   *   *

Even on its first release in 1937, *Maytime*, an MGM musical based upon an operetta first staged in 1917, was already a palimpsest of memory, 'a nostalgic thing set to music', according to its review in *Photoplay* magazine.[1] The film's narrative present harks back to the early years of the twentieth century; and as Marcia Mornay, the central character, embarks on her reminiscences, this gives way to yet further memorialisation – of events some fifty or more years before that. As this chapter's analysis of several fans' reminiscences seeks to demonstrate, the moment in *Maytime* when the young Marcia steps out of the old Marcia's dying body is emblematic of a mode of film reception that I shall call 'enduring fandom': loyalty to a star which continues throughout the fan's life, and even beyond the star's death.

John Fiske has suggested that fandom:

> selects from the repertoire of mass-produced and mass-distributed entertainment certain performers, narratives or genres and takes them into the culture of a self-selected fraction of the people. They are then reworked into an intensely pleasurable, intensely signifying popular culture that is both similar to, yet significantly different from, the culture of more 'normal' popular audiences.[2]

While all forms of fandom are, in Fiske's term, 'semiotically productive', enduring fandom adds something of its own to the usual repertoire of fan productivity. For enduring fans of particular film stars, distinctive modes of cinema memory are proposed and enacted in fans' discourses and practices. Ethno-historical study of these practices indicates that the enduring fan's past and present characteristically bear a relationship to each other markedly different from that observable in the 'ordinary' film-goer. For the enduring fan, the cinema-going past is no foreign country but something continuously reproduced as a vital aspect of daily life in the present.

By drawing mainly on oral history interviews with British cinema-goers of the 1930s, conducted as part of a larger ethno-historical study of film reception,[3] and by treating the transcripts of these interviews as memory texts, I propose to look at some distinctive forms of discursive productivity associated with enduring fandom.[4] Taking as a case study a group of admirers of the singing star Nelson Eddy and analysing the film *Maytime* (in which Eddy co-starred with Jeanette MacDonald) in similar terms as a memory text, I shall also explore some parallels between the film's articulation of memory and the memory productions of enduring fans of one of its stars.[5]

Interviews for the study were conducted across Britain between 1994 and 1996 with a total of 78 core informants, divided between a majority who volunteered themselves in response to appeals in local media and to local history societies and Workers' Educational Asssociation groups, and a smaller group in residential care or day-care centres for the elderly. The oldest informant was born in 1897, the youngest in 1928, with 1919 the median year of birth. Most informants were, then, over the age of seventy at the time of interview, and many would have been adolescents or children in the 1930s.

As might be expected, the recollections of informants who volunteered were, on the whole, more vividly recalled and recounted than those of the others'. It was, however, somewhat surprising to discover that few informants gave the impression of having been avid devotees of particular stars. Fewer still were enduring fans. Rather, the impression is of a group of men and women for whom cinema-going was an everyday activity for a brief but significant period of their lives. During this period, popular cinema became for them a topos of cultural competences honed, shared and reinforced with others, peer group members in particular.[6]

While every informant had his or her own style of storytelling, what came across from the interviews as a whole (including those with non-volunteers) was a ready recollection of people's earliest cinema-going experiences, along with quite detailed accounts of where and with whom this activity took place. Memories of film stars were usually less vivid and less seamlessly incorporated into the thread of informants' life stories than those relating to the experience of 'going to the pictures'. Also, such memories tend not to emerge spontaneously or in response to questioning, but rather as a result of visual prompts (the interviewer showed informants – often to their great delight – a 1930s film annual). Moreover, other than in stories of early cinema-going individual films are rarely discussed in any detail.

A number of informants recalled having been keen followers of 'the pictures' in a general way – reading the magazines, keeping scrapbooks, making lists of films seen, and so on – but activities of this kind are usually regarded as very much a thing of the distant past, allusions to them in the present being in the service of current relationships and activities. For example, two sisters interviewed together in Glasgow offer vivid accounts of their youthful picture-going and fan behaviour: their talk involve no regression, however, but rather provides a thread of continuity between past and present, sustaining their ongoing relationship.[7]

To the extent that 'cinema memory talk' is fostered through interaction with contemporaries, it may have certain qualities in common with the kinds of remembering characteristic of enduring fans. In both cases, memory talk is about the present as much as, if not more than, about the past; and in both cases it provides an occasion for certain forms of sociability. However, as I shall argue, enduring fandom embodies distinctive modes of remembering.

Dorris Braithwaite (hereafter DB) from Bolton, Greater Manchester, was one of the project's volunteer interviewees. She introduced herself in a letter to the Director written in early 1995:

> I am 73 yrs of age and have been a film fan all my life until the last ten years or so. The Cinema in my young days was a source of joy. We lost ourselves in the thrilling stories we watched on the screen. I loved the musicals and remember so well seeing 'Naughty Marietta', a new kind of musical and introducing Nelson Eddy who became the well loved singer and super star of that era. He and Jeanette MacDonald created a magic never before seen or since. They became known as 'The Singing Sweethearts' and a fan club for each of them still flourishes today. I know because I belong to the Nelson Eddy Appreciation Society. I fell in love with him at the age of thirteen when I saw him in his first starring role. I wrote to him and have many letters and Xmas cards from him, plus autographed photos and five albums. I bought every record he made and now through writing to friends in America have a number of his radio shows on cassette.[8]

In her letter, DB not only offers an account of her youthful enjoyment of 'the pictures' in general (phrases like 'we lost ourselves' are quite frequently used by informants) but also more unusually – and certainly more significantly for the informant herself – she describes her lasting attachment to one film star in particular. She records a lifetime's devotion to Nelson Eddy, baritone singer and star of a series of MGM musicals, from the day she first 'fell in love with him' to her current involvement with a fan club and her contacts with fellow fans overseas.

It appears to be characteristic of the written memory accounts of enduring fans not only that the defining moment of 'falling in love' with the star is vividly recalled, but also that this moment is accorded motivating status in a narrative of lifelong devotion.

Informants in Jackie Stacey's study of female film-goers of the 1950s include a number of enduring fans of Universal Studios' juvenile singing star Deanna Durbin. Writing of the occasion when she first saw Durbin on the screen, one fan recall:

> In 1940 at the age of twelve, I was evacuated from my home in South London to Looe in Cornwall, and it was there that I was taken to the pictures for a special treat. There at last I saw her. The film, a sequel to her first, was *Three Smart Girls Grow Up*. The effect she had upon me can only be described as electrifying. I had never felt such a surge of admiration and adoration before ... My feeling for her was no passing fancy. The love was to last a lifetime.[9]

Another key feature of this form of fandom is that devotion to its object is sustained through relationships in the present. So, for example, DB establishes her credentials as a potential informant by mentioning her membership of a still-flourishing fan club, an organisation which provides plentiful opportunities for networking both at home and abroad.

DB has two women friends, Vera Entwistle (VE) and Kath Browne (KB), whom she has known for many years and with whom she sustains her appreciation of Nelson Eddy in everyday conversation as well as through more obviously 'fannish' activities, such as writing essays and articles about her favourite star and attending fan conventions. The three friends were interviewed together, and this encounter was followed a few weeks later by a second interview in which only DB and VE took part, and in the course of which the informants and the interviewer (Valentina Bold [VB]) watched *Maytime*.[10]

The first interview opens with informants' accounts of their early film-going, then moves quickly into recollections focused more specifically on Nelson Eddy and his films. In the latter, the informants move freely between past and present, reliving their feelings as young women ('They were romantic'; 'Oh, I'm gone!'; 'It was sheer beauty') as they talk about those occasions now when they deliberately stage a re-entry into the past by viewing Eddy's films on videotape. A detailed resumé of the plot of *Maytime* gives way to more general fan talk about Nelson Eddy, and a disagreement between DB and KB about Eddy's acting skills:

VB: I've never seen *Maytime*, actually.

DB: Oh you must come!

VE: You'll have to come.

DB: Next time you come I'll put it on for you. You must! I've got every film.

VB: What's the storyline? Don't spoil the ending for me then. What happens in these films?

DB: Well, she's an opera singer. And this chap, who's John Barrymore, is her teacher.

VE: Teacher.

DB: And he's given all his pupils up just to, you know, see that she can get to the top. And she eventually gets to sing with the, what would you call him Louis of eh? No, Napoleon, wasn't it? Of, not Napoleon. The song. Napoleon Joseph or something like that. What was his name? It wasn't Napoleon and Josephine. It was the other one. Louis Napoleon.

KB: Yes.

DB: Louis Napoleon. And she gets to sing with him and that's the highlight, you know. And he asks her to marry him. And she's so excited. She accepts. She doesn't love him and he knows that. But she's so grateful that he's got her to where she wanted. And she's so excited, she can't sleep. So she decides she'll get a carriage to take her just riding round the park.

And the horse breaks loose. And she's left while the feller goes running after the horse. And from a little cafe you can hear this voice singing. There was like a party going on. Of course it's him, you see, singing. And he sings *The Fat Prima Donna*, doesn't he? [*Laughs*]. And of course, she's the Prima Donna, you see. So she goes in, listening. And, he gets carried to where she sat. Starts a conversation. And, then there's a raid by the police. And he runs. He makes her promise that she'll have lunch with him the following day. And he shows her where he lives. And said, you must come.

So, she turns up. And then, he goes to see her in the opera. Of course, he's fallen in love with her by this time. And then he asks her to go to this May Day fair. And that was, it was a lovely scene that.

VE: Beautiful.

DB: You know, it's all the typical old-fashioned May Day fair. And, of course, they finish up by singing *Will You Remember*. And, then he finds out that she's going to marry the other feller. So I won't tell you any, [*laughs*].

[*General laughter*].

VB: Oh, I'll have to see it now.

VE: Oh, you'll have to see that. It really is a nice film.

DB: Well, it's all the blossom.

VE: Yeah. The May blossom.

DB: You know, the blossom.

VE: It's beautiful.

[. . . .]

VB: Right. You were saying that you preferred *Naughty Marietta*.

KB: Yes, I think I did.

VB: Yeah.

KB: But that was the first one I saw. Well, I mean, I know it's heresy to . . . but I have expressed that before. I thought Nelson Eddy was a bit of a wooden actor.

DB: You're a —

VB: [*Laughs*].

DB: You can't say that because he wasn't wooden at all! [*Laughs*]. He wasn't wooden at all. [*Voice rises*]. You want to see him, his whole body's going when he's singing! His whole body is going!

KB: Is it?

DB: Yeah.

KB: Right.

There is constant movement here between past and present as memories of past activities and feelings are brought back into the present in a manner which appears to mimic the informants' behaviour outside the interview situation, such as viewing films again and again and repeating conversations about the star's life and personality. In the first interview, too, the informants recollect enjoying photographs of Eddy in magazines like *Film Weekly*; but then looking at one of DB's albums of photos of the star prompts VE to remind DB that when Nelson married, DB had, in a fit of pique, cut his wife out of the wedding photo that appeared in one of the magazines:

> VB: His wife's not unlike Jeanette MacDonald, is she? In some ways. She's not as attractive as Jeanette MacDonald but,
> VE: No, not really, no.
> DB: She was nice.
> VB: Yeah.
> DB: She was a nice person.
> VE: She was so nice that a friend of mine cut her off the picture.
> DB: I were jealous! When he got married, I couldn't! That was in the *Picturegoer*. [*Laughs*].

They laugh off their youthful folly ('We all thought we were in with a chance, you see')[11] and start to look back again at Nelson's entire career. This is neither regression, nor is it a reliving of the past; rather it is a use of memory to bridge past and present from the standpoint of the present.

The second interview, begun in earnest after the interviewer had been shown part of DB's substantial collection of Eddy memorabilia, focuses almost exclusively on Nelson Eddy and his co-star Jeanette MacDonald, and is very much about enduring fandom and its continuing meanings throughout the lives of the fans themselves. The interview includes a number of passages of 'insider' gossip about Eddy – anecdotes that the informants must have shared with each other on numerous previous occasions and yet whose retelling now appears to be only partly for the interviewer's benefit: they talk about collecting Eddy memorabilia, about DB's writings on Eddy in fanzines and nostalgia magazines, and about networking with fellow fans.

The interview then moves into more profound issues as the informants struggle to put into words their feelings about Nelson Eddy's special qualities and their fantasies about the star:

> DB: It comes over. And I mean, to have come over on the screen, it must've been, you know, you're not seeing them personally. So to see that or feel that on screen, there's something there.
> VE: Oh yes.
> DB: And it's not just odd ones. Everyone, especially Nelson Eddy. Everyone that likes him have all experienced the same feeling. That there was something there behind his handsome looks and his good voice. That there was a ... well a spiritual —
> VE: Yeah.
> DB: Kind of a spirituality. A good feeling.

VE: I was telling Val coming up on the bus, our Hilda used to sit there absolutely gone and think he was just singing to her!

DB: Well, you did!

VE: And you know, she was.

DB: Yeah, yeah.

VE: I used to keep watching her, you know. And when he was smiling she was, as though he was,

DB: [*Laughs*].

VE: Actually smiling at her. Any minute he would come off the screen and she would . . .

DB's talk here expresses considerable closeness to the feelings evoked, while her friend – who talks in the past tense about a third party's (our Hilda's) fantasy that Eddy was actually smiling at her – adopts a more distanced stance. Talk of emotions and fantasies leads into accounts by both informants of dreams they have had about Nelson Eddy, the telling of which suggests that they have been recounted many times before. The interviewer's unsuccessful attempt to move the informants back into the past (the question 'Did you used to dream about him when you were seeing the pictures as well?' is answered by DB, after some hesitation, with a denial that she can remember) supports the view that the dream narrations are non-regressive, in the sense that informants' talk is very much in, and indeed for, the present moment of narration.[12] Indeed the informants themselves make a distinction between dreams (which for them are still alive in the present) and the fantasy they had when watching the films as young women that they were 'the female in the film': their acting this out in real life is laughingly dismissed as a piece of girlish foolishness.

VB: Did you used to dream about him when you were seeing the pictures as well?

DB: Eh. [*pause: 2 seconds*] I can't really remember that far back.

VE: No, I don't think we actually *dreamt* it so much as, sort of imagined, you know. You could actually see the whole thing. And you would probably be saying the female's part, you know, to him, sort of thing. Just imagining that you was the female in the film.

VB: Yeah.

VE: Well, I did. I don't know about you.

DB: Oh yes! Well, my friend and I used to act them out. We used to act the films out. Because she liked Cesar Romero. Have you seen Cesar Romero? 'Tache and very dark. Well, she was blonde. So if she went for the dark, I went for the fair, you see. And we used to act them in her cellar. We used to act the film. And she was Nelson Eddy because she was blonde and she had a deep wave. And she used to deepen it and draw her hair back. I wish I could find that photo. I took a photo of her once. And she's doing, like that, [*demonstrates friend deepening hair*]. She's looking like him on it. Drew her hair back. And she was Nelson Eddy, see. And I acted Cesar Romero. [*Hilarious laughter*].

These observations are interesting for the light they shed not only on the operations of cinema memory but also on the potentially embodied quality of spectatorial engagements with cinema, what Vivian Sobschack describes as the way in which significance and the act of signifying in cinema 'are *directly* felt, *sensuously* available to the viewer'.[13]

The interview soon moves off this tricky ground, however, returning to 'safe' insider fan gossip, some of which repeats material in the first interview; and DB then shows the interviewer some newsletters of the Nelson Eddy Appreciation Society and letters received from the star between 1937, when she first wrote to him, and 1961. Informants and interviewer then view *Maytime* on videotape. DB, who does this quite often, makes a special occasion of the screening by drawing the curtains and offering servings of tea and cake throughout the proceedings. The interviewer notes that during the screening,

> [E]veryone was enthralled although there were certain bits where it was thought all right to interject a ... humorous comment. Especially at the expense of John Barrymore, who's ... Nelson Eddy's love rival in the picture .... So certainly they didn't feel they had to be totally uncritical of the film.[14]

*   *   *

These observations are of interest in light of Henry Jenkins's definition of fandom, which 'recognises that part of what distinguishes fans as a particular class of textual consumers is the *social* nature of their interpretive and cultural activity'.[15] Jenkins contends that fans adopt a *distinctive mode of reception*, involving conscious selection and repeated consumption of material; and translation of the material, and its reception into a social activity (for example, through talk with other fans, membership of fan clubs, attendance at conventions, exchanges of letters, and so forth). Fandom also constitutes a *particular interpretive community*, according to Jenkins – fan club meetings, newsletters and fanzines all offer a forum for collective negotiation of the meanings of texts – as well as an *alternative social community* ('the fans' appropriation of media texts provides a ready body of common references that facilitates communication with others scattered across a broad geographic area').[16] Jenkins also suggests that fandom constitutes a *particular 'Art World'* wherein fans use their selected texts as bases for new cultural creation.

Each of these aspects of fandom is of relevance to an understanding of the enduring devotion of DB and her friends to Nelson Eddy. DB often listens to Eddy's songs and repeatedly watches the films, both alone and in the company of others (indeed the interview itself provided further occasion not only for this activity but also for the enjoyment of a wealth of fan talk). This is clearly, in Jenkins's terms, a distinctive mode of reception. DB's devotion to Nelson Eddy, having brought her into contact with people from various parts of the UK and around the world, also secures her membership of an alternative social community. However, to the extent that debates between his fans centre on Eddy's star persona and personal qualities rather than on interpretations of 'Eddy texts', Eddy fans may constitute a social community more than an interpretive one. Nelson Eddy fandom also embodies some aspects of what Jenkins terms an 'Art World': mention is made of a sculpture of Nelson Eddy crafted by an American fan, and DB herself has produced a book-length manuscript about the performer. That DB and her friends' fan behaviour emphasises social more than interpretive activities may have to do with their gender and generation: Jenkins's definition emerged from his study of devotees of *Star Trek*, a group of people which is relatively young and male-dominated. Nevertheless, common structures seem to underlie a range of actual instances of fan behaviour and objects of fandom.

Jenkins's remarks refer to contemporary media fandom, however, whereas here we must bear in mind the historical dimension of the 'fannish' reception and use of media texts, as well as the role of memory in enduring fandom. What specific productions of memory are at stake in enduring fandom, especially where, as in the present instance, it involves near lifelong devotion to a star who is no longer living? And in what ways do these productions relate to the definition of fandom discussed above? To what extent are the enduring fan's orchestrations of past and present peculiar to this mode of reception? What specific continuities and discontinuities between past and present are proposed in the memories of enduring fans? And how do the present-day imaginings of such fans continue to engage cultural products first consumed many years ago, texts which indeed outlive the object of the enduring fan's devotion?

*   *   *

Although Nelson Eddy died in 1967, he remains very much alive for DB and her friends, and undoubtedly for his other enduring fans as well, in part at least because the element of fantasy in star worship does not necessarily require the sustenance of a living person's presence. The films, the photographs, the recordings remain as memorials, just as during the star's lifetime they were substitutes, standing in for something deeply desired and in the end unattainable. As DB says of Eddy's voice: 'It just did something. It still does to this day.'[17] This 'something', deeply felt and impossible to put into words, transcends the passage of time. In a discourse which speaks very much in and from the present, DB's statement, like the dying words of the Eddy character in *Maytime* ('That day *did* last me all my life'), connects past and present, weaving a thread of continuity between them.

But if this is a mode of memory production characteristic of enduring fandom, it is not the only one. Loss is always already present in the enduring fan's investments – investments not only in the star's persona but also in the tangible objects, the memorabilia, which stand in for the star. Loss is ever present, too, in *Maytime*: loss anticipated and loss relived pervade the story and its telling. From the standpoint of old age, Marcia Mornay, the Jeanette MacDonald character, mourns a lost opportunity, a lost love, and the lost Maytime of her youth. She remembers the love of her life as something that never quite was, something which could only be lived in the anticipation of remembrance ('Will You Remember?'): love as loss, love as memory. Likewise, from the vantage of her own advancing years, the enduring fan may adopt a similar narrative standpoint as she looks back upon, and weaves into her own life story, a lifetime's devotion to 'her' star.

Writing of her admiration for her favourite star, the Deanna Durbin fan quoted above recalls the 'electrifying' moment when, decades earlier, she first saw the singer on screen. With the insistence that 'the love was to last a lifetime', however, she makes a smart shift into the present, suggesting that her devotion has been carried on unbroken through all the intervening years. In an exemplary statement, whose complex subjectivity and temporality exactly replicate those of *Maytime*'s 'Will You Remember?' duet, the future anterior ('was to') at once looks forward to looking back and locates the anticipated recollection in a past time. There is the future, then, and there is the past that will be remembered in the future. In this discourse, the present is always somewhere else.

If death is a central theme of *Maytime* (both the central characters die in the story), in this instance it offers possibility rather than closure, hope rather than defeat. Although the two deaths are many years apart in the world of the film's story, they are contiguous in its plot: the scene in which Paul, the Eddy character, dies marks the conclusion of Marcia's flashback and thus the point at which the film's enunciation returns to the narrative present as, with a reprise of 'Will You Remember?', Paul's ghost appears before a Marcia exhausted to the point of death by her reminiscences. The young Marcia then steps out of the old woman's dying body; and the couple, reunited and restored in death to the springtime of their youth, finally grasp the love which had eluded them in life.

This literal putting into the image of what has already been proposed through the film's narrative discourse – that Marcia's aged appearance is no more than a cloak for the young woman she remembers herself to have been – echoes a point made by many of our interviewees: that, outward appearances notwithstanding, 'inside' they are still the young people they once were. For the enduring fan, though, this has a particular inflection: just as one's youthful self does not die as one ages, so the enduring fan's devotion survives the death of its object. In an essay in the newsletter of the Nelson Eddy Appreciation Society, DB conveys something of this transcendence: 'Now Nelson is gone and so is my husband. But I play records and videos and they are both with me again and I feel just as young and in love as I was all those years ago.'[18]

Youth lives on in old age, then, and love conquers death. The enduring fan's devotion, too, embodies something of this transcendent quality: DB speaks, for example, of a kind of spirituality lying behind Nelson Eddy's handsome looks and good voice. The tributes in a fanzine that appeared soon after Nelson Eddy's death eloquently convey this sense of 'higher things; their tone uncannily echoes that of the transcendent closing moments of *Maytime*:

> In the last, lingering note of the voice all of us knew and loved so well, there is an
> undying chord, a sound almost too exquisite to be borne, which will go on sounding
> through all the years so long as we who hear remember and cherish it.[19]

In the repeated re-viewings of *Maytime* by DB and her friends, the film – already in itself multi-layered in its enunciations of memory – accrues yet further layers of memory-meaning. Enduring fans of the film and its stars will perhaps recollect first seeing *Maytime* in the 1930s, and sixty years on might have memories of that first viewing to recall. But, true to the distinctive modes of reception associated with fandom, these fans will have viewed the film many times over since that first occasion. Memories of subsequent viewings will overlay each other and become informed by events and changes in the fans' own lives: DB, for instance, hints in the passage quoted above at a renewed mode of reception, new readings of Eddy texts, which became available to her after her husband's death.

In both theme and narrative discourse, *Maytime* is already saturated in memory, 'like lavender in a long unopened drawer'.[20] As the text is appropriated and used by enduring fans, further layers of inter-textual and extra-textual memory – meaning continuously accrue. On all levels, *Maytime* speaks a very specific type of memory: nostalgia, that bittersweet longing for a lost or otherwise unattainable object. In the film, the scene of memory constantly retreats into an ever more distant past – from whose vantage point the future itself is anticipated with nostalgia.

The same is true, perhaps, of the enduring fan's use of media texts, especially if the performer who is the object of devotion is no longer living. The case of *Maytime* suggests that in this mode of reception the death of the star may be mapped onto the deaths of the film's central characters, and love produced as triumphing over death. Thus, like Paul and Marcia, the enduring fan remains forever young in an eternal Maytime, bearing witness to a devotion that lasts not merely 'all my life', but beyond life.

Notes

1 *Photoplay* vol. 51 no. 5, May 1937, p. 53.

2 John Fiske, 'The cultural economy of fandom', in Lisa A. Lewis (ed.), *The Adoring Audience: Fan Culture and Popular Media* (London: Routledge, 1992).

3 Cinema Culture in 1930s Britain: Ethno-history of a Popular Cultural Practice, ESRC Project R000 23 5385, directed by Annette Kuhn (hereafter: CCINTB). Interviews were conducted by Valentina Bold and transcribed by Joan Simpson; extracts from transcripts in this chapter were revised, with the author's and the informants' consent, by the editors of the present volume. For an overview of the project, see *Cinema Culture in 1930s Britain: End of Award Report*, CCINTB Working Paper 2, 1997. I use the term 'ethnohistory' to suggest that the project's objective of investigating the ways in which cinema and film-going figured in people's daily lives in the 1930s both draws on and critiques some of the methods and objectives of contemporary media ethnography (see, for example, James Lull, 'An emerging tradition: ethnographic research on television audiences', in *Inside Family Viewing: Ethnographic Research on Television's Audiences* (London: Routledge, 1990), pp. 1–27) and also concerns itself with the texture of informants' own accounts (see, for example, James Clifford, 'On ethnographic authority', in *The Predicament of Culture: Twentieth-Century Ethnography, Literature, and Art* (Cambridge, Ma.; Harvard University Press), pp. 21–54). For a fuller discussion of these issues in relation to the overall project, see Annette Kuhn, *Cinema Culture and Cultural Memory* (London: I. B. Tauris, forthcoming).

4 The term 'memory texts' refers here to cultural production in various media which stage the activity of remembering in their 'writing' strategies. For a discussion, with examples, of various forms of memory text, see Annette Kuhn, 'A journey through memory', in Susannah Radstone (ed.), *Memory and Narrative* (London: Berg, 1999). Also see M. J. Fischer, 'Ethnicity and the post-modern arts of memory', in James Clifford and George E. Marcus (eds.), *Writing Culture: the Poetics and Politics of Ethnography* (Berkeley: University of California Press, 1986), pp. 194–233. For discussions of oral history interviews broadly in these terms, see, for example, Alessandro Portelli, 'The peculiarities of oral history', *History Workshop Journal* no. 12 (1981), p. 99; Luisa Passerini, 'Memory', *History Workshop Journal* no. 15 (1983), pp. 195–6.

5 During the 1930s, films featuring MacDonald and Eddy, both separately and as a team, were major box-office attractions in Britain – much more so than in the US: one or both performers was ranked among the *Motion Picture Herald*'s top ten money-makers on British screens in every year between 1937 and 1942. On *Maytime*'s British release, during Coronation week in May 1937, exhibitors were preparing themselves for a big hit. See *Kinematograph Weekly*, 13 May 1937, front cover and p. 25; *Today's Cinema*, 7 May 1937.

6 See also 'Cinemagoing in Britain in the 1930s: Report of a Questionnaire Survey', *Historical Journal of Film, Radio and Television,* vol. 19 no. 4 (1999).

7 Margaret Young and Molly Stevenson, CCINTB archive T94–16, T94–17, T95–12, T95–13.

8 Dorris Braithwaite to Annette Kuhn, 17 February 1995, CCINTB 95–38–1. In the late 1930s Bolton, as 'Worktown', was the subject of a number of Mass-Observation investigations of cinemagoing: see 'Cinema-going in Worktown', in Jeffrey Richards and Dorothy Sheridan (eds), *Mass-Observation at the Movies* (London: Routledge and Kegan Paul, 1987); Jeffrey Richards, 'Cinemagoing in Worktown: regional film audiences in 1930s Britain', *Historical Journal of Film, Radio and Television*, vol. 14 no. 2 (1994), pp. 147–66. Filmgoing in Bolton is also discussed in Leslie Halliwell's autobiography, *Seats in All Parts: a Lifetime at the Movies* (London: Grafton Books, 1986); and by John Sedgwick, 'Film "hits" and "misses" in mid-1930s Britain', *Historical Journal of Radio, Film and Television*, vol. 18 no. 3 (1990), pp. 333–47. A Bolton cinema manager, interviewed in late 1938, mentions that *Maytime* had by then achieved eight runs in the town: see *Mass-Observation at the Movies*, p. 29.

9 See Jackie Stacey, *Star Gazing: Hollywood Cinema and Female Spectatorship* (London: Routledge, 1994), p. 139.

10 The first interview took place on 11 May 1995 (T95–27, T95–71), the second on 5 June 1995 (T95–42, T95–43).

11 A photograph of DB's late husband suggested to VB that Mr Braithwaite actually bore a marked resemblance to Nelson Eddy. Interviewer's field notes, 11 May 1995, CCINTB T95–71.

12 This issue is discussed in greater detail in Kuhn, *Cinema Culture and Memory*. Also see Alessandro Portelli, ' "The time of my life": the functions of time in oral history', in *The Death of Luigi Trastulli and Other Stories: Form and Meaning in Oral History* (Albany, N.Y.: State University of New York Press, 1991), pp. 59–76.

13 Vivian Sobchack, 'Phenomenology and the film experience', in Linda Williams (ed.), *Viewing Positions: Ways of Seeing Film* (New Brunswick, N.J.: Rutgers University Press, 1994), p. 40.

14 Interviewer's field notes, 5 June 1995, CCINTB T95–43.

15 Henry Jenkins, ' "Strangers no more, we sing": filking and the social construction of the science fiction fan community', in Lisa A. Lewis (ed.), *The Adoring Audience: Fan Culture and Popular Media* (London: Routledge, 1992), p. 209. My emphasis.

16 Ibid., p. 213.

17 CCINTB T95–27.

18 Spring Supplement to 'The Golden Star', p.8. CCINTB 95–38–21.

19 Marguerite Malatesta in *The Shooting Star*, memorial edition 1967 (published by the Nelson Eddy Music Club), p. 10, CCINTB 95–38–26.

20 Nelson Eddy obituary, (London) *Evening Standard*, 7 March 1967.

8 'Desperate to see it': Straight men watching *Basic Instinct*

Thomas Austin

Straight white men, the normative, unmarked identity category of western culture, have tended to remain a given, beyond scrutiny in much empirical work on media audiences.[1] Furthermore, text-based analyses have often assumed that popular culture texts both inculcate and reinforce patriarchal and heterosexual attitudes among their male readers and spectators in a relatively straightforward way. Little work has as yet been devoted to examining the complexities of actual heterosexual male media users' engagement with popular texts. In this chapter I shall examine some of these processes by interrogating male heterosexual readings, knowledges and pleasures derived from viewing the erotic thriller *Basic Instinct* (1992).[2] This film follows San Francisco detective Nick Curran (Michael Douglas) as he becomes sexually involved with bisexual millionairess and glamorous murder suspect Catherine Tramell (Sharon Stone).

In the process, I will be exploring some ways in which real straight male spectators negotiated the film's images of women and men.[3] My primary purpose in examining such viewing practices is not to judge them, but to try to understand how they are produced. I assess the uses to which *Basic Instinct* was put by male adolescents in particular; the discursive and social contexts in which they viewed the film; and the role played by advertising, media coverage and gossip in the formation of expectations of, and orientations toward, the film. My aim is to trace some of the ways in which *Basic Instinct* acquired meanings by triangulating between text, contexts and audiences. Paying attention to the ways in which contexts and intertexts bear upon the reception of film may help to prevent the researcher falling into a simplistic trade-off between textual power on the one hand and spectator freedom on the other.[4] Moreover, emphasising the industrial procedures of market research, textual assembly and promotion corrects the implication in some studies that audiences read or 'activate' texts in scenarios unshaped by such practices. Film texts do not simply precede moments of viewing, but are designed and positioned in the marketplace with those moments in mind. There is no straightforward fit between marketing assumptions and audiences' diverse everyday encounters with films, but it is essential to consider how strategies of production, distribution and exhibition inform certain specific instances of consumption.

In the first place, I propose to sketch how *Basic Instinct* was assembled and sold as a 'dispersible text' – that is, as a package of component parts designed to both facilitate and benefit from promotional and conversational processes of fragmentation and diffusion. The concept of the dispersible text derives from the work of Barbara Klinger. According to Klinger, marketing, merchandising and media 'hype' operate to pluralise a mainstream film by 'raiding' the text for 'capitalizable' features that can be commodified and can circulate in their own right.[5] This elaboration and dissemination of images, ideas and interpretations of the film extends its presence in the social arena occupied by potential spectators. Crucially, such operations do not work on a finished film, but shape its assembly in the first place. Thus, advertising and media coverage amplify the capacity of the dispersible text to address a coalition of diverse audience fractions.

The dispersible text became institutionalised in Hollywood with the increasing financial importance of aggressively promoted blockbusters in the 1950s and 1960s, intensified in subsequent decades by the expansion of cross-marketing and the shift to saturation release patterns. Since the mid-1970s, the studios have either become absorbed within or expanded into horizontally integrated entertainment conglomerates, selling film 'brands' across multimedia product lines in pursuit of an audience fragmented into heterogeneous constituencies. As Thomas Schatz notes, this economic setting 'favours texts strategically "open" to multiple readings'.[6]

While *Basic Instinct* did not benefit from the 'multimedia reiteration' deployed around 'toy movie' blockbusters like *Jurassic Park*, it was pluralised instead in terms of potential meanings via the media space it was granted.[7] The film was assembled and marketed as an aggregate of disparate attractions which would sell to both men and women, to mass market and upmarket sectors, and to a range of taste formations. *Basic Instinct*'s populist aim was apparent in its target audience, which its British distributor Guild defined as: 'age 18–35, sex: male and female; class: B, C1 and C2'.[8] Industry surveys suggest that, in the event, 56 per cent of the film's cinema audience was male, and 44 per cent female.[9] The construction of *Basic Instinct* as a relatively open dispersible text is most clearly apparent in the casting of Douglas and Stone to play two 'strong' and competing protagonists, and in its equivocal ending, where Catherine reaches for, but refrains from using, an ice pick hidden under the bed she shares with Nick. The film's multiple address across genders and diverse sexualities was amplified, and its commercial and social reach extended, by a proliferation of secondary texts.[10] Canonical references to film noir and Hitchcock were stressed in the press pack circulated to journalists, and were picked up in some magazine and broadsheet press reviews. The film's sex, violence and stars were pitched at a wider audience, flagged in television spots, cinema trailers, press advertising and poster art. Invited to approach the film in various ways, prospective spectators were promised these attractions and others, such as a 'whodunit' thriller plot, auteurist touches, glossy visuals, the topicality of Stone's character as a 'post-feminist' New Woman for the 90s, or the 'must-see' appeal of a controversial film which 'everyone' was talking about. The interpretations and uses made of *Basic Instinct* by its audiences often drew on these popular media readings and on criticisms of the film. But real spectators' reactions were far from being confined by such frameworks. The array of secondary texts worked to cue, inform or guide spectatorial interpretations and responses, but never simply determined them.

In much of its promotion and critical reception in Britain, *Basic Instinct* was treated as noteworthy because of sex scenes unprecedented for a big budget mainstream production. The popular film magazine *Empire* lauded its 'justifiably celebrated humping scenes' and *The Daily Mirror* called it 'probably the most sexually explicit and violent thriller you are ever likely to see in a public cinema'.[11] Press commentary, both approving and disapproving, often labelled this sexual content 'pornographic'. The notorious scene where Catherine uncrosses her legs to reveal to detectives that she is wearing no underwear functioned both as a star-making moment for Stone, and to underscore the film's sexual explicitness. One of the most commonly reproduced publicity stills for the film was of Catherine with her legs crossed, prior to the exposure. A crucial intertext for *Basic Instinct* was the direct-to-video erotic thriller. Critics compared the film directly to this genre, or to upmarket variants. According to *Time Out* magazine it was 'like *Jagged Edge* with sex'; *The Sun* newspaper called it '*Fatal Attraction* Part Two'.[12]

Basic Instinct became a source of controversy on both sides of the Atlantic, variously accused of homophobia, misogyny and immorality. It was also a huge commercial success, achieving 'event film' status by selling beyond its core markets to attract infrequent cinema-goers. In the United Kingdom, it was seen at the cinema by 3.9 million people in 1992, grossing £15.5 million and out-performing *Batman Returns* to become the first '18' certificate film to top the annual box office since the similarly controversial *Fatal Attraction* four years earlier.[13] Its subsequent 3.4 million rentals placed it at number 2 in the national video chart.[14]

The Audience Research Project

I conducted an audience research investigation into *Basic Instinct* in late 1994 and early 1995, around two and a half years after the film's theatrical release in Britain. I wrote to a dozen magazines and newspapers, asking them to publish an invitation for readers to tell me their views on the film, after which they would be sent a questionnaire. Five publications printed my request: *Empire* magazine; the lesbian and gay newspaper *The Pink Paper*; *Gay Times* magazine; *The Guardian* (women's page); and the feminist monthly *Everywoman*. I received letters from 89 people, of whom 60 subsequently returned completed questionnaires. Of these, 26 were men – 19 heterosexuals, six gays, and one of unspecified sexual orientation. A further 15 men wrote letters but did not return the questionnaire. The questionnaire sample was entirely white, with the exception of one self-described 'black Indian'. A large majority of respondents were aged between 18 and 35 when they returned the questionnaire, but they could have watched the film up to two years before responding. Thus, several had apparently watched the film when 'under age'.[15] My research sample was entirely based on self-selected readers of five publications who were sufficiently motivated to write to me. Such a partial sample can have no pretensions to being either statistically representative or completely random. Nevertheless, a number of suggestions about general patterns in film consumption can be derived from it.

It should also be noted that respondents' accounts cannot be regarded as giving transparent, unmediated access to their opinions. Close attention has to be paid not only to the content of statements, but also to the use of language, which is both *constructed* according to specific repertoires and *constructive* of social relations and identity.[16] As Ien Ang has cautioned:

> What people say or write about their experiences, preferences, habits, etc., cannot be
> taken entirely at face value ... we must search for what is behind the explicitly written,

for the presuppositions and accepted attitudes concealed within them. In other words, [respondents'] letters must be regarded as texts.[17]

Approaching viewers' statements as texts does not entail disbelieving them, but it does require situating these texts within the social contexts of their production.[18]

Heterosexual Pleasures and Knowledges

Basic Instinct's sexual content was part of a package of disparate textual elements intended to appeal both to men and women. My audience research reveals diverse and often competing interpretations of the film. Women's views of Stone/Catherine ranged from seeing her as an empowering figure to regarding her as an oppressive male sexual fantasy. The accounts of heterosexual male respondents also varied, but many afforded primacy to the sight of the female body. These accounts typically suppressed the narrative agency of Catherine in favour of positioning her as erotic object.

For some straight males, *Basic Instinct*'s appeal lay in sexual and pornographic elements offered in combination with markers of cultural prestige, such as high production values, major stars and a 'quality' thriller plot. These additional features presented pleasures hitherto absent from their experience of porn films. The viewing protocols employed by these spectators commonly drew on their previous consumption of screen pornography in general and/or erotic thrillers in particular:

> I adore a little scene or two of tits and arse. Usually you have to sit through some B type film, XXXX rated to get a glimpse of a nipple. For me this was a new experience. A major film, good story and the sexy scenes. A joy. (Tony. Letter.)

> I found myself, like most hot-blooded heterosexual males ... titilated by the lesbian sub-plot and the infamous 'flash' by Ms Stone. I actually enjoyed the film almost guiltily in fact due to its a) gratuitous sex b) gratuitous violence. Overall I would say it was a perfect example of its genre: the 'Erotic Thriller'. (Mick. Letter.)[19]

The second account displays an awareness of possible disapproval of 'gratuitous' sex and violence, and treats the film as a guilty pleasure.

Linda Williams has defined film pornography as the 'representation of living, moving bodies engaged in explicit, usually unfaked, sexual acts with a primary intent of arousing viewers'.[20] Central to Williams' work on pornography, and to my own use of the term, is the understanding that this genre offers pleasures in and of sexual knowledge. Thus, pornography 'seeks knowledge of the pleasures of sex'.[21] *Basic Instinct* can be seen to offer a soft-core replication of certain pornographic scenarios, including the oscillation that Williams sees in the primitive stag film between 'the impossible direct relation between a spectator and the exhibitionist object he watches in close-up and the ideal voyeurism of a spectator who observes a sexual event in which a surrogate male acts for him'.[22] The first viewing pleasure is provided by Stone/Catherine's 'flash' in the interrogation scene, a genital show offering a glimpse of the secrets of the female body, what Williams terms 'the wonders of the unseen world'.[23] The second is provided in the sexual events between Catherine and Johnny Boz (her first victim),

Nick and his sometime lover Beth, and Catherine and Nick. A third pleasure, although somewhat less explicit, is that of the 'lesbian sub-plot' between Catherine and her female lover, Roxy.[24]

The first two pleasures in particular were referred to repeatedly in male accounts of *Basic Instinct*. These typically located Catherine as a sexualised object of vision, reduced in the everyday language of heterosexual males to body parts such as 'a great leg'. In objectifying readings of Catherine, the threat that this assertive and autonomous woman posed to men (a threat celebrated by some commentators and female respondents) was thus contained. Males often saw Catherine's bisexuality as titillating, or else appeared to elide it entirely, effectively rewriting her as a heterosexual.[25] In these readings, spectatorial agency and productivity are not necessarily progressive in their social effects, as some work on media audiences has tended to imply.

Respondents stressed the pleasures of looking at the female body both in isolated close-up (the interrogation scene) and in (sexual) motion. Stone/Catherine's was not the only body viewed in this way. One spectator compared the bodies of three women in the film, stressing them as its prime attractions:

> The reason I watched [was] Sharon Stone, but after viewing the film I found Jeanne Tripplehorn [Beth] far more sexy and with a better figure than Sharon Stone. At the beginning of the film the violent love scene involving a sumptuously built blonde (whose body doesn't quite resemble any one of three main suspects) who was that body double? (Basil. Letter.)[26]

This account privileges sights of the female body over narrative developments such as the murder of Johnny Boz in the opening scene, or Nick's 'rape' of Beth, whose semi-clothed body is 'on display' in a scene which moves from kissing and foreplay to the 'rape' itself.[27] I would suggest, however, that the female body could also be consumed as an enjoyable sexualised spectacle at moments when it was not unclothed or engaged in sexual activity, if the viewer was watching with what I shall call an appraising gaze. Such objectifying ways of looking at women have become naturalised in everyday heterosexual male culture.[28] A single film text should not be regarded as an isolated source of 'sexist' ideology; the film and its spectators should be situated according to prevailing social and cultural conditions, including the range of (dominant and marginal) interpretative frames which shape the text's reception. The film is not, however, without textual power. When watched for heterosexual pleasures, *Basic Instinct* effectively reinforces certain viewer dispositions. Thus, viewing practices do not simply emanate from a particular text, but are also learned and reproduced (and negotiated, reworked, even resisted) through the social and discursive contexts in which spectators and films take their places.[29]

The male reactions to the film's construction of femininity, with which I am principally concerned, contrasted with those of several female commentators and respondents, who interpreted Stone/Catherine as a positive representation of a financially independent and sexually desiring woman.[30] If men often wrote about moments of sexual display and activity as the highlights of the film, women were more likely to stress their enjoyment of the narrative, which they saw as being driven by the *femme fatale*,

Basic Instinct (Paul Verhoeven, 1992).

Catherine. Some even 'rewrote' the open ending so that she murdered Douglas's detective.[31] For several female respondents, *Basic Instinct* was an enjoyable (and erotic) celebration of female agency and desire, and a warning to men about women's power. However, rather than the male flight from Stone/Catherine suggested by female journalists and respondents, my research has uncovered male interpretative practices which derived sexual pleasure by viewing her as erotic object. One woman noted just such a process:

> It's erotic and so I watch it now with groups or just men on their own that I fancy ...
> also as the woman is always in control, but I think men always just want to see
> S. Stone's tits! (Bronwen. Student, age 22.)

Lynne Segal writes of 'the solace men seek from pornography' as a compensatory mythology, in the face of the limited social change brought about by second-wave feminism. In symbolising male power over women, pornography provides reassurance 'in these times of intensified struggle around gender and increasing insecurity about masculinity and male sexuality'.[32] I would make a similar suggestion about some pornographic readings of *Basic Instinct*. Catherine's sexual agency and murderous habits complicate, but do not preclude, such interpretations. Certainly, a dynamic of female assertion and male countervailing sexual aggression can be located in the actions of *Basic Instinct*'s competing but sexually involved protagonists. There is little overt evidence of Nick's appeal to male spectators as an embodiment of 'penile potency' (in Segal's phrase), an image of male supremacy in the face of the perceived social demands of women. However, such an impulse may be evident indirectly in some of those straight male responses which return Catherine to the position of sexualised object of desire, denying her sexual and narrative agency.

Adolescent Males

In considering male teenagers' consumption of the film, I shall examine the social and interpersonal relations at play in moments of viewing. According to this approach, the film text is seen as embedded within particular social locations, so that questions of context and of textual interpretations, pleasures and uses appear inextricably linked.

Among 'under age' males, the social act of viewing *Basic Instinct*, with its tally of sex and violence, endowed status or 'cool' in the peer group. This sixth-former watched the film on video with a male friend:

> I saw *Basic Instinct* for many reasons: – everyone was talking about it and I wanted to
> see what all the fuss was about. To see how far they pushed the boundaries of sex and
> violence. To tell all my mates how 'cool' I was for seeing it! To see if in the infamous
> interrogation scene, you really do see her private area.
> I was about 15 years old when I saw it. All my friends and I were crazy about Sharon
> Stone and all the hype surrounding it (because of the explicit sex scenes, it has to be
> said!) We were all desperate to see it. Since we were under age we tried many scams to
> get hold of a copy of it. Eventually I got around to renting it, one morning ... I thought
> it was a really entertaining trash thriller. Unlike most films of this genre or tackiness
> which promise lots of sex, but don't deliver the goods (so to speak) *Basic Instinct* gave
> what the viewer wanted. The script was so awful, it was funny and it brought up many
> interesting topics of discussion – such as 'What does it all mean' and 'Did they really
> DO IT' (!) (Paul. Questionnaire; letter.)

A key motive for seeing the film is male sexual curiosity about, and pleasure taken in the sight of, the female body. *Basic Instinct* constitutes an important source of information about 'doing it' for this teenage spectator. Gossip and expectation centre on the Catherine/Stone figure – notably the intimate knowledge and scopic pleasures provided by seeing 'her private area', and the question of whether sex really took place as a pro-filmic act.[33] These private, individual motives coexist simultaneously with the negotiation of social relations in the peer group and a public presentation of self as 'in the know' about the film and its illicit pleasures. Media consumption is not simply and directly structured by pre-existing identities.[34] As Liesbet van Zoonen notes, identity is never finished, stable, or 'true', but is always to some extent in process: '[B]eing a "woman" or a "man" does not come easily and requires continuous work … Media reception is one of the practices in which the construction of (gender) identity takes place.'[35] This observation applies not just to the media encounter, but also to the discussions mentioned by the above respondent to the survey, and to other written accounts sent to me. In these activities, 'masculinity is actively produced and sustained through talk', as David Buckingham expresses it.[36] In case of Paul, cited above, the consumption of sexualised images of women not only produces private pleasures, but is also part of an attempted public articulation of an 'adult' heterosexual male identity. This example and others like it indicate the fragility of adolescent male identities. Insecurity can be traced in the ongoing efforts made to 'fix' a stable, 'cool' identity and to claim status in the peer group. Harry Brod's concept of 'fratriarchy' is useful here in emphasising the gaps between the public face of male power and individual male anxieties, and highlighting the 'sibling rivalry' among straight men.[37] These transactions are worked out around self-image and social hierarchies such as that suggested in Paul's account. The act of viewing *Basic Instinct* can be seen not simply as an attempt to find pleasure and to claim an 'adult' identity but also, simultaneously, as a sign of immaturity. Being 'desperate to see it' can mean more than enjoyable anticipation. It also suggests the desperation of the sexually inexperienced male who consumes pornography as a substitute for 'real' sex.

My research request offered adolescents a space in which to speak, a chance to share their pleasures in the excitement of seeing a violent and sexually explicit film when 'under age'. For some, it also provided a further opportunity to occupy and project an 'adult' masculine identity. In the following account, the respondent appears unfazed and 'cool' about both the film's sex and its violence. This is not a fictional or dishonest statement, but it does show the respondent displaying his own viewing history and presenting a normative image of 'unshockable' masculinity which may mirror that undertaken for the benefit of his peer group:[38]

> I was 16 at the time (I am now 18) and to tell the truth it did not shock me. Having seen *Reservoir Dogs* eight or nine times and Marlon Brando's performance in *Last Tango in Paris*, I have to confess that the 'action' in *Basic Instinct* was what I would consider par for the course in today's movie terms. (James. Taking year off before university. Letter.)

Research into (male) teenage viewing practices has suggested that video classification functions as 'an index of desirability', with 18-rated videos at the summit, operating as both a forbidden pleasure and 'something "to test yourself out on" '.[39] For adolescents of both sexes, *Basic Instinct* had an 'adult' status as a forbidden text. Through the social event of viewing, such a status could be imparted to its spectators, as long as they remained ostensibly unshockable. However, while Paul, quoted above, focused enthusiastically on heterosexual desire for the female body (perhaps too enthusiastically to be really 'cool'), he admitted to discomfort at the film's depiction of 'nasty' violence. This appeared to be an 'adult' pleasure he was not expecting, particularly in the opening scene, which shifts from heterosexual sex to the woman's bloody stabbing to death of her male partner:

> You are witnessing this beautiful sex scene, then you are experiencing the most disgusting bit of bloodshed in a long time. The violence was really nasty — Hard to watch. (Paul. Questionnaire.)

There is a problem for the male viewer in adjusting to the relocation of woman from sexual object to assailant during this scene.

Home Video

For straight male viewers of various ages, watching such a sexually explicit film in a crowded cinema, in the presence of women as well as men, could be a source of discomfort and embarrassment:

> I would be lying if I said that an unclothed Miss Stone wasn't a factor in me seeing the film, but I always find that watching sex or erotic scenes in the same room as a hundred or so other people is, for me, just plain uncomfortable ... That, of course is watching the film in a crowded ODEON MULTIPLEX, watching the film at home is another kettle of fish. (Sean. Student. Letter.)

As this respondent indicates, watching *Basic Instinct* on home video, either alone or in select groupings, could avoid such problems. It also offered the possibility of repeated playback of 'highlight' sequences of violence and, in particular, of sex. This mode of viewing clearly relocates *Basic Instinct* as a soft porn erotic thriller on video – the very genre from which the film derives.

Basic Instinct was most commonly viewed on video among the adolescent age group in my sample. For teenagers, a further advantage of the video format could lie in the avoidance of age restrictions at cinema screenings. For adolescents of both sexes, watching *Basic Instinct* on video typically entailed finding a 'private' social space to escape the threat of parental interference. This resulted in the spatial and/or temporal separation of teenage viewing from parental presence in the home. For instance, one male teenager bought the video unseen at the age of 16 and watched it after his parents had gone to bed:

> I'm 17 years old, and my parents would not have been too happy that I'd bought such a film! (David. Student. Letter.)

Another respondent watched *Basic Instinct* on video in his bedroom between three and five in the morning, at the age of 14. In his account, there is a confession of the 'desperation' of the sexually inexperienced:

> I want to help you with your studies. But I won't give my address because you know
> what parents are like! 'I hope you didn't watch filth like that' etc. Well, I got out *Basic
> Instinct* last year from my local V[ideo] shop. I've got a video in my room so I stayed up
> until 5:00 am and watched it with earphones on desperate heah!
>   Well that's all about the hype. You hear everyone talking about it and you see pics
> of Sharon and you just have to watch it. I'm sure you felt the same at 14! (Shane.
> Letter.)

Shane appears aware that the lengths to which he went to watch the film free from parental regulation could easily be mocked. Anticipating this, he tries to regulate the addressee's interpretation. As Jackie Stacey argues, in such an attempt we can see a 'trialogic' relationship between respondent, imagined reader and that 'imagined other's fantasy of the [respondent's] self'.[40] In an attempt to govern this assumed production of his identity, Shane stresses commonality with the addressee and asserts that the 'mature' researcher was once like him, a sexually inexperienced male teenager consuming sexual images as a substitute for the 'real thing'. Shane's suggestion temporarily closed the gap between researcher and researched, and proved an unexpected source of (empathetic and nostalgic) pleasure. I recognised in him a part of my younger self.[41]

Analysing spectators' accounts as texts enables the researcher to uncover revealing blanks in these stories of film viewing. For example, Michael Douglas's naked body remained a structuring absence in the vast majority of male responses. The problem of the male body on display is that it may imply homoerotic desire, or the presence of a female audience inclined to look at men and evaluate them physically, much as men do to women. Shane provided a rare exception to this revealing silence in his refutation of any possible pleasure in looking at the male star naked: 'M. Douglas' ass turned me off my popcorn.'

'Hype'

Media coverage ('pics of Sharon') and gossip ('everyone was talking about it') play important roles in the formation of expectations and spectator orientations in the above accounts. In addition to its package of attractions, *Basic Instinct*'s considerable popular cultural and social presence was shaped by economic and discursive mechanisms: a concerted marketing campaign, extensive journalistic exposure, a saturation release across more than 300 screens, and wide video availability. Among respondents, these processes were commonly understood and represented by the term 'hype'. Advertising, publicity and delivery procedures do not entail the straightforward determination of spectatorial wants and decisions, however. Rather, audiences' established preferences and everyday talk mediate these practices and so influence their efficacy.

Even if disapproving at times, widespread media exposure can translate via gossip into diffuse social pressure to watch, overriding the distastes and disinclinations of some viewers: the film becomes 'unmissable'. Only by seeing *Basic Instinct* could one join in conversations about it. Having watched the film, the viewer is 'socialised' into the (heterogeneous and transient) collectivity formed around a shared visual event and so becomes able to participate in debates over it.

It appears that media coverage of *Basic Instinct's* sexual content, in particular the exposure scene, raised the next viewer's expectations to a level which the film could not meet. This respondent saw the film on video when he was 15:

> It had a good mix of sex and violence (which made it a good film), plus an interesting plot. . . . There is one small snag though, the scene where Sharon Stone gets interviewed by the police. The media makes out that Sharon keeps her legs open for longer than 10 seconds. I myself, was very disappointed at the fact that she only keeps her legs open for 2 seconds. I bought a copy of *Basic Instinct* to keep. This letter makes me out to be a complete pervert but I'm not. (Jason. Letter.)

Here again I note that the speaker anticipates a certain interpretation of his account, which is reflected in his anxiety about being thought a 'pervert' by the addressee and, in consequence, he attempts to pre-empt any judgmental reading.

Identification and Negotiation

I have discussed the way in which some straight male viewers derived sexual knowledges and pleasures from watching *Basic Instinct* and suggested that the social act of viewing can be a means of establishing identity and status in the adolescent peer group. I have also argued that an assessment of male teenagers' reasons for using the video of *Basic Instinct* can contribute to an understanding of how adolescents learn to behave as heterosexual men through the consumption of images of women. However, the account of Paul quoted earlier manifests not so much a monolithic acceptance of the film's construction of what it is to be male, as a series of negotiations of a particular masculinity represented as anti-social and violent as well as sexually active. Consequently, while this viewer shared Nick's curiosity about and desire for Catherine, enjoying vicarious pleasure in the 'sexual event' between them, he criticised Nick's treatment of Beth:

> [Nick was] A real stupid gullable bastard with no will power. A real 'fuck up'. [Beth was] a very intelligent sensible woman who gets treated badly by shitheads like Michael Douglas. (Paul. Questionnaire.)

The first comment here appears to refer to Nick's sexual attraction to Catherine, which he follows against the warnings of his partner, Gus. It may also refer to Nick's consumption of alcohol, which is coded as problematic in the film. The second statement appears to be a reference to Nick's 'rape' of Beth. The convergence of surrogate sexual agent and violent 'fuck up' in the figure of Nick raises questions about spectatorial identification. Is the spectator complicit in Nick's violence against women, as well as in his lust for them? Another teenager, James, called Nick 'an obscene, uncaring, selfish man who is someway meant to be "the hero" '. These two cases suggest one way in which straight male viewers negotiated their way through the film, both in the act of viewing and in the process of forming and writing responses retrospectively. They picked and chose elements, focusing on some (what we might call 'good sex') and filtering out others (such as violence and 'bad sex'). Splitting images of 'bad sex' off from the spectrum of 'legitimate' male heterosexual activity may be necessary for some men to enjoy the portrayal of 'good sex' as exciting and arousing, but also as ultimately consensual and 'non-violent'.

The violence inherent in Nick's sexuality is negotiated in the above two cases through attempts to divorce it from the heterosexual desire that the spectator shares with the character, and to expel it as 'sickening' and 'obscene'. These accounts demand a flexible model of identification, rather than the total and unquestioning spectatorial absorption into voyeuristic and sadistic pleasures proposed by some paradigms of 'male' spectatorship. (A further problematisation of identification between male adolescents and Douglas' character could stem from the significant age gap between spectators and star.)[42] Other straight male respondents appeared to negotiate the film's construction of a sexually-aggressive masculinity by attempting to evade it. Nick's 'rape' of Beth, for example, was absent from many accounts.

Conclusions

Some heterosexual male respondents rejected *Basic Instinct* as a violent and exploitative example of the objectification of women. I have chosen to concentrate here, however, on a type of response which remains relatively under-examined in studies of film and mass media, that of male heterosexual readings which locate woman as object. These objectifying looks, with their pleasures, subtleties and uses, are socially embedded in a range of everyday situations, including – but not limited to – those of watching film, video and television. It is tempting, but erroneous, to assume that the men making such interpretations passively imbibe heterosexist and patriarchal ideologies from popular culture texts in a straightforward, monolithic and ultimately fairly uninteresting way. Instead they actively inhabit and engage with elements of such ideologies via the dominant, everyday norms of masculine identity and behaviour, which shape the decoding as well as the encoding of films such as *Basic Instinct*. Any return to a hypodermic needle model of transmission which 'explains' straight male pleasures and interpretations should be avoided. This model has long since been abandoned in connection with other groups of media users, including heterosexual and lesbian women and gay men. Heterosexual men, too, actively negotiate their self-images and the meanings of the texts they consume. In the case of *Basic Instinct*, this can mean eliding Catherine's narrative autonomy to position her as a female sexual spectacle, or grappling with the film's construction of a masculinity which is violent and unstable but driven by an all too recognisable heterosexual desire. Or it can mean deriving visual pleasures and knowledges from female physical display, along with the kudos of seeing an 'adult' film 'under age'; or encountering costs such as the perceived social disapproval of the 'pervert', or the embarrassment of watching sex scenes in a public cinema. Sexual pleasures here are not simply 'read off' from the film text, in which a fixed meaning resides. Instead, interpretations, pleasures and uses are produced in the interactions between text, viewers and contexts.

Notes

Thanks for comments and advice to Andrew Higson, Peter Krämer, Charlotte Adcock, Lee Grieveson, Mike Hammond, Linda Ruth Williams and the reception studies reading group at Southampton Institute, Martin Barker, Mark Jancovich and Pam Cook.

1 On whiteness as a normative category, see Richard Dyer, *White* (London: Routledge, 1997); on whiteness and audience response, see John Gabriel, 'What do you do when minority means you? *Falling Down* and the construction of "whiteness"', *Screen* vol. 37 no. 2, Summer 1996.

2 This is not to suggest that all straight men found the film (sexually) pleasurable, or that no women did. See Thomas Austin, 'Gendered (dis)pleasures: *Basic Instinct* and female spectators', *Journal of Popular British Cinema*, vol. 2 (1999), pp. 4–21. On gay male responses, see Austin, *Industry, Intertexts and Audiences: The Marketing and Reception of Contemporary Popular Film in Britain* (PhD dissertation, University of East Anglia, 1997). For related discussions, see Chris Holmlund, 'Cruisin' for a bruisin': Hollywood's deadly (lesbian) dolls', *Cinema Journal*, vol. 34 no. 1 (Fall 1994), pp. 31–51; Charles Lyons, *The New Censors: Movies and the Culture Wars* (Philadelphia, Temple University Press, 1997), pp. 107–45.

3 I use the terms 'real spectator' and 'viewer' interchangeably to describe actual consumers of films, as studied through empirical audience research. This differentiates them from the essentially ahistorical 'ideal' or 'implied' spectators constructed by the critic or assumed to be inscribed by the text in certain structuralist and post-structuralist theories of viewing. See also Janet Staiger, *Interpreting Films: Studies in the Historical Reception of American Cinema* (Princeton: Princeton University Press, 1992), pp. 8–32.

4 See John Corner, 'Meaning, genre and context: the problematics of "public knowledge" in the new audience studies', in James Curran and Michael Gurevitch (eds), *Mass Media and Society* (London: Edward Arnold, 1991), p. 271.

5 Barbara Klinger, 'Digressions at the cinema: reception and mass culture', *Cinema Journal* vol. 28 no. 4, Summer 1989.

6 Thomas Schatz, 'The new Hollywood', in Jim Collins, Hilary Radner and Ava Preacher Collins (eds), *Film Theory Goes to the Movies* (New York: Routledge, 1993), p. 34. As Peter Krämer argues, the present state of Hollywood should be understood in some ways as 'an intensification of past structures ... rather than as a radical break with them'. Peter Krämer, 'The lure of the big picture: film, television and Hollywood', in John Hill and Martin McLoone (eds), *Big Picture, Small Screen: the Relations Between Film and Television* (Luton: John Libbey Media and University of Luton Press, 1997), pp. 9–46. The most celebrated example of a dispersible text selling across diverse taste formations is James Cameron's *Titanic* (1997).

7 Merchandising for *Basic Instinct* in Britain was limited to a music soundtrack by Jerry Goldsmith and a novelisation of the film published by Signet, a Penguin imprint; Schatz, 'The new Hollywood', p. 33.

8 Guild Film Distribution Ltd, Marketing and Publicity Department, letter to the author, 10 July 1992.

9 Of the cinema audience, 54 per cent were from classes ABC1, and 46 per cent from classes C2DE. Cinema Advertising Association. Class codings are as follows: A = Upper

Middle Class; B = Middle Class; C1 = Lower Middle Class; C2 = Skilled Working Class; D = Working Class; E = Lowest Level of Subsistence.

10 Whether or not *Basic Instinct* is an example of straight culture's incorporation of lesbian and bisexual lifestyles has been hotly contested. On the reactions of lesbian, bisexual and gay male spectators and critics, see Austin, *Industry, Intertexts and Audiences*.

11 Barry McIlheney, 'Basic Instinct', *Empire*, 36, June 1992, p. 20; Pauline McLeod, 'Pretty suspect', *Daily Mirror*, 8 May 1992, p. 22.

12 Steve Grant, 'Divide and conquer', *Time Out*, 22, 6 April 1992, p. 21; Peter Cox, 'Douglas earns his strips', *The Sun*, 8 May 1992, p. 15.

13 Attendance figures provided by the Cinema Advertising Association. These figures include repeat visits. 'UK top 10 films', *Screen International*, 18 December 1992, p. 2. *Basic Instinct* was the sixth biggest film at the North American box office in 1992, grossing $117 million. 'US top 30 releases, Jan 1–Dec 31, 1992', *Screen International*, 29 January 1993, p. 15. The film headed box office charts in Germany, France, Italy, Spain and Japan, taking a global gross of $328 million in 1992. Ralf Ludemann, 'Full frontal assault', *Screen International*, 29 January 1993, pp. 13–15.

14 'Top 10 video rental titles, 1992', *BFI Film and Television Handbook 1994* (London: British Film Institute, 1993), p. 63. The terrestrial television premiere on ITV attracted 7.3 million viewers. While relatively low compared to the most successful film broadcasts, *Basic Instinct*'s ITV audience still easily exceeded the audience for its theatrical release. 'Top 10 films and TV movies', *Broadcast*, 9 December 1994, p. 19.

15 CAA figures show that 77 per cent of *Basic Instinct*'s cinema audience was under 35. They list 0 per cent as under 18.

16 David Buckingham, 'What are words worth? Interpreting children's talk about television', *Cultural Studies* vol. 5 no. 2, May 1991, pp. 229–30.

17 Ien Ang, *Watching Dallas: Soap Opera and the Melodramatic Imagination* (London: Routledge, 1989) , p. 11.

18 Jackie Stacey, *Star Gazing: Hollywood Cinema and Female Spectatorship* (London: Routledge, 1994), p.76. For a defence of analysing 'the spectator as text', see pp. 71–8.

19 Names have been changed where requested. All accounts here are from readers of *Empire*.

20 Linda Williams, *Hard Core: Power, Pleasure, and the 'Frenzy of the Visible'* (Berkeley: University of California Press, 1989), p. 30.

21 Ibid., p. 31.

22 Ibid., p. 80.

23 Ibid., pp. 59, 80.

24 One commentator likened the film to 'the "lesbianism" of *Playboy*'. Lucinda Broadbent, 'Basic Instinct', *Harpies and Quines*, August-September 1992, pp. 33–4.

25 Several reviewers accused the film of repositioning Catherine as heterosexual. See Simon Barnett, 'Basic Instinct', *Northern Star*, 14–21 May 1992, p. 21; J. Hoberman, 'Fantastic projections', *Sight and Sound* vol. 2 no. 1 (NS), May 1992, p. 4.

26 The opening scene was shot using Stone, not a body double, according to Verhoeven, quoted in Douglas Thompson, *Sharon Stone: Basic Ambition* (London: Warner Books, 1995), p.124.

27 While I interpreted Nick's aggressive sex with Beth as rape, not all press and audience

accounts did so. (More women than men in the sample did.) I have placed the word in quotation marks to indicate its contested status. In the film, Beth protests mildly. As the 'rape' is not mentioned by Basil, it is impossible to say whether or not he derived pleasure from it.

28 As Marcia Pally argues, a knee-jerk rejection of objectification *per se* should be queried: 'It cannot be a goal of feminism to eliminate moments during the day when a heterosexual man considers a woman, or women as a class, to be sexually desirable … It is a feminist goal for women to recognize the objects of *their* desire.' Marcia Pally, 'Out of sight and out of harm's way', *Index on Censorship*, 1 (1993), p. 6, cited in Brian McNair *Mediated Sex: Pornography and Postmodern Culture* (London: Arnold, 1996), p. 95.

29 Carol Clover notes that 'There is no single "right reading" of pornography.' However, some readings may be more socially and culturally sanctioned than others. Carol Clover, 'Introduction', in Pamela Church Gibson and Roma Gibson (eds), *Dirty Looks: Women, Pornography, Power* (London: British Film Institute, 1993), p. 4.

30 Suzanne Moore, untitled, *The Guardian*, 7 May 1992, p. 34; Fiona McIntosh, 'Woman: the sexual tiger', *Daily Mirror*, 27 April 1992, pp. 16–17.

31 See Austin, 'Gendered (dis)pleasures'.

32 Lynne Segal, *Slow Motion: Changing Masculinities, Changing Men* (London: Virago, 1990), p. 229. As Segal makes clear, to note male resentments and feelings of insecurity is in no sense to ignore the material and gendered power that men, and heterosexual men in particular, still enjoy in contemporary society.

33 In hard-core pornography, the 'meat shot' answers this question, providing 'irrefutable, visual evidence of penetration'. Linda Williams, 'Pornographies on/scene or Diff'rent strokes for diff'rent folks', in Lynne Segal and Mary McIntosh (eds), *Sex Exposed* (London: Virago, 1992), p. 241.

34 Ien Ang and Joke Hermes, 'Gender and/in media consumption', in Curran and Gurevitch (eds), *Mass Media and Society*, p. 319.

35 Liesbet van Zoonen, *Feminist Media Studies* (London: Sage, 1994), p. 123.

36 David Buckingham, 'Boys' talk: television and the policing of masculinity', in Buckingham (ed.), *Reading Audiences: Young People and the Media* (Manchester: Manchester University Press, 1993), p. 97. Other respondents used my research as an opportunity to display their knowledge as film buffs.

37 Harry Brod, 'Pornography and the alienation of male sexuality', in Jeff Hearn and David Morgan (eds), *Men, Masculinities and Social Theory* (London: Unwin Hyman, 1990), pp. 132–4.

38 On the performance of masculinity, see Julian Wood, 'Repeatable pleasures: notes on young people's use of video', in Buckingham (ed.), *Reading Audiences*, pp. 184–201.

39 Ibid., p. 188.

40 Jackie Stacey, 'Hollywood Memories', *Screen* vol. 35 no. 4, Winter 1994, p. 326. Stacey is drawing on theorisations of dialogics by Volosinov and Bakhtin.

41 There are also voyeuristic pleasures (of course) to be had in audience research. See Valerie Walkerdine, 'Video replay: families, films and fantasy', in V. Burgin, J. Donald and C. Kaplan, (eds), *Formations of Fantasy* (London: Methuen, 1986), pp. 167–99.

42 Douglas's age was mentioned by several women, largely aged under thirty, who found him physically unattractive and too old to be paired sexually with Stone.

9 Bleak Futures by Proxy

Martin Barker and Kate Brooks

Kate Brooks (KB): What did you think of it as a kind of vision of the future, this film?

Chris: It was pretty accurate, really.

Anthony: I don't think I'd want to live if that was the future. Everyone's running around either taking drugs [or] being shot ...

Gerard: ... or shooting somebody else ...

Anthony: or shooting somebody else ...

Martin Barker (MB): So ... do you ever think about that when you're watching a film like that? You know, this is showing a world that I wouldn't want to be in, but I'm still enjoying it?

Anthony: Sometimes you're sat there, and you're imagining yourself in that place, and in that situation, and you sort of sit there and you watch it on the screen and you think, oh cool ... wouldn't like to be in their shoes, and you sort of sit there and think about it and you think ... nah, no way would I like to be there.

KB: So why do you think you enjoy these kinds of films, then?

Gerard: 'Cos of the effects ...

Others: ... yeah ...

Chris: I came out of some films feeling queasy, thinking if that happened, if I had to live there ... like *Alien*, that is one film ... I can watch ... and enjoy [but] I can't finish watching it ...

Anthony: No way![1]

This exchange comes from an interview conducted as part of an eighteen-month research project into the audiences of the film *Judge Dredd* (1995), which was based on a character and storyworld derived from the British comicbook *2000AD*. The project explored the different ways people make meanings from popular films such as *Dredd*. But this and other responses led us to outline a way of thinking about the historical significance of these films which was, frankly, startling. To get there, we had to discard many existing assumptions and theories about films and audiences.

Why do people go to the cinema? What do they get out of the experience? Most importantly, what are the connections between these two things? 'Action' films such as *Dredd* are particularly interesting for a number of reasons. They are immensely import- ant to Hollywood, as one of the main genres to generate real financial blockbusters in recent years. They have been one of the significant factors in the rise of the multiplex cinema, which has in turn underpinned recovery in the numbers of people attending cinemas in the last decade. They are a largely derided part of our culture; seen at best as 'trash' and 'junk food for the eyes', they are often dismissed as unworthy of serious attention. They are also the occasion of regular scares in the popular media over possible 'bad influence'.

If we answer our opening questions from the basis of cultural 'common sense', the first – why go? – would surely make reference to such standardised concepts as 'entertainment', 'fantasy' and 'escapism'. The trouble with these is their essential vagueness. 'Escape' from what, toward what, with what success, for instance? These terms substitute for investigation and suppress the need for it.[2] The second question might be answered in terms of putative 'effects': what *harm* might be done by these films? Answers to the first two questions framed in such terms would, between them, make any answer to the third question about how people's reasons for going to the cinema might relate to what they gain from it meaningless.

The recent regrowth of qualitative audience studies seems to offer grounds for hope. This tradition has strongly criticised the evaluative classifications of cultural forms into 'better' or 'worse', 'higher' or 'lower', 'educational' or 'entertainment', 'worthy' or 'junk'. Much useful work has been done to rescue despised forms, such as soap operas and popular romances, and to explore their significance for their audiences. Coupled with the growth of sophisticated ways of analysing textual meanings, this has promised much, although academic interest has so far concentrated heavily on women as audiences. This has not only led to the neglect of boys and men, but – worryingly – has insisted on treating them almost as a 'known problem'. After all, was it not the apparently predominantly male patterns of cinema-going that led researchers to examine the neglected subject of women audiences?

In reality, there is a strange and paradoxical illness abroad within audience studies. Informed by cultural studies, empirical studies of audience response have delved into various media and genres. We should surely delight in their insights and achievements. They also seem to offer an unparalleled opportunity. One of the promises this tradition offers is to locate cultural forms socially and historically. Might not this allow us to construct histories of audience-ing?[3]

Yet, at this very moment, we find audience studies largely trapped within a set of disabling theoretical parameters which *prevent* a fully historical understanding of audiences' responses. This has occurred because, alongside the recent will to gather and generate empirical materials, there runs a set of theoretical metaphors and research strategies which limit both *what* is researched and *how* research materials are analysed. The problems derive from three sources: (1) the centrality accorded to psychoanalytic ways of understanding films and other media – which then suggest a way of *knowing in advance* their relevance to audiences, and also of *knowing the categories* into which films must fall, ahead of asking audiences; (2) metaphors of audiences which talk in terms of 'limits', 'constraints' and 'horizons', all implying boundaries and barriers; and (3), overarching these, a uni-dimensional model, running between textual determinism and audience freedom. Linda Williams's introduction to a recent collection of essays on the spectacular in cinema opens with just such a self-limitation:

> The issue that now faces the once influential sub-field of spectatorship within cinema –
> and indeed all visual – studies is whether it is still possible to maintain a theoretical
> grasp of the relations between moving images and viewers without succumbing to an
> anything-goes pluralism.[4]

Both poles in this are problems. If these images do have power over the spectator, audiences must be *vulnerable and invaded by the cinematic experience* – though empirical audience research has not managed to find these people yet. If there is no textual or spectatorial determinism, can there be any 'limit' on what audiences can do with films? Or, as it is often put by locating this approach within Stuart Hall's 'encoding' model, are there no limits to 'polysemy'? If not, then it appears that current film theory has run out of useful things to say.

We propose to abandon these theories and their attendant metaphors, in order to start elsewhere. Consider, first, the implication behind Williams's question, that if audiences are *not* determined or constrained by the filmic apparatus or text, they must be *inventing meanings for themselves*.[5] This is strange. For the most striking thing about fans is *how much they care about their chosen materials*. They are moved by them, learn from them and about them, love to talk about them, debate them, categorise them, collect and swap them – and, of course, are often disappointed by them. This last point draws attention to something central – committed audiences *make demands on* their chosen media materials.

We want to break through this limitation in theory by reversing its central proposition. Instead of asking what are the limits of polysemic interpretation (with its attendant image of texts as tethers, holding in the wild horses of interpretative freedom), we want to ask: what common elements might we find *within the diversity* of audience responses? How might we differently understand the 'text' if we begin from the range of audiences' uses and responses? We start from audiences' own judgements of our film, examined through the lens of discourse analysis. Discourse analysis, which we utilise here as a set of procedures for disclosing the operation of social processes, categories and relationships within people's talk, has enormous potential for audience research.[6] In this chapter we can only hope to illustrate a number of these potentials.

Ideas of Modality

Our difficult third question asked: how might people's reasons for going to the cinema relate to what they gain from it? This invites thinking about the place of cinema among other aspects of people's lives. How separated from, or integrated into, work, leisure, domesticity, sense of self, cultural valences, personal 'career', and so on, is the cinema? One advantage of discourse analysis is its ability to explore *modal judgements*. Modality refers, firstly, to the manner in which people assert beliefs – with confidence, with reservations, or other qualifications (tentativeness, hesitancy, hope, fear, unwillingness, for example). It refers, secondly, to the ways people's beliefs are accorded 'reality'.[7]

Discourse analysis, then, can help us investigate people's talk for the modal relations that films have to the rest of their lives.

In principle, we are doing nothing new. A number of important empirical studies have explored audiences' modal responses. Ien Ang has analysed the ways different audiences judge *Dallas* 'realistic' or 'unrealistic', and demonstrates the operation of two quite opposite meanings in this connection: empirical versus emotional realism.[8] Robert Hodge and David Tripp have argued that children watching cartoons are practising skills of making modality-readings. Far from being 'harmful', they argue, such fantasy materials are essential to children becoming competent in understanding the relations between the real and the fantastic.[9] Elizabeth Bird has examined the manner in which readers of American supermarket tabloids (with their rich diet of stories about UFOs and revelations of the current whereabouts of President Kennedy and Elvis Presley) believe their stories. She argues that, commonly, such readers combine belief with desire ('you know it's not, but you wish it was true').[10] In their cross-cultural study of *Dallas*'s audiences, Tamar Liebes and Elihu Katz argue that different cultures seem to attribute differing versions of 'reality' to the programme.[11] David Buckingham demonstrates that even quite young children confidently distinguish between what is true as presented on television and what is true in their lived world.[12]

Valuable though these studies are, each poses difficulties. Ang, for instance, wishing to affirm the interpretative authority of her female fans of *Dallas*, treats the critics who measure the programme for its 'empirical realism' as effectively making a mistake because of their attachment to a 'mass culture discourse'. Hodge and Tripp, concerned to demonstrate that cartoons help children to tell the 'real' from the 'fantastic', thereby assume that we should keep 'reality' and 'fantasy' compartmentalised – a strange notion, as we will try to show. Elizabeth Bird aims to show that fans of her tabloids do not 'really' believe that Elvis is alive, they just use a different notion of belief. Liebes and Katz claim that a distanced reading of *Dallas* that treats it as a 'text' is somehow safer, and evidences less textual 'influence', than an engaged and involved reading – a claim for which there is no evidence at all in their study. Buckingham wants to allay the fears of cultural administrators that children might need more protection from 'risky' materials.[13] Central to all these are questions of the *truth and adequacy* of modality judgements, because of the presumed importance of *maintaining a clear distinction between the 'real' and the 'non-real'*. We want to change this, for two reasons. Firstly, politically if you will, we question the need – or the possibility – of a clear demarcating line between what is real and what is not. Secondly, methodologically, this preoccupation with reality and non-reality is effectively blocking other questions: what do people *do* with their filmic experiences? What kind of an encounter is it between what people gain from going to the cinema, and their other projects, hopes, dreams, understandings, models, and memberships of groups?

Spectacular Futures

Consider, then, the extract at the beginning of this chapter, taken from one of fifty interviews with groups of audiences for *Judge Dredd*. Our schedule of questions had ranged across the issues of how people choose films, and cinemas; who they choose to go with and what constitutes a typical trip to the cinema; how they had heard about *Dredd* and what, if anything, they knew about the character or the film in advance; what sort of film they had expected it to be, and how it turned out; what they thought were the most important features of the film, good or bad; and what they did after seeing it. So when Chris judges *Judge Dredd*'s future to be 'accurate', what is involved? He and his mates, all working-class boys aged fourteen or fifteen, agree: *Dredd* may prove to be 'accurate', although this is something that disturbs them. A paradox emerges from this discussion: the idea of accuracy is undercut by the 'special effects', but without such effects, there could be no depiction of the future.

Compare next how a group of fourteen- and fifteen-year-olds from a boys' club in Bristol, who were interviewed both before and after seeing the film, dealt with the same topic:

KB: So what sort of things do you expect there to be in it?
John: Violence . . .
Turtle: Violence, yeah . . .
John: Bashing people over the head with a big stick thing . . . truncheon . . .
Mike: Yeah, his truncheon thingy . . .
John: There's loads of posters up where he's got this big . . .
Turtle: And I like [the] bad side of everything . . . all the baddies and stuff . . .
KB: Yeah . . .
John: I like watching futuristic films 'cos you see peoples' ideas of the future, weapons and . . . stuff . . .
Turtle: And you get ideas of like what it's gonna be and you think, 'well, can't wait till it gets to . . . that year'.
KB: Right . . .
John: Like *Back to the Future 2*. I . . .
Mike: That [wasn't] really violent, though, was it?
John: Yeah, but that still gave you a pretty good idea of the future I thought . . .
KB: Right . . . obviously it's set in the future, and what do you think about that kind of view of the future?
John: Well, stuff like the bikes and everything that was good, but all the lives and everything was tat. I didn't like that.
KB: And what didn't you like about that?
Mike: Well it was . . . all horrible, wasn't it and . . .
John: You would have thought it would be like nice where everything was like nice and everything. But it was a state, really, for the common people.

Part of the pleasure these boys seek is to live on that cusp between envisioning technologies which look good (the bikes) and future conditions which are 'tat'. It is strange to see that phrase 'common people' – a phrase resonating with class feelings, but utilised almost inarticulately, perhaps expressing a need to reach back to old terminology. These boys also spelled out their delight in the pace, and the effects, of 'Actions', a singular term which depicts a whole genre of films.[14] They offer them a 'pretty good idea of the future'. 'Realism', then, is a combination of extrapolations from the present, along with a bleak imagery of the future which is recognised, but not liked. These notions were also addressed by a slightly older group:

KB: What about the city?

Martin: A dump ... [Pause]

KB: I mean, were there any parts of it that made you kind of think, I wonder if it'll be like that in the future or ...?

Johnny: Yeah, the first bit, when they fire across the street ...

Lee: The riots, yeah ...

KB: Why did it make you think that?

Lee: 'Cos that's what it's gonna get like ...

Johnny: 'Cos it's getting like that [isn't it]!

Lee: With all the guns and that, so, it probably will be like that ...

KB: What do you think, then, about the idea of having these, kind of, Judge people who are judges and executioners ... all in one?

Martin: 'Cos just say, if I was a policeman, and I didn't like someone, then I could just ... charge up to them and that and say 'I don't like you so you'll be killed'. That's ridiculous, so ...

KB: Do you think that will happen?

Martin: Dunno ... [Pause]

Johnny: Yeah ...

Martin: [*Laughs*] You reckon it'll happen?

KB: Why do you think it will happen?

Johnny: 'Cos the police will get bored [with]... locking people up so they'll just go round shooting people instead ...

KB: Does it worry you, then, what's going to happen in the future?

Johnny: No, I'll be dead by then.

Here, even more than previously, the line between present and future, between image and prediction, is blurred. When Martin says 'A dump', does he mean that *filmically* it was inadequate, that it was *ugly* as a place, or that to *conceive of living there* would be bad? The flow of conversation suggests it is a combination of all three. *Judge Dredd* disappointed them as a film: it was, again, too 'slow', though in its opening vision of Block Wars, they could glimpse a real future. But John, who feels most strongly that this is a possible vision, can at least rhetorically forestall any personal implications by simply saying 'I'll be dead by then'.

Notice that these are very much group-responses – as these entire interviews were. For a few moments, the interviews gave access to their group's ways of looking at films. A disagreement hardly ever appeared, to the point that they regularly finished each other's sentences. At the same time, they emphasised that the point of going to the cinema was to have a 'mass' experience. When others laughed or screamed, you could join in uninhibitedly. Not only, then, is their talk about films as a group process, but they define film as a group experience. The core of that experience is to be 'done to', to be hit hard by the sound, the visuals, the spectacular images. Hence their disappointment with *Dredd*, that it was too 'slow': you had to pay attention to the plot. From the spectacular effects comes the excitement, but at the same time, like a glimpse through a gap in time, that sense of a future.

Another striking thing which illuminates the boys' club extract is the ambivalence towards authority.[15] It is 'ridiculous' that police might just turn up and kill someone because they did not like them. What is the force of 'ridiculous' here – does it say that the *action* would be stupid, or that the *idea of conceiving it thus* is stupid? Again it seems to straddle the two, marking the boys' ambiguous attitudes. The same ambivalence showed up in another extract, from a group of bikers, again interviewed in advance of seeing the film. Some of them were long-standing fans of *2000AD*, to which Gary is referring in this first sentence:

> Gary: You got a city with something like 800 billion people in it, and none of them have got jobs, you know . . .
> Herb: Yeah, it would be really nice if they could get . . . all walks of life in there?
> KB: Yeah . . .
> Herb: In the future, you know, you got the vagrants, you got people homeless, this that and the other . . . I'd love to see how they portray it, in, X amount of years' time, in this film, that'd be interesting, because, you've got them all, haven't you?
> Gary: I mean if you stick to the comic, you haven't really got that, sort of thing, they're all just like street gangs, aren't they, there's no . . .
> Herb: Yeah . . . I'm, thinking that, if you look at the pictures, though . . . there's always some scum, somewhere . . .

It is realistic to have depictions of the unemployed and vagrants, because these are phenomena that relate to the present, and this has also been part of their pleasure in *2000AD*. And the pleasure will be to see that writ large on a huge screen. But whose side are they on? If on any, they are on the side of *seeing what it might look like*.

The Safety of Non-involvement

As a contrast, consider the comments of several other kinds of viewers. First, two women in their twenties, who had enjoyed *Dredd* because it was 'escapist':

> KB: What's your . . . definition of escapist films?
> Teresa: I don't like action macho kind of stuff . . . Robin Hood . . .
> KB: But what is it that makes you kind of lose yourself in them in ways that you can't with other films?
> Teresa: Because they are just there to entertain you . . .
> Alison: And they are sort of completely unrealist as well aren't they? . . . I wouldn't go to see anything that . . . represented violence in a very realistic way. I think that's the attraction . . . [of] *Judge Dredd*. It is violent if you look at what happens to people, it's just . . . far removed that it is . . . easy to watch. But something like *Reservoir Dogs* which I . . . ended up watching . . . on video having watched *Pulp Fiction* [which] I thought . . . was brilliant [yet] . . . I watched *Reservoir Dogs* and actually had to leave . . . because I found that too realistic and . . . so films like that I wouldn't watch.

These two draw a different distinction. *Judge Dredd* is violent *if* you look at what happens to people. But they simply will not really bother, because it is too 'removed', 'unrealist'. What they simultaneously admire, but have great trouble watching, are films which by their complexity cannot be bracketed off in this way. This is a quite different viewing strategy from those we have considered so far. Here *Dredd* is just 'entertainment', measured by its unpassable distance from the rest of their lives. They, therefore, view it without preparation, without commitment, and without any strong demands.

Another meaning of 'realism' altogether emerges from the responses of a middle-class group of viewers:

MB: How did you feel about its image of the future? ...

Richard: Well, it wasn't one ... that I connected at all ... with any sort of vision that I have of the future, which I felt was completely fantasy, it was like complete make-believe. ... I must admit ... I don't tend to buy into any vision of the future that *Star Trek* ... which I love watching, [offers] and ... I feel the future is so unpredictable and it always goes a completely different way than you expect ... that you never end up having anything like what you think it was [going to be like]. If you look back, say, thirty years, [at] ... science fiction films ..., what they think the 1990s are [going to be] like, it's absolutely hilarious.

Fabian: In 2050 people will still be living in this house ... .and people forget that they make science fiction films and everybody's living in stuff that's ... thirty, forty, fifty storeys up in the air. But ... people will still be living in semis, and terraced houses, and ...

Richard and Fabian adopt a 'knowing and weighing' attitude to the image of the future. Even though Fabian has been a fan of *2000AD* and wished for a 'darker' Dredd, this was strictly for filmic purposes. The vision of the future is just that: a vision or 'a complete fantasy', because futures are about making predictions based on knowledge. To indulge in fantasies like this is to 'buy into' something, and their sceptical attitude will not allow that. The same happens in a different way in an interview held with an individual scientist:

KB: What did you think of its view of the future?

Mike: Personally I think it's unrealistic ... it is a view of the future that somebody drew twenty years ago, or approximately, so if you think of the way the future was viewed, back in the early 70s, it was probably a very orthodox view, but I think with what we've learned in the last twenty years, it would be regarded as unrealistic.

KB: Do you find the ... scientist bit of you coming out then, when you're watching films with ...?

Mike: Yes, yes!

KB: In what way?

Mike: There are certain bits of, I can't remember specifically, there are bits of technology you see in films such as that, that you ... now understand could never happen. You understand that there are technical reasons why that's not possible. ... The flipside of that, with something like *Judge Dredd* that was thought up a long time ago, is that you see a bit of technology that [has] happened that you regard as old hat. ... Although I'm trying, I'm struggling to think of an example. It's things like those computerised fingerprints scans they had. They can be done, it's not well publicised but it can be done! [But] things have gone [on], there are far better approaches to identifying people than that now. For example, retinal scanning is much more precise.

Mike had been taken in tow by a friend while convalescing with a broken leg. *Dredd* meant almost nothing to him. It simply fell foul of his scientific credentials, from which he would not depart. On those grounds, the film simply was 'unrealistic', since its extrapolations could have no basis in known science.

Commitments and Judgements

What we are suggesting is, in essence, that viewers perform a series of manoeuvres around a central pivot. There is agreement between them as to *what* the future in *Judge Dredd* looks like, but disagreement as to *how and from what point it should be evaluated*. Those who have least involvement in the world of *Judge Dredd*, for whom the experience is most detached and ephemeral, are at the same time most likely to judge the image of the future to be 'unrealistic', and least likely to be disappointed with the film. Because they made no demands of the film, they were easily satisfied. Those who are committed to the project of a film like this, on the other hand, engage richly with it. For our young working-class groups this meant attending fully to the 'hype', even if that meant being disappointed:

> Joe: The film didn't live up to the hype, I don't think. It was a good film, but it just didn't live up to the hype. All the clips you saw just happened to show the most dramatic bits, you know, boom, bang . . . Most of the film . . . wasn't like that, it was more realistic than what I expected. . . . I didn't expect them to be shocked or anything or ever to be even scratched. I just thought [Dredd]'ll be invincible. I didn't think he'd be sentenced to life, or anything, and there was a plot to it as well, actually.

The trouble is, they had gone for the plot; that was not what they had been led to expect. Here, 'realistic' is not a compliment, but an impediment, for it refers to plot-complexities. This lack of interest in plot was an important feature of our working-class groups' accounts of their experience. They accept that films have to have a plot, but their attention lies elsewhere. 'Plot' is like a carrier-wave, a means to take them from action to action, from effect to effect. Rather than dismiss this as an inadequate or ill-educated mode of attending, we believe it has its own logic and direction.

This is the exact opposite of the one other group that shared the working-class groups' double-interest in the future: the fans of *2000AD* or, more accurately, those who carry their fandom into the cinema with them (for some told us that they made a conscious decision to 'leave my Dredd-head at the door'). For these, the future represented in *Dredd* is about plot-depth, as exemplified by two fans who also worked as artists on (different) comics:

> MB: How do you feel about the future that's portrayed both in the comic book and maybe differently in the film? You know, what sort of future, how do you feel about it?
>
> David: Ironic dystopia, isn't it? . . . It's presented as a hell-hole, full of citizens who

accept their lot and deal with it rather than attempt to ... do anything about it. The only way of challenging the system seems to be to resort to crime. The way it's dealt with, though, is a little verging on the ironic – that's what attracted me even as a young reader 'cos Dredd was far and away the best thing in *2000AD*, it just had some kind of depth compared to *Harlem Heroes* and *Flesh*, which are straight sports and straight monster story. Whereas Dredd was something new. Very [...], very odd, very weird, and the humour, yeah. Very ... very humorous.

It is not just that the points of comparison are different (comic book stories, as opposed to other films), but the sense that this is not merely glimpses through cracks into the future. *Dredd*'s is a whole world, with its own logic, and with depths and layers of 'irony' to make it odd, weird and humorous. To be a fan of *2000AD* is to have participated in an intensive fan-world of discussions of the 'meanings of *Dredd*', of the ironies of the comic, of the bleak bizarreness of the world of Megacity One through which it laced its many narratives.

Hoping through Bleak Futures

In essence, we propose a way of thinking about film audiences which turns on two features: firstly, a general *strategy of viewing* which shapes how people prepare for viewing, what they demand of a film, and thus how they attend to and use the experience of viewing; secondly, a 'wild card' of personal or group commitment to the act of viewing – how far spectators follow through and stick by their strategy. When they do commit to the act, to that extent are they simultaneously demanding *and* fascinated? To understand the importance of films such as *Dredd* to these audiences would require both a new way of thinking generally about the significance of the 'special effects' movie and, at the same time, a close investigation of the particular historical moment when this variety of them emerged. We think these things might take us in a number of directions.

In an enlightening essay, Albert LaValley has discussed recent uses of 'effects'. Examining the differences between 'trickery' in science fiction films and in other genres, he comments that 'science fiction and fantasy films hover between being about the world their special effects imply – i.e. about future technology and its extensions – and about special effects and the wizardry of the movies themselves'.[16] LaValley bases his remarks on a survey of science fiction films generally, without distinctions or periodisations. We are examining particular audiences at a particular historical moment. A tradition of bleak, futuristic action films developed from the end of the 1970s. Exemplified by films such as *Blade Runner, Terminator* and *Terminator II, Robocop* and *Total Recall*, this tradition built on but differentiated itself from that of the earlier but 'sweeter' *Star Wars*.[17] Their 'moment' was a period of political conservatism and relative working-class quietism (not forgetting explosive confrontations such as the 1983–4 British miners' strike). We suggest that, for young working-class males growing up in this period, these films offered a way of imagining their class situation, in the virtual absence of any languages or coherent experiences of class.

Most current commentaries on these films stress only the masculinity of their central figures – and therefore ponder, ambivalently, cases where the central figure is female.[18] Our interviews reveal something curious here. Working-class boys do see these films as an opportunity to practise and perform their masculinity in public. Repeatedly in our interviews, subjects talked of cinemas as places to muck about as a group, and spaces they could claim for themselves. They also spoke of their horror of being 'policed' by parents who might embarrass them.[19] But not one of the boys' groups we interviewed had any difficulty with the idea of female heroes in such films – as long as the hero, who-ever s/he was, was adequate to the dangers and tasks set. And the mucking about itself is primarily a challenge to authority, rather than about being boys in front of girls.

This suggests a fusion of several elements into one modality of how cinema is used. It is not just the films themselves, but their aura of 'danger' as well – these films are defi-nitely not part of 'approved' culture. They combine action in which heroes are tested to their limits by grotesque and often official forces with special effects that are simul-taneously attractive as spectacular images and disturbing as glimpses of possible futures. The new multiplexes permit spectators to play public games in relatively 'safe' ways. Our evidence, of course, is tentative, and further research is required. For instance, what different relations to these films are taken up by older working-class men, and especially for those with experiences of direct working-class struggles? What differentiates the minority of working-class girls who share the boys' relation to these films from the majority who dismiss them as 'boys' rubbish'. What other materials, if any, play an equivalent role in giving them glimpses of possible futures? We are not sure that the methodological tools to conduct such research yet exist, but we believe our existing evidence suggests that it is definitely worth trying.

Notes

1 We record our thanks to the British Economic and Social Research Council for their support for this project, in the form of research grant R000221446.

2 Hence the frequency of saying things such as 'it's just a bit of entertainment', signifying 'I don't wish to discuss it further'. For an example of this kind of 'excusing' talk, see Linda Grant, *Guardian*, 25 November 1997. Writing in response to a damning Social Affairs Institute report on women's magazines, she puts her case defensively, arguing that 'underlying every women's magazine is the notion that this publication represents in some way or other an indulgence, an escape'.

3 A number of notable scholars have begun this process. Perhaps the most important is Janet Staiger's *Interpreting Films: Studies in the Historical Reception of American Cinema* (Princeton, N.J.: Princeton University Press, 1992), which offers a series of striking case-studies which draw on reviews and other contemporary responses to illustrate the formative discourses shaping responses to films. A useful summary of the potentials of such research directions is given in Barbara Klinger's 'Film history terminable and interminable: reviewing the past in reception studies', *Screen* vol. 38 no. 2, 1997, pp. 107–28.

4 Linda Williams, 'Introduction' to her ed., *Viewing Positions: Ways of Seeing Film* (New Brunswick, N.J.: Rutgers University Press, 1994), p. 4.

5 The type-case of such people in recent research has been female fans of science fiction. See, for instance, Constance Penley, 'Feminism, psychoanalysis and cultural studies', in Larry Grossberg, Cary Nelson and Paula Treichler (eds), *Cultural Studies* (London: Routledge 1992), pp. 479-93; Henry Jenkins, *Textual Poachers* (London: Routledge,

1995); and Camille Bacon-Smith, *Enterprising Women: Television Fandom and the Creation of Popular Myth* (Philadelphia: University of Pennsylvania Press, 1992).

6 'Discourse' has, by dint of a series of largely separate developments, become one of the central terms of a great deal of cultural debate. These developments include: the decline in post-Stalinist versions of Marxism, resulting in loss of confidence in the concept of 'ideology', for which 'discourse' now offers a safer substitute; the acceptance of Michel Foucault's paradigms of historical analysis of institutions as sites of productive knowledge; a reaction within mainstream psychology against treating people's talk as symptom of internal 'attitudes', moving instead toward understanding talk as situationally produced and determined; two separate developments within linguistics – one, concerned to take sociolinguistics towards the study of the rules and patterns of naturally occurring language, the other, concerned with the idea of 'social grammars'; and a rediscovery of the work of Valentin Volosinov, as a source for thinking how people use language as a means of social action. The differences between these sometimes get lost in generalising talk about a 'turn to language' in social theory. We say more both about the general approaches to 'discourse', and about the resultant varieties of discourse analysis, in Chapter 5 of our book *Knowing Audiences: Judge Dredd, Its Friends, Fans and Foes* (Luton: University of Luton Press, 1998).

7 For a clear introduction to the role and relevance of modality judgements, see Robert Hodge and Gunther Kress, *Social Semiotics* (Cambridge: Polity Press, 1988).

8 Ien Ang, *Watching Dallas: Soap Opera and the Melodramatic Imagination* (London: Methuen, 1985). See, in particular, Chapter 1.

9 Robert Hodge and David Tripp, *Children and Television: a Semiotic Approach* (Cambridge: Polity Press, 1990).

10 S. Elizabeth Bird, *For Inquiring Minds: Supermarket Tabloids* (Knoxville, Tenn.: University of Tennessee Press, 1993).

11 Tamar Liebes and Elihu Katz, *The Export Of Meaning: Cross-Cultural Readings of Dallas* (Cambridge: Polity Press, 1993).

12 See, for instance, David Buckingham, *Moving Experiences* (Manchester: Manchester University Press, 1996).

13 It is worth saying that this has consequences. Buckingham seems to concur with the judgement that, because one programme *did* confuse and worry a number of children, it was unacceptable. This was a mock-horror show which did not overtly announce its fictionality, with the result that some children were frightened. This is a very risky argument, especially when one remembers that this is the same argument used against other 'border-challenging' materials, such as drama-documentaries, and that such border-breaking is one way in which, under oppressive regimes, cultural producers have carved out space for satire, social comment and opposition.

14   KB: What kind of film do you think *Dredd* will be?
         Toby: Action. Definitely an Action.
         Others: Yeah! (eleven-year-old boys)

15 This ambivalence showed in some surprising ways. These boys told repeated tales about fiddling their way into '18' films, yet often coupled that with a moral condemnation of the cinemas for letting them.

16 Albert J. LaValley, 'Traditions of trickery: the role of special effects in the science fiction

film', in George Slusser and Eric S Rabkin (eds), *Shadows of the Magic Lamp: Fantasy and Science Fiction in Film* (Carbondale: Southern Illinois University Press, 1985). This quote is from p. 144.

17 *Robocop* was rightly seen as partly a 'steal' of the concepts behind *Judge Dredd*, and resulted in a ten-year delay in the latter's arrival on screen.

18 See, for instance, Pat Kirkham and Janet Thumim (eds), *You Tarzan: Masculinity, Movies and Men* (London: Lawrence & Wishart, 1993), and their *Me Jane: Masculinity, Movies and Women* (London: Lawrence & Wishart, 1995); and Steve Craig (ed.), *Men, Masculinity and the Media* (London: Sage, 1992). See also the extensive discussions about *Alien*, where the need to produce a feminist reading has led to some remarkable interpretative contortions. A number of these are reproduced in Annette Kuhn (ed.), *Alien Zone: Cultural Theory and Contemporary Science Fiction Cinema* (London: Verso, 1990).

19 The nightmarish quality of parental presence is captured in a story whose truth is surely more mythical than literal:

> KB: Right. So what's the difference, what, how is it different from say, going
> with your mum and Dad, what ways is it different?
> Nick: It gets embarrassing! Cos like, there's all girls around you.
> KB: Yeah.
> Nick: And they're like, they're like, chatting to you, and then your mum goes, 'Oh,
> you got a bit of dirt there!' and spits on a bit of tissue and wipes your face!

10 Risky Business: Film violence as an interactive phenomenon

Annette Hill

Watching film violence is a social activity. It is also a 'risky' activity. In this chapter I will consider how both of these factors play an important role in viewers' experience of watching violent movies. My evidence comes from a series of self-contained focus groups in which men and women discussed why they chose to watch violent films that had been deliberately marketed as extreme and disturbing, such as *Natural Born Killers* (1994), or *Reservoir Dogs* (1992).[1] In examining the perceived 'risks' of violence in this type of popular entertainment, I shall refer to John Adams's 'risk thermostat hypothesis' as a way of understanding the way in which participants in the focus group discussions respond to film violence.[2]

Participants are aware of film violence as a form of entertainment that is identified as a social 'problem' and perceived negatively by certain sections of society.[3] Their awareness of media violence allows participants to categorise themselves in relation to what we can call 'risk-takers' (for example, young males) and 'risk products' (for instance, action movies). Participants gauge their responses to film violence, in part, by their awareness of types of movies and types of viewers. Viewers watching a film such as *Reservoir Dogs* have actively chosen to associate themselves with a particular category of product and consumer, in this instance a film that participants identify as part of a new breed of violent, realistic and intelligent movies attracting intelligent and sophisticated audiences.

Participants are aware that certain violent movies are marketed as 'risky' entertainment, and they use categories such as 'Hollywood action movies' to distinguish between different types of film violence. This decision-making process leads to a distinctive social awareness of other viewers, and to a shared social knowledge of the types of responses considered appropriate to the viewing experience. Participants regulate their responses according to perceptions of other people and their reactions to film violence. This social awareness of perceptions and categories of film violence, together with the importance of personal experience of watching violent movies, sheds light on the relations between the public and private sphere. Participants regard viewing film violence as a social activity, but they also express a concern with individual responses. The private experience is part of a public understanding of risk and film violence.

The Risk Thermostat Hypothesis
The risk thermostat hypothesis proposes that every person has a propensity to take

Reservoir Dogs (Quentin Tarantino, 1992)

risks, and every person balances their perception of risk in relation to the benefits and drawbacks of certain risk-taking activities. John Adams explains the risk thermostat as follows:

- everyone has a propensity to take risks
- this propensity varies from one individual to another; this propensity is influenced by the potential rewards of risk-taking
- perceptions of risk are influenced by experience of accident losses – one's own and others'
- individual risk-taking decisions represent a balancing act in which perceptions of risk are weighed against propensity to take risk
- accident losses are, by definition, a consequence of taking risks; the more risks an individual takes, the greater, on average, will be both the rewards and losses he or she incurs

Adams maintains that risks are part of our everyday lives, and that we take risks because there are 'potential rewards' to risk-taking activities. Thus, unlike 'zero-risk man', the rational and responsible person that most safety literature invokes, Adams asserts that people like to take risks: '*Homo prudens* is but one aspect of the human character. *Homo aleatorius* – dice man, gambling man, risk-taking man – also lurks within every one of us.'[4] Risk is also an interactive phenomenon. A person's propensity to take risks must be balanced with others who are also contemplating the rewards and dangers of risk-taking activities.

Adams suggests that there are 'degrees of volition in the taking of risk'. Some risks are imposed upon an individual, and others are taken by an individual.[5] A consumer of film violence actively chooses to engage with this risk-taking activity: viewing is a voluntary activity, in the sense that people pay to take part in this leisure activity in the same way that people pay to play squash or bingo. Film violence is not imposed upon members of the public. Consumers have the choice to watch or not watch representations of violence, and there are other leisure activities they can take part in if film violence is not to their liking.

Consumers are aware that, if they watch a film containing representations of violence, they are engaging with risk on a personal level. They are aware of the dominant discourse on film violence, and its definition of certain texts as hazards which can harm vulnerable viewers, especially children. A consumer of film violence, therefore, is actively engaging in a risk-taking activity. In what follows I shall look in more detail at the way in which watching violent movies can be an interactive phenomenon: participants are aware of how other people respond to the on-screen 'risks' of violent films, with some viewers setting their 'risk thermostats' at different temperatures, and therefore showing different degrees of response to representations of violence.

Types of Movies, Types of Viewers

Films such as *Pulp Fiction* (1994), *Reservoir Dogs*, and *Henry, Portrait of a Serial Killer* (1990, produced 1986) attract a specific kind of publicity which draws consumers to view them in order to satisfy a cultural curiosity. The release of *Reservoir Dogs* attracted controversial publicity that generated rumours and scandal in the media and more broadly. Derek Malcolm wrote in the *Guardian*: 'There is a point in *Reservoir Dogs* when it's difficult not to take the ultimate sanction against violence and walk out', while Shaun Usher, in the *Daily Mail*, advised his readers in a review of *Reservoir Dogs* to 'steel yourself, for this is even more shocking to read than witness'.[6] Similarly, advertisements for *Natural Born Killers* capitalised on its notoriety as a controversial film. One advert quoted *Empire* magazine as saying '*Natural Born Killers* succeeds in being the kind of risk-taking, all-out visual experience that comes along all too rarely', while Christopher Tookey in the *Daily Mail* reviewed it under the headline 'Why this film is a work of pure evil'.[7]

Evidence from the focus groups shows that participants were very aware of the hype and cultural significance of the target films in their immediate society. The films were discussed, praised and vilified by the media and peers alike, and although spectators did not claim they chose to see the target films because of their violence, a heightened awareness of the controversy surrounding them was a contributing factor in their decision to see the films. As these viewers explained, the publicity made them curious to see these 'new brutalism' movies for themselves:

> You hear all these rumours and scandals about these films and you think, what's the fuss all about? You go and see the films just to find out whether it's worth all the hype and bullshit. (twenty-year-old male)

> I'm swayed by media hype. Films like *Reservoir Dogs*, everyone's talking about it, and if you haven't seen it you're not in the gang. (32-year-old male)

Finding out about these films isn't too hard because any violent film gets a lot of publicity. If a film is getting a lot of publicity then I'll try and make an effort to see it; if it's making that much of a difference to other people it must be worth seeing. (25-year-old male)

Films such as *Natural Born Killers* or *Reservoir Dogs* are marketed as 'dangerous', and their promotion in adverts, trailers, reviews, interviews and front page news items normally ensures that people who choose to see them are aware of the controversy surrounding them. Evidence from the focus groups suggests that consumers of film violence choose to see such films, in part, because they wish to watch 'risky' entertainment. This does not, however, mean that viewers are only interested in violence. Their choice is influenced by their interest in directors, actors, soundtracks and dialogue, but the sense of 'danger', albeit fictionalised, attached to them is a significant factor influencing their decision.[8]

As the following comments suggest, some viewers are also curious to see just how violent and disturbing such controversial movies really are. These two participants discuss how they deliberately test their response to infamous representations of violence:

I'm interested in my reactions to violent films because I think I don't like them. So, I put myself through it to see if I can tolerate the violence. It's a purposeful position. I adopt this kind of bunker mentality, like I'm steeling myself to not be shocked. (37-year-old male)

Yeah, I think I would agree with you there as well and quite often with violent films or movies like this I sort of put myself through seeing the film, to see can I brave this, you know. Everyone else has gone to it, you're a wimp if you don't sit through it. '*Reservoir Dogs* oh yeah, very very violent, you know', like you have to get ... (32-year-old male)

Yeah, it definitely feels like a bit gruelling ... I feel like I've got to see if I can tolerate it ... (37-year-old male)

These comments highlight the preparation and conscious desire of certain male participants not to be shocked by violent content. These viewers monitor their own responses, using such words as 'tolerate', 'steel', 'brave', to establish the position of the viewer as a reflection of a tough personality. They augment this vocabulary with phrases like 'steeling myself to not be shocked' and 'you're a wimp if you can't sit through it' in order to accentuate masculine traits. The second viewer follows up the comment made by the first, echoing his point about a 'bunker mentality', and inviting him to feel that he is not alone in his desire to monitor his own response. He emphasises the position of a masculine viewer, but the first viewer's rejoinder introduces a different approach to his position: he steels himself to tolerate the violence but admits that it can still feel 'a bit gruelling'. Indeed, he goes on to say: 'I think I'm not going to be shocked, whereas it does still get to me.' Thus, while this spectator chooses to see violent movies in order to monitor his own (masculine) response, he is at the same time aware that he is sensitive to film violence.

This example suggests that a complex series of negotiations takes place when some-one chooses to watch a violent movie. Spectators engage in a balancing act, where they weigh their perception of the 'risks' of film violence – the alleged risks of negative effects, such as desensitisation, and other risks, such as fear or nightmares – with the reality of their experience of watching film violence. In the next part of this chapter, I want to consider the way in which spectators construct categories of film-goers in order to position themselves in relation to the perceived 'risks' of film violence.

Hollywood Versus 'New Brutalism'

Spectators clearly differentiate between Hollywood action movies, such as the *Die Hard* series (1988, 1990, 1995), or *Terminator 2* (1991), and 'new brutalism' movies such as *Reservoir Dogs* or *Natural Born Killers*. The term 'new brutalism' usefully encapsulates social perceptions of film violence as a risk-taking activity: it is new, and therefore part of a specifically modern development within the entertainment industry that is seen by some as immoral and unethical; and it is brutal, implying that such new forms of enter-tainment brutalise innocent viewers.[9] This term therefore assumes that consumers of such movies will be well aware of the negative and 'risky' connotations that accompany such films.

All participants in the focus groups agreed that the quality dialogue is significant to their appreciation of 'new brutalism' films, as distinct from Hollywood action movies. In particular, Quentin Tarantino is praised for the witty, intelligent dialogue and characterisation in his films. One participant explained: 'Hollywood action movies are too cartoony at the moment. Something like the *Terminator*, it's just straightforward kind of kids' comic adventure. There is no sophistication in the text, in the dialogue. There's no irony' (37-year-old male). Action films are considered good fun, but 'new brutalism' films possess more thought-provoking and 'realistic' representations of viol-ence, which make them more disturbing and challenging:

> I went to see *Die Hard with a Vengeance* at the cinema. It was very, very violent but it was so funny, so stupid that it made me laugh. It didn't trigger the same as either *Reservoir Dogs* or *True Romance*. They scared me far more. (21-year-old female)

> *Die Hard with a Vengeance* or *Terminator 2* are very mainstream Hollywood films, whereas these films are more off-beat, more on the fringe, so they can get away with saying more. There's nothing that really, really makes you scream inside about those films, whereas *Reservoir Dogs* and *Man Bites Dog* definitely do. (twenty-year-old male)

Participants discussed their heightened levels of fear and adrenalin when viewing these films, as opposed to viewing Hollywood action movies. To be scared, or 'scream inside' is a response desired by the second participant above, and other group members imply they know what to expect from Hollywood action movies, whereas 'new brutal-ism' films can take them by surprise. These films are also seen to represent the conse-quences of violence more realistically, and this is regarded as a virtue:

> I think Hollywood movies are far more offensive personally because of the way they

portray violence. There's a total lack of reality. I mean – in *Pulp Fiction* compare John
Travolta, when he accidentally blows a guy's head off in the car. In *Die Hard* Bruce
Willis never gets covered in bits of bone and brain; his clothes fall off so we get to see a
bit more of his body, he gets beaten to a pulp and then gets up and scales an elevator
shaft or something. (31-year-old female)

People like Schwarzenegger or Stallone don't even look real. They look fantastical.
Whereas in *Henry, Portrait of a Serial Killer*, Henry is someone you could see walking
down the street. You don't know. (nineteen-year-old male)

'Realistic' representations of violence are praised because they cannot be anticipated,
because they are not formulaic, and because they are based on participants' perceptions
of real life experiences. Because of these factors, participants take these films more
seriously than their 'action movie' counterparts.

Although they consider the target films as different from other Hollywood action
movies of similar content, this does not mean that participants do not like to watch
action movies. As one participant states: 'The *Terminator* films are mainstream, but
they're still interesting and a lot of fun to play around with' (25-year-old male). The
phrase 'play around' serves to highlight the differentiation made by participants
between action movies as fun, playful and unrealistic, and other violent movies as the
direct opposite: serious, intelligent and realistic. Participants' repeated praise of characterisation, dialogue, direction and acting in the target films suggests that their aesthetic
appreciation of such films functions as an alternative form of response to the playful
engagement suggested by the idea of 'playing around' with the violence in action
movies.

Viewers' categorisation of 'new brutalism' movies as different from Hollywood action
movies ensures that those consumers who choose to see 'new brutalism' movies are
positioning themselves as a specific type of viewer. By saying that these films are intelligent, sophisticated and realistic in their representation of violence, these participants
are identifying themselves as intelligent and sophisticated audiences. The pleasure that
they gain from this type of entertainment is a pleasure that they share and agree with in
general terms; it does not involve 'playing around' with film violence so much as aesthetic appreciation.

In relation to Adams's risk thermostat hypothesis, this is a particular type of risk-
taker. These participants liked violent movies which are not predominantly mainstream, which are perceived to be independent and challenging, which do not cater for
the masses. Participants' perception of these films as challenging and controversial is
reflected in their own discussion about what type of viewer they perceive themselves to
be. Participants do not see themselves as strange, or disturbed or emotionally deficient
– the qualities often associated with controversial and violent movies.[10] Even though
some admit they are attracted to see such films because they are categorised as violent,
they do not regard themselves as violent and unable to function in society. On the contrary, viewers of film violence see themselves as *sensitised* to representations of violence.

None of this is to say that participants have offered their 'true' response to controversial films. As David Buckingham observes:

What we say is inextricably bound up with the context in which we say it: consciously or unconsciously, we adjust what we say in the light of how we perceive our listeners … and what we would like them to believe about us. Talk is, in this sense, an unavoidably *social* act.[11]

We can quite clearly see from the way in which participants respond to each other's comments that their talk is a social act and that they present a version of themselves that they feel is appropriate to this social context. Given the dominant social construction of these films and their audiences, it is significant that participants in this study are aware that there are acceptable and unacceptable responses to viewing violence and that specific types of viewers must be conscious of socially acceptable modes of response. In this respect, at least, popular discourses surrounding film violence have some influence on the way viewers of film violence perceive themselves. Since these participants wish to be perceived as intelligent and critically aware viewers, it is important for them to discuss their responses to 'new brutalism' films in ways that highlight their critical skills. When they discuss these films as a group, they share an awareness of types of films and viewers, the group dynamic re-enforces shared perceptions of 'new brutalism' films and socially acceptable responses to 'risky' entertainment.

Collective Responses

The focus on perceptions of 'risk' and film violence ensures that going to see a controversial film such as *Natural Born Killers* is a social activity. David Buckingham's research suggests that 'the social context of viewing is clearly a key factor in the pleasure of horror'[12] and we can see from the evidence of the focus groups that watching film violence also involves watching how other people respond to film violence. In the discussions, participants mimed audience response: placing hands over their eyes, turning away from the screen, squirming in their seats. One participant recalled: 'In *Pulp Fiction* when they do the insulin shot the whole cinema just erupted' (37-year-old male). Two participants discussed a collective response to *Reservoir Dogs*:

We spent the first hour waiting for the ear-slicing scene, then during this scene the entire cinema was saying oh, oh, this is it, and then after that everyone is oh no, wow. (22-year-old male)

The cinema was packed, there was definitely an atmosphere, like going to a gig or a play. There was a tangible tension and then people definitely relaxed a lot after the ear scene. (37-year-old male)

One spectator chose to watch *Natural Born Killers* in part to monitor his own reaction:

I think with these films, you go in the cinema and are very aware of other people's reactions, you're expecting it. Especially with *Natural Born Killers*. It was banned, and so you're watching the film partly for yourself and partly to see how others react because it has been hyped up. You want to see how your friends react to all the killings. (nineteen-year-old male)

Most participants recalled audience response to infamous scenes from movies such as *Reservoir Dogs*, *Natural Born Killers* or *Pulp Fiction* precisely because they were alert to the shared anticipation and excitement specific to viewing such films. They also considered how different types of people might respond to these scenes.:

> I don't think I've actually ever heard or seen anybody scream or stand up in the cinema and go, 'Ah no, look they've just cut his ear off' and run out the cinema. So, I think everybody's sort of socially prepared for these type of films, but obviously when you come out of the cinema you all have to shout all at once until you get to the pub as quickly as possible. I think everybody always starts talking about it and then they all get to the pub and they all start going, 'Oh yeah what about that bit', you know, like – when he was going to shoot him in the head or something like that … I think people tend to analyse films too much. They can't be real, but I think people's reactions – I think people do react differently. I think some people sort of say, 'Oh yeah, I didn't really like that and I wouldn't go and see it again or recommend it to anybody'; and then other people take it quite light-heartedly – aren't too bothered about violence, right. (32-year-old male)

> What about the person sitting next to you — what about [Participant 3] sitting next to you in the cinema? (Interviewer)

> Yeah, she has to cover her eyes occasionally because, perhaps, I don't know, in China it's a different culture so perhaps they don't have violent films like this. Although having said that I was going to bring in at this point that I've seen a lot of martial arts films years ago and they were pretty violent. (32-year-old male)

This viewer associates himself with a particular type of consumer of film violence: someone who is light-hearted, socially prepared, who does not react excessively to images of violence. His claim that he is unaware of other people's responses to scenes of violence is, in many ways, an indication of the type of viewer he does not wish to associate himself with. When asked to consider his female partner's responses to film violence, he explains her different response by the fact that she is not socially prepared for this type of excessive violence. However, he then goes on to discuss the gory violence in martial arts films, and his partner confirms this; she thinks that martial arts films are 'more gory' than the target films. There is clearly a contradiction here, which highlights this spectator's wish to align himself with socially prepared viewers who do not take representations of violence too seriously, and with whom this participant might wish to socialise. His contradictory explanation of his partner's different response suggests that he does not wish to acknowledge that she is a different type of consumer, who is 'bothered about violence', and therefore someone who is not 'right' in this context.

Other participants distinguished between the way men and women react to representations of violence. Men are perceived as having little reaction to violence, whereas women are more voluble and physical in their response to violence. Two participants explained:

> I pay a lot of attention to the way other people react in the cinema. I think there is a difference between the way men and women react to violence and I think a lot of it is a conditioned response. It's okay for women to scream but a lot of men don't feel comfortable doing that kind of thing. (31-year-old female)

> I really loved *Braveheart* (1995); it was very violent, very gory, but I really enjoyed it – we were hiding under our coats – it was very gory. I noticed other people, especially men, sit there and have to watch it. We were like this – 'Oh my god, that's disgusting' – they were like (*mimics serious expression, pursed lips*). I was looking around at people and they were half-watching me. (21-year-old female)

This conscious awareness of other movie-goers and the issue of gender became a subject of group debate. In one all-male group, one participant said he knew of a female friend whose response was noticeable because it was extreme, and other group members laughed at this comment, also citing examples of other women they knew who had similar responses when viewing violence. One participant claimed that, if he goes to the cinema with male friends, he is aware that their reaction to violence is positive ('that's cool'), whereas if he goes to the cinema with his girlfriend, or in mixed sex company, he is aware that female reactions are different: 'Girls don't like it when someone gets shot' (eighteen-year-old male).

Some male participants claimed that they do not notice audience response to violent scenes. On closer inspection, however, these admissions reveal how aware male participants really are of the shared activity of viewing violence. For example, one male participant commented:

> If I'm watching a film, I don't notice what other people are doing. The only time I do notice is when I feel something like a jump, you know, you feel everyone else doing the same thing. But other than that I don't actually look at what other people are doing. I get the impression they're not doing anything except watching the film. (23-year-old male)

This participant concentrates on his own non-responsive state when viewing violence. He speaks both as an individual member of the audience, and (apparently) for the audience as a whole. He claims not to notice audience response for the most part. But as soon as he claims *not* to notice other movie-goers, he shows just such an awareness by mentioning audience fear and shock.

One couple debated this issue. The male partner claimed:

> I don't find myself shocked very often by violence in films. I think if you're shocked you might look around for a reinforcement of your feelings. But, I'm not aware of why I should be looking to see other people's reactions if I'm not reacting myself. (28-year-old male)

In contrast, his partner responds verbally and physically to violence on screen. She commented:

> If I see something which is shocking then I'll yell out or laugh. It's the shock that makes me laugh. I'll bring my knees up or I'll hide under a coat and then I'll look around to see if anyone is looking at me or other people are doing the same. (31-year-old female)

These comments suggest that, despite what he actuallly says, the male participant is aware of his partner's different reactions.

When going to see a controversial film, participants have a heightened awareness of how they and other people respond to scenes which contain representations of violence, whether they themselves display their responses or not. This is, in part, because these viewers are aware of what they consider to be appropriate and inappropriate behaviour at the cinema. For example, one participant recalled seeing the film *Braveheart* with a friend who called out and laughed at the violence:

> What really annoyed me was that one of my friends sat through all the battle scenes saying: 'Oh yes, see his head come off, oh brilliant, oh look at all that blood', and I was thinking 'Shut up'. This is not the sort of film where you want to be doing this. You should be saying: 'Oh those poor people laying down their lives', not 'Oh cool, did you see his arm fly off'. (22-year-old male)

Laughter is a common response spectators notice and question. Certain movies, such as *Pulp Fiction*, generate acceptable laughter while others, such as *Henry, Portrait of a Serial Killer* or *Braveheart* do not, and to laugh at inappropriate places risks censure from other members of the audience. Two participants discussed how sensitive they become to unwanted noise and inappropriate laughter:

> I get hyper-sensitive when I'm watching a film and I can hear the slightest noise anywhere – it drives me absolutely mad. The worst film I ever saw was *The Texas ChainSaw Massacre* (1974). Everybody in the audience just seemed to be laughing constantly, as loud as possible, just to impress their mates; to say: 'I'm not affected by this, it doesn't upset me at all.' I wished they'd just shut up and watch the film. It is a social activity but, you know, keep your (social side) out. (25-year-old male)

> There's also something, for example in *Braveheart*. A guy falls to his death and everybody laughed at that and I felt as if maybe I should laugh with them, and I did. I can't understand why I did that. I suppose you try to fit in with everybody else so you're not left out. (twenty-year-old male)

The social context of the viewing experience sets up this understanding of appropriate/inappropriate responses to film violence. The first speaker wants to disassociate himself from normative responses to horror films. He is aware that certain viewers perceive such films as an opportunity to show how 'light-hearted' types of film violence can be and, significantly, how 'socially prepared' they are for the accepted response to such a horror film. For the first speaker, his identification of this type of young male horror fan who wishes to impress his mates with his light-hearted responses to film violence allows him to situate his own response as mature and sensitive, even 'hyper-sensitive', to the social activity of viewing violence. The second speaker also wishes to show that he is a sensitive and mature viewer, but he does so not by offering an example of his observation of others, but rather by showing his ability to recognise his own inappropriate response, and thus demonstrating that he has now learnt the 'right' response.

Inappropriate laughter signifies the fine line between legitimate and unacceptable responses to fictional violence. Aware of societal/cultural consensus on the part of consumers of violent films, and conscious of their own perceptions of movie-goers, participants become sensitised to how they should respond. They show an ability to monitor other responses and censure that which is perceived to be inappropriate to a specific category of viewer, or to the context of representations of violence. In all the examples cited, no participant compared an awareness of laughter and screen violence with laughter and other movie genres. This laughter is accompanied by a visually violent scene, and is recognised as different. Indeed, as the above example illustrates, even within the context of film violence, there are further distinctions to be made. As one participant notes: 'That kind of response is alright in *Pulp Fiction*, but if everybody starts going "Ah, please" in the middle of *Man Bites Dog* you'd go mental' (25-year-old male).

Conclusion

It is possible to see that consumers of film violence self-regulate their responses according to how other people react to the perceived 'risks' of film violence. Perceptions of risk influence how viewers perceive themselves and other people in the viewing environment and a delicate balancing act takes place, similar to the balancing act of John Adams's risk thermostat hypothesis, which postulates that 'risk is an interactive phenomenon', and that the way people balance their risk-taking behaviour has consequences for others.[13] In relation to film violence, this balancing act reveals a number of significant issues, such as public and private responses to violence, or trust of self and distrust of others, that help to illuminate why and how people like to watch controversial movies.

We can see from the way in which participants discuss appropriate and inappropriate behaviour in the cinema that to act inappropriately is to upset this balance. This is an example of 'social competence'.[14] Viewers understand that it is necessary to act correctly in social situations, and their competence depends on an understanding of acceptable methods of response to film violence. The negative, one-sided 'debates' about film violence that take place in newspapers such as the *Daily Mail* can be seen to have exercised some influence on the way in which participants perceive themselves in relation to film violence. There may be a cultural curiosity to see certain types of violent movies but, at the same time, viewers are careful to dissociate themselves from the types of 'problem' viewers who may be drawn to watch these films. Consequently, these consumers of film violence situate their own private responses in relation to the public arena of the 'risks' of film violence.

Notes

1 Annette Hill, *Shocking Entertainment: Viewer Response to Violent Movies* (Luton: John Libbey Media, 1997).

2 John Adams, *Risk* (London: University College London, 1995).

3 For recent discussion of the film/violence debate, see Martin Barker and Julian Petley (eds), *Ill Effects: the media/violence debate* (London: Routledge, 1996).

4 Adams, *Risk*, pp. 14–16. The model was originally devised by Gerald Wilde in 1976. It has been modified by Adams in ibid., p. 14.

5 Ibid., p. 66. Research by Fischhoff and others attempted to distinguish between voluntary and involuntary risk, and found that people were far more prepared to accept levels of risk from activities that are voluntary. See Baruch Fischhoff *et al.*, *Acceptable Risk* (Cambridge: Cambridge University Press, 1981).

6 Derek Malcolm, 'Dogs of gore', *Guardian*, 7 January 1993, p. 6; Shaun Usher, 'Deadly dogs unleash a whirlwind of violence', *Daily Mail*, 22 December 1992, p. 26.

7 The advertisement appeared in most film magazines and *Time Out* in February 1995; Christopher Tookey, 'Why this film is a work of pure evil', *Daily Mail*, 21 February 1995, p. 9.

8 See Hill, *Shocking Entertainment*, pp. 19–27.

9 So far as I have been able to ascertain, the term originates with Jim Shelley. See Shelley, 'The boys are back in town', *Guardian*, 7 January 1993 and 'Down these mean streets many men have gone', *The Times*, Saturday Review, 20 February 1993, p. 12. For discussion of the manner in which these movies are perceived to be hazardous and dangerous, see Barker and Petley, *Ill Effects*, and Annette Hill, *Natural Born Killer: social theories of risk and media violence* (Luton: University of Luton Press, forthcoming).

10 See Barker and Petley, *Ill Effects*.

11 David Buckingham, *Moving Images: understanding children's emotional responses to television* (Manchester: Manchester University Press, 1996), p. 57.

12 Ibid., p. 109.

13 Adams, *Risk*, p. 20.

14 Jonathan Potter and Margaret Wetherell, *Discourse and Social Psychology: beyond attitudes and behaviour* (London: Sage, 1987).

11 Refusing to Refuse to Look: Female viewers of the horror film

Brigid Cherry

Most studies of the horror film that have considered questions of gender and spectatorship have concerned themselves with a theoretical male spectator, usually identifying the monster's gaze as male, and the heroine-victim as the subject of that gaze.[1] From such a critical perspective, Linda Williams describes the female spectator's gaze at the monster as representing 'a surprising (and at times subversive) affinity between monster and woman' that acknowledges their 'similar status within patriarchal structures of seeing'.[2] Williams does not, however, regard this female gaze as a pleasurable one: despite their affinity, female spectators do not find pleasure in the figure of the monster, and the act of looking is punished. For Williams, this explains why the female viewer of horror films refuses to look, often physically blocking or averting her eyes from the screen.

Whether most female spectators actually behave like this is another question: in my own study of female horror film fans and followers, only 19 per cent of participants claimed frequently to avert their gaze in some way, while 67 per cent claimed they only rarely or never refuse to look. In some segments of the audience, then, there are female viewers who do take pleasure in viewing horror films and who, in what could amount to an act of defiance, refuse to refuse to look.

The horror film audience has long been regarded as completely 'other'. In his review of Hammer's *The Curse of Frankenstein* (1957) in the *Financial Times*, Derek Granger suggested that 'Only the saddest of simpletons ... could ever get a really satisfying frisson' from such material.[3] More recently, in an article entitled 'The best places to meet good men', the woman's magazine *Cosmopolitan* warned its readership against starting up a conversation with any man looking for horror films in the local video store, since such men might harbour 'questionable feelings about women. Whether buried deep within him or overtly expressed in his words and actions, his misogynistic tendencies make him a man to avoid.'[4] From being the 'saddest of simpletons', the horror fan has become a positive danger to women. In the 1950s, Granger acknowledged that women could also find gratification, or at least a simple escapism, in the horror film, which he saw as 'a rather eccentric and specialised form of light entertainment, and possibly a useful means of escape for a housewife harrowed by the shopping'.[5] By the 1990s, however, at least in *Cosmopolitan*'s imagination, the horror film could only represent a threat to women, in real life as well as on the screen.

Since the rise of the slasher film in the late 1970s, the horror film audience has been regarded for marketing purposes as consisting primarily of adolescent boys and men under the age of twenty-five. James Twitchell's observations of horror film audiences in *Dreadful Pleasures* led him to the conclusion that 'most of the audience are in their early to mid-teens', while Carol Clover claims that 'the proportions vary somewhat from subgenre to subgenre and from movie to movie ... but the preponderance of young males appears constant'.[6] The industry has made the same assumption: Miramax president Mark Gill told *Variety* that, prior to *Scream 2*, 'horror film audiences used to be heavily male. If they could drag their girlfriends along you were lucky'.[7]

In their empirical work on socialisation and horror film spectatorship, Dolf Zillman and James B. Weaver have suggested that adolescent males can use horror films to demonstrate to their peers that they can stand up to frights and shocks, and provide comfort and protection to their girlfriends, while adolescent females can demonstrate their fearfulness and need for protection. Their conclusions are based upon experiments in which 'male and female adolescents watch a horror film with an opposite-gender peer, ostensibly another research participant but actually an experimental confederate, who either displayed gender-appropriate, gender-inappropriate, or no emotions'.[8] The experiment measured enjoyment of the movie, liking of the cohort, romantic attraction to that cohort, and being intimidated by the cohort. Zillman and Weaver observe that 'enjoyment of the horror film proved to be greatly affected by the emotional displays of an opposite gender companion'. Male respondents enjoyed the film twice as much in the presence of a distressed female as when they were with a fearless female peer, while female respondents enjoyed horror the least in the presence of a distressed male. Female respondents were more attracted to a male companion when he exhibited mastery of fear than to the same companion when expressing distress, while male respondents tended to be more attracted to females showing acute distress than the same companion who exhibited fearlessness.[9]

Both the production industry and the majority of academic criticism assume that taking pleasure in horrific or frightening images is a masculine trait, not a feminine one. According to this model, while women may watch horror films, they do so only reluctantly and with displeasure, not least because of the representations of violence against women they contain.[10] Demographic profiles of contemporary cinema audiences, however, suggest that women can comprise up to 50 per cent of horror film audiences. The Cinema Advertising Association's audience profiles indicate that in Britain the female audience segment for *Scream*, *Silence of the Lambs* and *Alien³* was 48 per cent, 49 per cent and 42 per cent respectively.[11] As Carol Clover has acknowledged in *Men, Women and Chainsaws*, however, it seems inadequate to dismiss large numbers of women as 'male-identified' and account for their responses only as 'an "emasculated" act of collusion with the oppressor'.[12] Zillman and Weaver suggest that play-acting and pretence play a large part in the responses of viewers to horror films, because regular horror film viewers become habituated to the material they see, so that the emotional intensity of their initial distress reaction decreases with repeated viewings.[13] Female viewers, required by peer pressure to continue to exhibit fear, may be especially likely to exhibit pretended responses. It may be that in recent decades this peer pressure has lessened somewhat, and it may have become more acceptable for women to be seen to enjoy horror. They may have simply become less inclined to play-act feminine responses to horror, especially when they are not participating in a dating situation.

Critics such as Williams who observe displeasure in the female viewer may be under-estimating the pleasures inherent in this type of film for at least some female viewers. If female viewers do not always refuse to look, what kinds of horror film do they attend and what pleasures do they derive from seeing them? What is at stake for the female fans and followers of the horror film? These questions about the consumption of the horror film cannot be answered solely by a consideration of the text-reader relationship or by theoretical models of spectatorship and identification. A profile of female horror film fans and followers can be developed only through an audience study. Jackie Stacey's study of female film-goers of the 1940s and 1950s provides a useful model and high-lights the need to interpret generic films in relation to their audience.[14] Since the hor-ror genre is also the subject of fan discourses, my study also aimed to investigate female participation in fan practices, drawing on the work of Henry Jenkins.[15]

While heeding Tanya Modleski's warning of the dangers of producing a celebratory and uncritical account of popular culture and pleasure, the value of 'demonstrating the invisible experiences of women with popular culture' was demonstrated by the very large proportion of respondents in this study who expressed their delight and thanks in having an opportunity to speak about their experiences.[16] My study of female horror film viewers allows the voice of an otherwise marginalised and invisible audience to be heard, their experiences recorded, the possibilities for resistance (if any) explored, and the potentially feminine pleasures of the horror film identified.[17]

Given that this audience is largely hidden, the initial research problem was to ident-ify female horror fans and followers for recruitment purposes. Rather than trying to recruit participants from those attending film screenings, I sought to identify fans through the institutions of organised or casual fandom. The majority of participants were drawn from the memberships of horror fan groups and fantasy societies, and from the readerships of a cross-section of professional and fan horror magazines, with additional participants being drawn from attendees at horror film festivals and conven-tions.[18] A number of local groups were attended for direct recruitment purposes and word-of-mouth contacts from further afield were also included in the study, as were a few respondents contacted through newsgroups and electronic mailing lists.

This diversity of recruitment methods provided a mix of dedicated horror fans, more casual followers (some of whom did not even consider themselves to be fans) and those whose liking for horror was part of a wider range of genre and media tastes. Although the sample was inevitably self-selected, respondents represented a wide cross-section of the population in terms of age, education, employment, marital status and geographi-cal location. Participants' ages ranged from teenagers to women in their fifties and six-ties. They were predominantly white and mainly well educated; differences of race and class have not been examined. Qualitative data was collected through focus groups, interviews, open-ended questions included in the questionnaire and through the com-munication of opinions and experiences in letters and other written material. This approach to data-gathering provided information on the tastes and responses of the female fans, together with a demographic profile produced from the questionnaire's quantitative data as a supplement to what little demographic data exists about the horror film audience. This methodological pluralism may turn up contradictory evidence but, as in Ien Ang's study of *Dallas* viewers, the aim of this research was to explore the diversity of women's consumption of horror.[19] Rather than being a problem, conflicting information turned up by the different methods can be seen as evidence of viewers' negotiations with dominant ideology.[20]

The survey obtained information exclusively from self-selected British female horror film fans and followers; its results cannot, therefore, be taken to apply to casual horror film audiences. During the research, I also studied horror fan discourse in magazines, fanzines and Internet groups. The topics that concerned the respondents in this survey broadly reflected those within the wider arenas of fan discussion. It can be assumed, then, that the responses reported on here can be taken as fairly typical of female horror film fans and followers.

Earlier studies of gendered spectatorship have shown that the horror film's gaze is not as fixed and monolithically male as might once have been suggested. Carol Clover has explored the notion that cross-gender identification is a fluid process. She recognises that, although they form a minority of the audience, female viewers of horror who 'actively like such films' exist, particularly for mainstream horror films and occult films.[21] Clover suggests that 'female fans find a meaning in the text and image of these films that is less inimical to their own interests than the figurative analysis would have us believe'.[22] She also supposes that the female spectator may interpret horror films in a fundamentally different manner to the male. This chapter seeks to shed light on this mode of interpretation by focusing on actual audiences; it will attempt to position the female viewer in the context of women's increasing visibility as consumers of horror films.[23]

Mark Jancovich notes that 'despite claims that horror is primarily produced and consumed by men, and that it promotes patriarchal values, there has been an important and enduring tradition of horror produced and consumed by women'.[24] Women were the primary consumers of what Ellen Moers calls the 'female gothic' tradition: 'the willing audience of the literature of horror', according to Judith Halberstam.[25] Rosemary Jackson asserts that this tradition fantasises about 'a violent attack upon the symbolic order and it is no accident that so many writers of a Gothic tradition are women.'[26] Writers such as Nancy Collins, Lisa Tuttle and Anne Rice continue this tradition of female authorship, while the female readerships of horror fiction, including fiction aimed at children and teenagers, are high.

Although horror literature is recognised as appealing across the sex and age ranges, the widely held notion that the horror film is the preserve of the adolescent male has created a situation in which films are marketed and reviewed with a male youth audience in mind. Pandering to the perceived tastes of the majority audience limits the appeal of certain types of horror films to other segments of the audience. Women appear to have become a hidden audience for horror, repressing their liking for it because such a response is seen as unfeminine. Reading, on the other hand, is a private activity, and horror fiction can be consumed 'legitimately', or at least without attracting negative comment. Some recent horror films have, however, been marketed as Gothic romances, including *Bram Stoker's Dracula* with its poster line 'Love Never Dies', and *Wolf*, with a moody sepia-toned still of lead actors Jack Nicholson and Michelle Pfeiffer, hinting at sexual overtones to the werewolf transformation with the line 'The Animal Is Out'.[27] Films that are not easily classifiable as horror or do not conform to contemporary notions of what constitutes the genre, such as *Silence of the Lambs*, may be classified as mainstream, not least because of the economic need to maximise attendance beyond the relatively small horror film audience.

As Nina Auerbach observes in *Our Vampires, Ourselves*, the construction of a female exclusion zone around horror is a relatively recent development. Publicity surrounding the initial release of *Dracula* (Universal, 1931), for instance, emphasised its appeal to female viewers. In a fan magazine interview, Bela Lugosi declared,

> It is *women* who love horror. *Women have a predestination to suffering*. It is women who bear the race in bloody agony. Suffering is a kind of horror. Blood is a kind of horror. Therefore women are born with a predestination to horror in their very bloodstream. It is a biological thing.[28]

A 1996 market research survey found that Madame Tussaud's Chamber of Horrors was 'more popular with women than men, with over twice as many women than men liking it'.[29] The survey report echoed Lugosi's comments about biological predestination:

> Women tend to be more tolerant about visceral things because they have more direct personal experience of them. They cope with periods once a month, they go through childbirth and they are usually the ones who look after the bleeding and battered limbs when the kids take a tumble. They can put blood and gore in context and generally cope better than men.[30]

While it is simplistic to suggest that women enjoy horror solely or mainly because of their biology, these comments raise the possibility that some women may view horror films for more complex reasons than are suggested by the socialisation theories of Zillman and Weaver. There is, moreover, evidence to suggest that women have always reacted in pleasurable ways to some types of horror film. Auerbach explains that her own response to horror films led her to question some of the academic canon of horror film spectatorship:

> When I was twelve or thirteen, some enterprising ghoul began to televise 1930s horror movies on Saturday nights. These shadowy monsters were a revelation to my best friend and me ... we had found a secret talisman against a nice girl's life. Vampires were supposed to menace women, but to me at least, they promised protection against a destiny of girdles, spike heels, and approval. I am writing in part to reclaim them for a female tradition, one that has not always known its allies.[31]

Tanya Kryszynska likewise relates the lesbian vampire film to her exploration of her own emerging sexuality, and illustrates the potentially gender-specific pleasurable reactions that female viewers may have to horror films, especially to the vampire film.[32] Auerbach questions the masculine emphasis in the work of such critics as James Twitchell, David J. Skal and Walter Kendrick. According to her analysis, Skal 'quarantines' female viewers from 'vicarious bloodlust', while Twitchell relates the appeal of horror films down to a Freudian 'Ur-myth of adolescence' which is itself constructed within a patriarchal system and deals almost exclusively with the fantasies of boys.[33]

The common perception of the contemporary horror film viewer as an adolescent male also results from the research emphasis on the slasher film, a type less well liked by women. The female audience for vampire and supernatural/occult films, for instance, may well be proportionately larger.[34] Sierra On-line's 1996 market research found that 27 per cent of girls between the ages of thirteen and eighteen named horror as their favourite film type, compared to 14 per cent of boys.[35] J. B. Barclay's 1961 survey of viewing tastes indicated that more than half of all girls around the age of fifteen named horror as one of their most liked film genres, almost as many as boys of the same age.[36] Girls, however, professed an increasing dislike for the genre as they matured. This may be explained by patterns of socialisation: girls are dissuaded from liking horror because it is seen as unfeminine, whereas boys are encouraged to display their fearlessness and outgrow it more gradually. In my own study of audiences in Edinburgh, just under one-third of total horror film audiences were women.

Among the survey participants, the liking for horror persists well into middle age, but these women do not appear in profiles of the cinema audience because they largely view horror films in the home, either on television or video. The age profile of the respondents in the survey was much more evenly spread than might be expected: 68 per cent were over twenty-five, 30 per cent over thirty-five and 15 per cent over forty. The oldest person in the study was over sixty.[37] This indicates that while the primary cinema audience for horror films is young and male, the television or video audience contains higher numbers of older and female viewers. While these habitual viewers of horror comprise only a small proportion of the total audience, their presence raises important questions about gendered spectatorship and accepted models of femininity.

One proposition that this study confirms is that these horror film fans and followers tend to keep their liking for the genre private, and either view alone or with one or two people close to them who also like the genre. Cinema-viewing was the most infrequent format for viewing horror films. This may be related to the infrequency with which horror films are released as well as the less regular attendance of people over twenty-five at all forms of cinema, but the 11 per cent who never watched horror films at the cinema, together with the 67 per cent who watched at the cinema less than once a month, reinforced the idea of an invisible female horror film audience. These female horror film viewers watched horror films on television or, more frequently, on video cassette. Seventy-two per cent of the respondents watched a horror video at least monthly, while 56 per cent watched several times a month; 17 per cent watched a horror film on television at least once a week, 37 per cent two or three times a month and 19 per cent once a month. Overall, 12 per cent watched a horror film two or more times per week, 34 per cent once or twice a week and 41 per cent two or three times a month; thus, just under half of the participants watched a horror film at least once a week. Fourteen per cent viewed fairly infrequently, although only 1 per cent watched less than one horror film a month.

The survey confirms Clover's suggestion that there is a larger female audience for certain horror film types than for others.[38] By far the most popular type of horror film was the vampire film: 92 per cent of the respondents liked all or most vampire films. This was followed in popularity by occult/supernatural films (liked by 86 per cent), psychological thrillers (81 per cent), Hammer films (76 per cent), and science-fiction/horror films (74 per cent). The least well-liked horror film type by far was the slasher film, liked by only 25 per cent of the participants. It was also the most disliked horror film type. Fifty-four per cent of respondents disliked all or most examples of the type. The second and third most disliked types were the serial killer film at 25 per cent and horror-comedies at 22 per cent but these types were liked by 53 per cent and 59 per cent of participants respectively, so that the slasher film seems to be unique in its low appeal to female viewers.

The comments of respondents who liked this film type revealed a significant contradiction in the tastes and responses of these female fans. Surprisingly, perhaps, there was no significant difference between age groups in their preferences for these films. Those respondents classing themselves as fans, however, were more likely to admit to liking slasher films, suggesting that they may have more appeal to the more dedicated female horror film viewer. Many respondents tended to excuse their taste in some way, typically by stating that they like particular examples of the genre – *Halloween, Friday the 13th* and *Nightmare on Elm Street,* which they regard as being well made or original – and not others which were held to be formulaic or imitative. Some respondents preferred the funnier versions of the subgenre, while others said that they had to be in a particular frame of mind to watch slasher films.

Typically, many of those who stated that they liked slasher films made an attempt to argue against the criticisms made of the genre. A 39-year-old respondent argued:

> there is no predominance of females being killed. Most slasher films ... have nearly equal numbers of male and female victims. I think an actual census of horror movie victims would show that females tend to be threatened but escape or are rescued; males tend to be killed. But people only notice the threats to the females and simply shrug off the male deaths.

Others recognised the genre's violence toward women, but chose to ignore it:

> there's definitely some sexist treatment of women going on but at the same time, I enjoy the films, sometimes despite the fact that I'm protesting all these naked female bodies and stupid women who can't do anything but scream. It's foolish when it comes down to it.

As this comment suggests, respondents themselves frequently recognised that their responses were contradictory. This extended to feelings about the victims themselves: one participant described her feelings about characters she referred to as 'the stereotypical bimbo': 'I tend to find that I don't mind these women being victims – they deserve to be killed off!'[39]

Participants were also invited to name up to ten of their favourite horror films. In total, 336 individual films were named by 107 of the participants. The ten most frequently listed favourite horror films were:

		No. of times listed
1.	*Hellraiser* (1987)	33
2.	*Alien* (1979)	30
3.	*Interview With the Vampire* (1995)	30
4.	*The Lost Boys* (1987)	22
5.	*Aliens* (1986)	21
6.	*Bram Stoker's Dracula* (1992)	19
7.	*The Evil Dead* (1982)	17
8.	*The Hunger* (1983)	17
9.	*The Thing* (1982)	17
10.	*Night of the Living Dead* (1968)	15

The twenty most frequently selected films confirm the favourite film type selections with four vampire films,[40] three supernatural/occult films,[41] two psychological thrillers,[42] and three science-fiction/horror films[43] in the list. The list also contains three films adapted from the novels of Clive Barker,[44] and all three of the *Evil Dead* series.

Some films were undoubtedly selected because they were recent but, significantly, the majority are older. A number of the films most frequently selected have major female characters, a point that participants drew attention to when asked to explain their choice. By far the most frequently mentioned feature in the appeal of *Alien* (1979) was the enjoyment viewers obtained from watching a strong woman taking an active role. Many respondents felt that the representation of a strong, intelligent and resilient female was a major change from the vast majority of female roles they had previously seen. It has frequently been pointed out that this role was originally written as a male character and there has also been some criticism that Ripley (Sigourney Weaver) is stereotypically masculine. For some viewers, however, watching heroines who behave like heroes, in a masculine fashion, was itself attractive. In general, women appeared to enjoy strong, capable characters, regardless of sex, but were concerned that in the cinema few such characters are female. Other films with strong female leads, such as *Terminator 2* and *The Silence of the Lambs* were also often named by women as favourites.

Issues of 'quality' were also frequently mentioned in the evaluation of particular films. Quality for these viewers signified several aspects of cinema, including high production values in art direction, set design and costumes. Acting was frequently mentioned as being crucial, with individual actors (in particular Peter Cushing, Christopher Lee and Vincent Price) singled out as giving convincing performances or having star appeal. In the main, however, the quality of a film was determined by plot and character development, in ways that parallel Janice Radway's findings about the interpretative activities of romance fiction readers.[45] Radway demonstrated how a group of women united by their reading preferences actively responded to romance fiction, using it to help themselves deal with their everyday lives. Although there are demographic differences between Radway's readers and the group of horror films viewers discussed here (in addition to the obvious difference of nationality, the horror film viewers are far more likely to be in full-time occupations), their reactions to their chosen cultural texts show strong similarities. Like the subjects of Radway's study, female horror fans judge the quality of films on the basis of the relationships which develop between the characters. This explains the particular liking for vampire films among this group of viewers, since many seemed to read them in a similar way to romance fiction, identifying the relationships between the vampires or between the vampire and its victim as a major source of pleasure. Like Radway's readers, these viewers chose to ignore the events and actions in the narrative that contradicted their reading of the heroine as strong and independent.[46]

For many viewers, the appeal of vampirism seems to be tied into a romanticisation of the past. The taste for Gothic horror is often linked to a liking for historical and costume dramas, with Hammer and other horror films providing a key source of images for this imagined past, which one 23-year-old respondent described as 'a stylish image of dark beauty ... The classically Gothic full-length dresses and cloaks, the numerous high-ceilinged rooms full of dark wood and velvet curtains are now, without a doubt, for me synonymous with grace and charm.' A 41-year-old respondent commented that 'the vampire film is the closest the horror genre comes to the traditional romantic film. Vampires have most often been portrayed in literature and film as handsome, often foreign, exotic men who seem to have an uncanny knowledge of how to give pleasure. Not so different from the old ideal of a movie star: How do you think Valentino made it so big?' A 53-year-old participant suggested that 'tragic hero figures' such as Heathcliff or Lord Byron were similar to the 'magnetic vampire characters'.

Subtlety of horror was also mentioned as a reason for liking particular films or types of films (*The Haunting*, 1963, is commonly praised in this respect). The horror classics *Frankenstein* and *Dracula* were often cited as examples of 'quality' horror, along with films with a historical or costume-drama style and reflecting Gothic or Romantic themes. Quality in an individual film in a subgenre was given as a reason for liking that film when the subgenre was disliked as a whole. Lack of quality, defined in terms of weak or formulaic plots and stereotypical characters, was often cited as the main reason for not liking slasher films, which were regarded as boring and predictable. Viewers preferred to watch films they took to be imaginative, intelligent, literary or thought-provoking. Dislike was often expressed for films that revolved around excessive or gratuitous displays of violence, gore or other effects used to evoke revulsion in the audience. The women often preferred things left to their imaginations. A respondent in her early thirties claimed that 'those movies that allow me to use my imagination and offer the frame and some atmosphere are more scary to me than any other horror film'. Again, parallels can be identified with Radway's findings: lack of character development and relationships together with high levels of aggression and violence are very similar to the reasons that romance fiction readers gave for defining romances as bad.[47]

For most respondents, the pleasures of viewing horror films did not include the violence inherent in many examples of the genre. A few expressed a delight in the more violent forms of horror, but women who claimed to enjoy the visceral thrills of watching violence were a small minority.[48] In the main, those who claimed to select horror films with gory special effects preferred such films to be over the top, unrealistic or comic. Bad special effects were enjoyed precisely because they *were* bad and unconvincing. If a gory or violent film was thought to have a good story with interesting characters and to be well made, however, some respondents who otherwise disliked this type of film might enjoy it. Female viewers appeared not to reject gore or violence *per se* so much as the way these elements were used in the film. Sexual and erotic themes, on the other hand, were important to many of the participants, particularly in vampire films. Although sexual violence is commonly disliked, vampires are the most popular form of horror film monster, and blood is often mentioned as a crucial element. This may indicate that vampire films can function as a form of erotica for women, providing these viewers with sexual fantasy.

More generally, emotional or psychological responses were frequently deemed important in the enjoyment of a film. Tension and suspense were preferred over shock and revulsion. A writer in her forties declared: 'I have always enjoyed tense, thought-provoking films on what may be regarded as the edge of horror.' For a small number of women, being scared was identified as important (though equally as many claimed *not* to be scared by horror films). Generally, these viewers' discourses about their choices and tastes in horror films seemed to be at odds with the fact that horror films are widely regarded as low culture and viewed, as Jonathan Lake Crane observes, as 'the entertainment of the young, minorities, the working class, or the disenfranchised', and frequently criticised by mainstream critics and moral guardians.[49] In common with Radway's romance fiction readers, these women cannot easily be viewed as ignorant, dull, or misguided consumers of mass culture, nor can they be viewed as the impressionable, bloodthirsty viewers which the moral guardians of society associate with horror cinema.[50]

For many of these habitual viewers, the taste for horror often began well before adolescence – several reported that their first experience of horror involved being enjoyably frightened by Disney-animated films and other dark children's films based on fairy tales – and has persisted long after. Horror films share the frequent representation of distortions of natural forms – supernatural monsters with a human face, for instance – with children's fiction, and these representations were often mentioned by participants as a continuing source of fascination, suggesting that these viewers continue to be simultaneously drawn to, and repelled by, similar representations to those that had engaged them in childhood.[51] Part of the appeal appears to be sympathy or empathy with monstrous creatures. A typical comment was provided by a respondent in her late thirties:

> When I was very little, I used to collect 'monster cards' and one I remember was called 'the gormless blob'. It was a huge heap of green slime with one eye in the middle of its head, it was hideously ugly but it lived on love. If it wasn't loved, it died. I had that card on my bedroom wall, near my bed and told it I loved it every night before I went to sleep ... Monster films always make me cry – classic monsters such as Lon Chaney Jr., Karloff's monster, Charles Laughton's Hunchback, etc.

This empathy for the monster continues into adulthood and may be one of the reasons why some types of horror film – vampire films, versions of Frankenstein and films adapted from the work of Clive Barker, for example – are so popular with female viewers. Many respondents declared that they felt like loners or outsiders as children, describing themselves as 'school swot', 'introverted' or 'bookish', and their identification with the monster may be related to their not feeling part of a peer group.[52] Respondents reported that, as they got older, the very fact that they were fans contributed to their feelings of isolation. John Tulloch and Henry Jenkins describe the popular perception of the fan as other: 'The fan as extraterrestrial; the fan as excessive consumer; the fan as cultist; the fan as dangerous fanatic.'[53] In *Textual Poachers*, Jenkins observes that 'such representations isolate potential fans from others who share common interests and reading practices ... [and] make it highly uncomfortable to speak publicly as a fan or to identify yourself even privately with fan cultural practices'.[54] This status as outsider – seeing themselves or being seen as a 'geek' or as belonging to a distinctive subculture – continues well into adulthood for some respondents.

Fascination with monstrosity is an important factor in the continuing appeal of horror for women. Although respondents mention many different kinds of monsters when describing what they like about horror films, vampires are by far the most frequently mentioned, often in terms of their sexual fascination for women. As a 24-year-old respondent puts it:

> I have a particular fondness for vampire films, a fascination with the vampire, really. It originated as a sexual feeling evoked in me by the vampire character, and an admiration of his/her style – the elegance of their costume and their aristocracy. As I got older this became a real hobby for me, really, and I began to read a lot to discover the psychology at work behind that. I wanted to understand the evolution of the vampire and to unravel the intrigue surrounding its sexuality.

This fascination for the vampire and its sexuality is typical of many participants, often related to the sexuality and appeal of the male stars playing the dark, handsome, exotic and charismatic vampire popularised by Bela Lugosi, Christopher Lee, Gary Oldman and Antonio Banderas. The homoerotic theme of *Interview With the Vampire* seemed to be no deterrent to its appeal to a female audience. The 24-year-old respondent quoted above describes her use of the film as erotica:

> I've hired vampire videos which I find particularly erotic and sat with my partner at the time watching them in a darkened room – *Interview With the Vampire* is one that I found particularly sexy, there's something intriguing about the homoeroticism between those beautiful young men. I didn't say anything but I think that my partner took pleasure in how I couldn't take my eyes off the screen, and obviously initiated something because of this.

Both film and fictional vampires are often portrayed as polygamous and bisexual and it would appear that for many viewers the vampire film reflects a sexual fantasy.[55] A number of respondents reported fantasising about becoming vampires themselves, and some fans wear vampire costumes, including fangs, on a regular basis.

The physical attraction of the identifiably human monster Pinhead was also a major factor in the appeal of the *Hellraiser* films, again illustrating the sexual fascination with monsters for the female horror fans.[56] Although the extreme levels of violence and excessive special effects render these films problematic for some viewers, others were eventually drawn to his human qualities. The artist respondent typifies this response:

Interview With the Vampire (Neil Jordan, 1994)

When I first saw Pinhead I think that he really did scare me ... It wasn't until *Hellraiser* 3 that he showed any weakness at all, but to fans of the films I think that Pinhead finally revealing his hidden human depths was regarded merely as an insight into one of their favourite monsters. I'm certainly very fond of him now.

Clive Barker's source material was particularly well regarded for its sympathetic attitude to monsters. One respondent in her late thirties explained:

Clive Barker's films are so beautiful, and his vision of the dark side is so complete. *Hellraiser* I and II and *Candyman* are scary, well written and beautifully filmed, but I feel his vision is most beautifully portrayed in *Nightbreed*, where the monsters are the good guys. I think this may be a girlie film as most of the men I know don't like it much, but all the women do. A monster movie for people who love monsters.

This love of monsters was repeated by a 35-year-old respondent:

I have always enjoyed the imagination of Clive Barker because he takes a very obvious joy in the supernatural, the macabre and the downright weird ... I have never seen anyone else create quite such a variety of monsters. Some are ugly, some are beautiful, they are happy, confused and sad just like human beings.

Although many women felt it was socially unacceptable to express fantasies about stars or characters in horror films – perhaps because most of those surveyed were above the age at which fan attachments to stars are seen as acceptable – one 29-year-old respondent admitted to having crushes on horror film monsters, 'not only when in repose but when they change into their full monstrous forms, fangs bared, blood flowing ... It is the entire image that I find attractive, not just the stars when they're looking human.' Such comments highlight a particular form of identification to emerge in this study – a 'subversive affinity' with the monster.

Many respondents also appear to have adopted deliberate interpretative strategies to accommodate the films' representations of women, either ignoring and making excuses for what they see as negative representations or condoning feminine behaviour in strong female characters. As one 24-year-old respondent explained,

> I think Ripley's strength in *Alien* is very female – a very female level of practicality that movies like *Predator* don't have. And I love the female lead in *Nightmare on Elm Street*. She knows what is going on and doesn't fall for all of the typical 'crazy female' coddling that everyone around her tries.

Other respondents excused the sexism of older horror films as reflecting a gender stereotype common at the time they were made, which one eighteen-year-old respondent called the 'pathetic female victim syndrome'. She added that 'there are a lot of old horror films where the women have the upper hand, for example, they become vampires and men are attracted to them and led to their deaths which seems like justice to me!' A 29-year-old respondent agreed: 'men get the raw deal in horror – a woman killed by a vampire tends to be seduced, a man is more likely to be savaged'. While these remarks do not indicate any depth of feminist belief or activism, they might suggest that the films fulfil some kind of revenge fantasy. Other respondents, however, did not overly concern themselves with issues of sexism and stereotyping, not allowing the representations of gender to overwhelm their viewing pleasures. As a nineteen-year-old participant said: 'I object to these women who scream every five seconds but I don't think women have to be the strong lead to make it a good film.'

On the evidence of their comments in this survey, female viewers of the horror film do not adopt purely masculine viewing positions, nor do they simply, as Clover suggests, respond to the literal level of the text.[57] When given the opportunity, as in *Alien*, female viewers strongly identify with the feminised hero because she is literally female. While Clover argues that 'the fact that we have in the killer a feminine male and in the main character a masculine female would seem to suggest a loosening of the category of the feminine', the participants' responses to films like *Alien* and *Hellraiser* suggests that for the female spectator the category of the feminine can be strengthened by adopting particular viewing strategies. Gendered identification for the female viewer may not be as fluid a process as Clover proposes it is for the male viewer.[58]

The similarities between these viewers' interpretative activities and the reading strategies of romance fiction readers revealed in Radway's study suggest that the pleasures and responses of female horror fans may be categorised as feminine. But these female viewers do not react as might be expected: they do not flinch, block their view or turn away from the screen, nor do they appear as the emasculated viewers one might expect if they were adopting a male gaze or colluding with the male oppressor. This audience segment's preferences for Gothic horror film types and for the thrills and adrenalin rush of the shiver sensation combine with their liking for strong female characters and their most prevalent and frequently mentioned viewing pleasure, an erotic or romantic identification with vampires and other sympathetic or attractive monsters to provide a distinctively feminine viewing strategy. Like the readers of feminine genres such as romance and historical fiction, these viewers exhibit a tendency to elide those narrative aspects of the films which conform to patriarchal repression or oppression of these characters. These feminine interpretative strategies suggest that if the horror film remains a predominantly masculine genre, it nevertheless continues to incorporate some of the feminine aspects integral to the literary forms of Gothic horror. Most significantly, perhaps, the pleasure that these viewers find in images of terror and gore and, in particular, in the body of the monster belies Linda Williams' assertion that the female spectator of the horror film can only refuse to look. In the words of the 24-year-old respondent:

> I was always touched by the immense tragedy and sorrow of the vampire, and I suppose enjoyed the vicarious pleasure of the female sexual excess and expression in [vampire] films. As a rather shy, mousy and introverted youngster it really filled a void in me. They were never so much role models, that style was far beyond me, but characters I could escape with into a fantasy world of glamour as I watched these films. I really found them arousing, exploring a sexual life which I had never had any contact with before – one that seemed otherworldly, and was glittering slick and soft focus on the screen, but beyond my imagination, confidence and certainty in real life.

Refusing to refuse to look is, for such viewers, an act of affinity with the monster more subversive than Williams imagined.

Notes

1 See, for instance, Barbara Creed, 'Horror and the monstrous-feminine: an imaginary abjection', in James Donald (ed.), *Fantasy and the Cinema* (London: British Film Institute, 1989, pp. 81–2, 87.

2 Linda Williams, 'When the woman looks', in Mary Ann Doane, Patricia Mellencamp and Linda Williams, (eds), *Revision: Feminist Essays in Film Analysis* (Washington, DC: American Film Institute, 1984), p. 89.

3 Derek Granger, film review, *Financial Times*, 6 May 1957.

4 E. Lederman, 'The best places to meet good men', *Cosmopolitan*, June 1992.

5 Granger, *Financial Times* film review.

6 James Twitchell, *Dreadful Pleasures: An Anatomy of Modern Horror* (New York: Oxford University Press, 1985), p. 70; Carol Clover, *Men, Women and Chainsaws: Gender in the Modern Horror Film* (London: BFI Publishing, 1992), p. 6.

7 Mark Gill quoted in Andrew Hindes, 'Scream 2 showcases demographic power', *Variety*, 16 December 1997.

8 Dolf Zillman *et al.*, 'Effects of an opposite-gender companion's affect to horror on distress, delight, and attraction', *Journal of Personality and Social Psychology*, no. 51, 1986.

9 Dolf Zillman and James B. Weaver III, 'Gender socialisation theory of reactions to horror', in James B. Weaver III and Ron Tamborini (eds), *Horror Films: Current*

Research on Audience Preferences and Reactions (Mahwah, New Jersey: Lawrence Erlbaum Associates, 1996), p. 86.

10 Williams, 'When the woman looks', p. 83.

11 The figures provided by the Cinema Advertising Association are used to sell cinema advertising slots. Film profiles undertaken by the CAA are from representative samples of the British population highlighting age, sex and class.

12 Clover, Men, Women and Chainsaws, p. 54.

13 Zillman and Weaver, 'Gender socialisation theory of reactions to horror', in Weaver and Tamborini, Horror Films, p. 86.

14 Jackie Stacey, Star Gazing: Hollywood Cinema and Female Spectatorship (London: Routledge, 1994).

15 Henry Jenkins, Textual Poachers: Television Fans and Participatory Culture (New York/London: Routledge, 1992).

16 Tanya Modleski, Feminism Without Women (London: Routledge, 1991); Liesbet van Zoonen, Feminist Media Studies (London: Sage Publications, 1994), pp. 128–9.

17 Brenda Dervin, 'The potential contribution of feminist scholarship to the field of communication', Journal of Communication, Autumn 1987, pp. 107–20.

18 Fan clubs and societies either circulated their female membership with questionnaires directly or together with a letter explaining the research; smaller groups passed on details at meetings. Flyers explaining the research and calling for participants were circulated at conventions and film festivals and magazine recruitment was via letters published on the letters page, small ads, or mention in an editorial column.

19 Ien Ang, Watching Dallas: Soap Opera and the Melodramatic Imagination (London: Methuen, 1985).

20 See also Stacey, Star Gazing, pp. 44–5.

21 Ibid., pp. 6, 54, 66.

22 Ibid., p. 54.

23 See, for example, Auerbach, Our Vampires, Ourselves (Chicago: University of Chicago Press, 1995) and Norine Dresser, American Vampires: Fans, Victims, Practitioners (New York and London: W.W. Norton and Company, 1989).

24 Mark Jancovich, Horror (London: Batsford, 1992), p. 18.

25 Ellen Moers, Literary Women (London, 1977), pp. 90–110; Judith Halberstam, Skin Shows: Gothic Horror and the Technology of Monsters (Durham, North Carolina: Duke University Press, 1995) , p. 165.

26 Rosemary Jackson, Fantasy: The Literature of Subversion (London/New York: Methuen, 1981), p. 103.

27 With the exception of Nicholson's glowing yellow eye, not unlike a photographic image from a Häagan-Daz advertisement.

28 Text reproduced from 'The feminine love of horror' in Motion Picture Classic, reprinted in David J. Skal, Hollywood Gothic: The Tangled Web of Dracula from Novel to Stage to Screen (London: Andre Deutsch, 1990), p. 149. Skal, making reference to this interview in Skal, The Monster Show, pp. 126–7, believes it to have been Tod Browning who was being quoted, not Lugosi.

29 David Cantor and Saw Associates, Horror: Continuing attraction and common reactions (a report to coincide with the re-opening of the Chamber of Horrors) (London:

Madam Tussauds, March 1996), p. 13. Survey conducted by MEW Research in March 1995.

30 Cantor and Saw Associates, *Horror*, p. 13.

31 Auerbach, *Our Vampires, Ourselves* p. 3.

32 Tanya Krzywinska, 'La Belle Dame sans Merci?', in Paul Burston and Colin Richardson (eds), *A Queer Romance: Lesbians, gay men and popular culture*, (London: Routledge, 1995), pp. 99.

33 Auerbach, *Our Vampires, Ourselves*, p. 4; David J. Skal, *The Monster Show: A Cultural History of Horror* (London: Plexus, 1993); Walter Kendrick, *The Thrill of Fear: 250 Years of Scary Entertainment* (New York: Grove Press, 1991).

34 See Twitchell, *Dreadful Pleasures*, p. 70.

35 Guy Cumberbatch and Gary Wood, *Phantasmagoria: a survey of computer game players* (unpublished report, September 1996), p. 6.

36 J. B. Barclay, *Viewing tastes of Adolescents in Cinema and Television* (Glasgow: Scottish Educational Film Association and Scottish Film Council, 1961).

37 While only two respondents are under eighteen and only one over sixty, this is most probably due to the recruitment methods. I am not claiming that this sample is a statistically accurate representation of habitual female viewers of horror films.

38 Clover, *Men, Women and Chainsaws*, p. 66.

39 These ambivalent attitudes may be related to the response given to victims of domestic violence that they 'deserve it'. See Philip Schlesinger, R. Emerson Dobash, Russell P. Dobash, C. Kay Weaver, *Women Viewing Violence* (London: BFI Publishing, 1992).

40 *Interview with the Vampire, The Lost Boys, Bram Stoker's Dracula* and *The Hunger*.

41 *The Exorcist* (1973), *The Omen* (1976) and *The Haunting* (1963).

42 *The Silence of the Lambs* (1991) and *Psycho* (1960).

43 *Alien, Aliens* and *The Thing*.

44 *Hellraiser, Hellbound: Hellraiser II* (1988) and *Nightbreed* (1990).

45 Janice Radway, *Reading the Romance: Women, Patriarchy and Popular Literature* (Chapel Hill: University of North Carolina Press, 1984).

46 Ibid., p. 79.

47 Ibid., p. 159.

48 This aspect of horror film enjoyment is typified by a group of women in Brighton who formed 'Women Into Violent Movies' to watch horror, kung fu, and other similar films.

49 Jonathan Lake Crane, *Terror and Everyday Life: Singular Moments in the History of the Horror Film* (Thousand Oaks, California: Sage Publications, 1994), p. vii.

50 Ibid., p. 3.

51 Joanne Cantor and Mary Beth Oliver have described the kinds of material which frighten or otherwise affect children as varying with age. See Joanne Cantor and Mary Beth Oliver, 'Developmental differences in responses to horror', in Weaver and Tamborini, *Horror Films*, pp. 63–80.

52 Cantor and Oliver, 'Developmental differences', p. 71, discussing C. Hoffner and J. Cantor, 'Developmental differences in responses to a television character's appearance and behaviour', *Developmental Psychology* vol. 21, 1985, pp. 1065–1074.

53 John Tulloch and Henry Jenkins, *Science Fiction Audiences: Watching Doctor Who and Star Trek* (London/New York: Routledge, 1995), p. 4.

54 Jenkins, *Textual Poachers*, p. 19.

55 The Goth subculture too models a desired sexuality along similar lines.

56 Pinhead has become a pin-up and sex symbol in Japan, for instance.

57 Clover, *Men, Women and Chainsaws*, p. 54.

58 Ibid., pp. 62–3.

Index